"Although Egbert makes it clear that nobody but a long-distance hiker can truly understand what it's like to tackle a thru-hike, her book provides an overarching picture of a hike that comes as close to conveying understanding as any second-hand account can. Her 10-year-old daughter Scrambler's enthusiasm for the trail is apparent and contagious. That Scrambler is the youngest person on record as having completed the PCT is an extraordinary feat in itself, but what is truly inspirational about 'the Blighs' is their ability to take on this adventure as a family, and stay together through sun and snow, blisters and mosquitoes, and even too much togetherness. This is a great read for anyone who has ever thought of hiking the PCT, or of introducing a child to backpacking."

—**Liz Bergeron**,
Executive Director,
Pacific Crest Trail Association

"*Zero Days* is a fascinating account of the thrills and challenges of long-distance hiking, but the true joy of the book comes from watching a family grow closer to each other while spending six months together on the trail. Ten-year-old Scrambler's ceaseless optimism is especially inspiring to parents like myself who dream of long backpacking trips with their children."

—**Tim Hauserman**,
author, *Monsters in the Woods:
Backpacking with Children*

"This is the story of an epic adventure by uncommon and wonderful people. It is a peek into the world of long-distance hiking along the Pacific Crest Trail. It inspires, educates, and entertains. For families or individuals who aspire to attempt such a hike, it provides a reality check and many insights."

—**Donna Saufley**,
owner of the PCT hostel Hiker Heaven

ZERO DAYS

*The Real-Life Adventure
of Captain Bligh, Nellie Bly,
and 10-Year-Old Scrambler
on the Pacific Crest Trail*

Barbara Egbert

 WILDERNESS PRESS · BERKELEY, CA

Zero Days: The Real-Life Adventure of Captain Bligh, Nellie Bly, and 10-Year-Old Scrambler on the Pacific Crest Trail

1st EDITION January 2008

Book, cover, and map design: Larry B. Van Dyke
Book editor: Eva Dienel

ISBN: 978-0-89997-458-3 (cloth)
UPC: 7-19609-97458-1 (cloth)

ISBN: 978-0-89997-438-5 (paper)
UPC: 7-19609-97438-3 (paper)

Manufactured in the United States of America

Published by: **Wilderness Press**
               1200 5th Street
               Berkeley, CA 94710
               (800) 443-7227; FAX (510) 558-1696
               info@wildernesspress.com
               www.wildernesspress.com

Visit our website for a complete listing of our books and for ordering information.

Cover photos: Scrambler on the PCT in southern California *(front, main photo)*;
               Captain Bligh, Scrambler, and Nellie Bly on top of Mt. Whitney *(front,
               inset)*; Scrambler celebrates her successful PCT thru-hike at the
               U.S.-Canada border *(back, main photo)*; View from Packwood Glacier in
               southern Washington state *(back, banner photo)*

Library of Congress Cataloging-in-Publication Data
Egbert, Barbara, 1951-
   Zero days : the real-life adventure of Captain Bligh, Nellie Bly, and
10-year-old Scrambler on the Pacific Crest Trail / by Barbara Egbert. -- 1st
ed.
       p. cm.
   ISBN 978-0-89997-458-3 (hardcover) -- ISBN 978-0-89997-438-5 (pbk.)
1. Backpacking--Pacific Crest Trail. 2. Egbert, Barbara,
1951---Travel--Pacific Crest Trail. 3. Pacific Crest Trail--Description and
travel. I. Title.
   GV199.44.U82P333 2008
   917.94'9--dc22
   [B]
                                                        2007036438

ZERO DAYS is the story of my family's backpacking trip along the Pacific Crest Trail. My family—my husband, Gary, our 10-year-old daughter, Mary, and I—started hiking the trail on April 8, 2004, and finished on October 25, 2004. I named my book *Zero Days* after the phrase long-distance backpackers use to describe a short break from hiking. It's a "zero day" because a backpacker racks up zero mileage on the trail itself that day. For weary, footsore, and half-starved backpackers, a Zero Day is a Very Big Deal.

NOTE ABOUT JOURNAL ENTRIES: Throughout our PCT trek, Mary kept a daily journal with illustrations and thoughts about our journey. Several of her illustrations and journal entries are included in this book.

TRAIL SONG

(Sung to the melody of "Git Along, Little Dogies")

One morning as I was out driving for pleasure,
I saw a thru-hiker come walking along.
I pulled my car over and opened my window,
And as she drew closer I sang her this song:

> Chorus:
> Yippee ti yi yo, get along little hiker,
> It's your misfortune and none of my own.
> Yippee ti yi yo, get along little hiker,
> For onward to Canada is where you must roam.

It all started out way back down south in Campo,
Where the cactus grow and the yucca bloom.
She wanted to fatten on ice cream and pizza,
Yet before Jeff and Donna's, she was just skin and bones.

> Chorus

At Kennedy Meadows she climbed the Sierra,
With lightning and thunder and mountains that loom.
She finally got to Vermilion Valley,
Where she could get burgers and a motel room.

> Chorus

Into Yosemite her PCT took her,
Where the streams and rivers are deep, cold, and wide.
She fooled the bears and the backcountry rangers,
But from the mosquitoes there was no place to hide.

> Chorus

She sweated and swore through Section O's bushes
In the miserable heat of the Hat Creek Rim.
Then Oregon came with cold nights and downpours,
And she thought she would never have dry feet again.

Chorus

At the Bridge of the Gods, Washington beckoned,
And she thought for the border she'd make a mad dash.
But wait—what's this white stuff falling from the heavens?
Is that simply snow—or volcanic ash?

Chorus

—by Scrambler, Captain Bligh, and Nellie Bly

1. Campo—Mexican border
2. Warner Springs
3. Idyllwild
4. Big Bear City
5. Cajon Pass
6. Aqua Dulce
7. Mojave
8. Kennedy Meadows
9. Mt. Whitney
10. VVR on Edison Lake
11. Tuolumne Meadows
12. Sonora Pass—Bridgeport
13. Echo Lake
14. Peter Grubb Hut
15. Highway 49
16. Belden Town Resort
17. Drakesbad—Lassen Volcanic NP
18. Old Station
19. Burney Falls
20. Castella
21. Seiad Valley
22. Hyatt Lake Resort
23. Mazama Village—Crater Lake
24. Bend
25. Seventh-Day Adventist Big Lake Youth Camp
26. Detroit
27. Olallie Lake Resort
28. Timberline Lodge—Mt. Hood
29. Cascade Locks
30. White Pass—Packwood
31. Snoqualmie Pass
32. Skykomish
33. Rainy Pass—Mazama
34. Canadian border

CONTENTS

FOREWORD

IN MAY, just as the summer heat begins to soar, they arrive, dusty from the trail and ravenous. Their shoes are worn and their clothing tells the tale of life in the rugged southern California mountains and deserts, caked with dirt and salt. They've hiked hundreds of miles to get here. Up the road and in the gate they come, seeking rejuvenation and respite from the trail. For them, we open our hostel door and hearts. Ours is a place where hikers take zero days.

Driven by dreams and desires to experience something that is difficult to convey to the uninitiated, most who come through our gates are seeking the same goal: to walk the entire length of the 2,650-mile Pacific Crest Trail from Mexico to Canada. Many will make sacrifices to take this journey, and many will suffer bodily and mentally to reach the trail's northern terminus. Obstacles and challenges will be presented to all. The trail will humble and elate them, luring them onward with the invitation to see what is around the next bend or mountain. Hundreds will start out, but only the luckiest and most determined will make it. A handful return again and again, finding their truest happiness in the rugged simplicity of trail life.

The Pacific Crest Trail's remoteness and the wildness of the lands it passes through make hiking it in one season a daunting endeavor. The timing of the season is dependent on snow and weather, limiting the typical season to five or six months. Those who intend to complete the trail must carry food, gear, and supplies across mountains and deserts and through rivers and streams. In the long, dry reaches, they must add to their burden the weight of precious water. They endure insects, physical discomfort, and extremes of temperature. Feet and muscles rebel. No bed or hot shower will wait at the end of each day, and a week or more may pass before resupply opportunities. Proper equipment, logistical planning, and preparation are required. So are the rarest of all gifts: good health and free time. It is a determined and fortunate group of individuals that attempts this lengthy trek.

Stereotyping these seemingly unemployed bohemians is a fruitless endeavor. They may be world-class or first-time adventurers. You'll find grandmas, construction workers, veterinarians, airline pilots, lawyers, waitresses, and firefighters. Liberal doses of musicians, writers, and engineers walk alongside college students and retirees, from trail-wise veterans who've walked tens of thousands of miles to high schoolers on a lark. Couples, relations of all combinations, or simply single and on their own, each hiker may have a home and family who provide support, or may be alone and homeless for the duration of the hike.

The trail is the Great Equalizer, removing all vestiges of status, wealth, or occupation, giving each the appearance of a vagabond traveler, the vocation to which they seemingly aspire despite their diverse economic backgrounds and points of origin. What one does, drives, or possesses is meaningless and invisible, as the trail cares nothing for such things and exposes the inner character of each soul to its owner.

This great river of humanity flows through the doors of our trail retreat, Hiker Heaven. Since the first hosting of thru-hikers in 1997, thousands of them have found respite here on their way north and south.

In this sea of hikers who have stopped at our hostel, the rarest sight of all is a family as defined by mother, father, and child. Many families may hike and camp together, but precious few of them thru-hike.

The reasons families don't attempt thru-hiking are evident in all that is said above; it is rigorous and rife with challenge. As much as the hardships and shared passion can forge social bonds, it can also break them. Relationships both begin and end on the trail because of the shared difficulties encountered. Life on the trail is definitely not for everyone, so an entire family that possesses the dream, motivation, and fortitude to attempt such a feat is uncommon, even in this community of uncommon individuals.

Thru-hiking young children are rarer still. Few children would be willing to forgo every imaginable creature comfort, be separated from friends, and muster the courage and perseverance to walk 2,650 miles for fun. An unwilling child dragged along on such a journey is a formula for a nightmare.

The uncommonness of the thru-hiking family isn't the only thing that sets Nellie Bly, Captain Bligh, and Scrambler apart, however. Their love, support, protection, and encouragement of one another through their hiking joys and travails are inspirational. They survived the challenges as a unit rather than merely individuals, which requires the additional aspects of compromise and cooperation. They were a team of problem-solvers, cheerleaders, and doers for their common cause.

Barbara and Gary (before they were Nellie Bly and Captain Bligh) gave their daughter, Mary, a precious gift. They introduced her to the wonders of the backcountry. They painstakingly cultivated skills and sought to bring enjoyment to backpacking for their child, always with safety paramount. The result is amazing. At age 10, Scrambler was the youngest child ever to complete the Pacific Crest Trail in a single hiking season. That amazing record still stands.

Amazing is the word for Scrambler. She not only hiked the 2,650 miles, she hopped, skipped, read, and still had time to play. Wanted to play, after grueling days of hiking up and down mountains! At 10, Scrambler could hold court with adult thru-hikers on any topic related to the trail. Though she for all the world played and behaved like the child she was, peering into her eyes, one encountered the depth of a soul who had trod many miles, learned many lessons, and absorbed the beauty of the places wandered.

What follows is the story of an epic adventure by uncommon and wonderful people. It is a peek into the world of long-distance hiking along the Pacific Crest Trail. It inspires, educates, and entertains. For families or individuals who would aspire to attempt such a hike, it provides a reality check and many insights.

Enjoy!

—**Donna Saufley** and her husband, Jeff, have lived in Agua Dulce since May 1996, and began hosting PCT hikers at their hostel, Hiker Heaven, in May 1997. Since then, Donna has been active in the Pacific Crest Trail Association in many ways, including chairing the 2006 Trail Fest and working on volunteer trail crews.

CHaPTeR 1

IN THe BeGiNNiNG

Day 3: *Today was not all that interesting. We walked through a burned area and walked 16 miles.*

—from Scrambler's journal

JUST NORTH OF KITCHEN CREEK, 30-some trail miles from the Mexican border, the Pacific Crest Trail crosses a clearing near a campground. A small PCT marker guides thru-hikers on their way north; a side trail to the left leads down to a dirt road. As Mary, Gary, and I entered the clearing through tall, fire-scorched brush on a warm April morning, a woman wearing a bright red shirt watched us curiously. She and her husband and their two children—boys about 7 or 8 years old—had walked up the small hill to the trail intersection.

"Hello," Mary greeted the young mother as we approached. Always friendly, Mary is eager to socialize with everyone she meets. "Hello," the woman responded. "Where are you going?"

Mary pointed to the trail sign: "We're hiking the PCT." The woman had obviously never heard of the PCT, and she looked at me with the quizzical expression of an adult confronted with a completely nonsensical statement from a child. "We're hiking the Pacific Crest Trail," Gary explained. "It goes from the Mexican border to Canada, 2,650 miles. We're on our third day."

At this point, the woman's expression changed to something between disbelief and fear. I assured her we were sincere. She looked at her husband and children, then at Gary and me, with our sweaty faces, big packs, and little kid in tow. "You're kidding," she said. Then she said it again, "You're kidding." Finally, she turned to Mary and exclaimed, "You're not going to let them make you do this, are you?" Mary folded her arms, stuck out her chin, and replied, "They're not leaving me behind!"

As the magnitude of our endeavor sank in, I could picture what was going through this woman's mind. A hike of the Pacific Crest Trail is an impressive feat, especially for a child. Beginning in southern California's Mojave Desert at a modest monument near the wall along the southern border of the United States, the Pacific Crest Trail runs from Mexico to Canada, ending at a matching monument on the northern border, at the edge of British Columbia's Manning Provincial Park. Along the way, the trail rises and falls through the San Jacinto, San Bernardino, and San Gabriel ranges (and the desert valleys in between) before ascending to the crest of the Sierra Nevada. Its highest point, at 13,180 feet above sea level, is at Forester Pass in the southern Sierra. Continuing north over a succession of lofty mountain passes through Sequoia, Kings Canyon, and Yosemite national parks, the trail takes in views of Lake Tahoe in central California and then winds its way north through the mountains toward Lassen Volcanic National Park in northern California. Following the crest of the Cascade Range, the PCT offers views of Mt. Shasta before continuing into Oregon and Washington on a route punctuated by more volcanoes, including Mt. Jefferson, Mt. Hood, Mt. Adams, the still-smoking Mount St. Helens, and the mighty Mt. Rainier. At the Canadian border, as if ushering jubilant hikers back to civilization, there is a broad, 7-mile trail to the nearest paved road.

The PCT zigzags along ridgelines, meanders through public property, and follows wandering rights-of-way across private lands. The trail is more than twice the length of the highways that travel the same route from south to north; indeed, if you wanted to drive a distance equivalent to the trail, you would have to take your car from Los Angeles to Baltimore. Because of its length, PCT thru-hikers typically allow five to six months to hike the entire distance. Our own PCT adventure lasted from April 8 to October 25, 2004.

It's not surprising that most people who encountered our threesome reacted with disbelief. Even if they had heard of the trail—and many had not—it's rare to see a pair of 50-something parents and their 10-year-old cheerily saddled up with big packs for the trip. The people least likely to believe we could do it—much less would want to do it—were adults engaged in a weekend camping trip, complete with RV, generator, running water, and television set. It's hard enough explaining to sympathetic friends and relatives why we would want to spend an extended vacation lugging heavy loads up steep hills, sleeping on the ground, and digging holes for trailside latrines. But parents whose children have to be cajoled to move more than a few feet away from their video games cannot imagine a 10-year-old girl who can walk 20 miles a day with a full pack, and get into camp still capable of climbing trees and making up games with twigs and pinecones.

We found ourselves constantly responding to the kinds of questions that day-hikers and car campers are prone to ask upon meeting a trio of hard-muscled, razor-thin, scruffy-looking hikers intent on racking up a 20-mile day: How do you get food? How often do you take a shower? How come your daughter's not in school? But the biggest question everyone asks, which is even more important than how much weight has been lost and how many bears have been seen: *Why are you doing this?*

· · · · ·

THE STORY OF WHY we attempted to hike the Pacific Crest Trail as a family—and in the process gave Mary an opportunity to become the youngest person to finish—begins even before Gary and I met. While I spent my childhood exploring the high desert and lonely mountains of east-central Nevada, Gary was rambling around rural Maryland, 2,000 miles to the east. We both grew up comfortable in the wilderness and felt a strong need to escape into it frequently. We were in our 30s when we met in the spring of 1988. I was living in Baltimore doing a year of volunteer work, and because I had no car, I jumped at a friend's offer to join a hike and get out of the hot, humid city. That's where I met Gary, along the banks of the Gunpowder River. Soon, he invited me on our first date; rock climbing at Annapolis Rocks, along the Appalachian Trail in Maryland, I learned how to belay with no difficulty, but when it was time for me to rope up and ascend a fairly easy climb, I froze. I was maybe 6 feet off the ground and I panicked. Couldn't move up, down, or sideways. Gary had to coax me down like a police negotiator talking a desperate stockbroker off a 20th-story ledge. To my surprise, Gary invited me on a second date, my very first backpacking experience. We hiked into Virginia's Shenandoah National Park on a Friday evening, and I thought I would collapse from the heat and humidity. But otherwise it was wonderful, and I discovered that I loved backpacking as a novice just as much as Gary did, with his 20 years of experience.

Gary drove out to California the next year so that we could get married. The bridegroom's present to the bride: Hi-Tec hiking boots (still my favorite brand) and a pair of convertible pants—the kind with zippers around the legs that allow you to change them from trousers to shorts without taking off your boots. We took care of the important stuff first—a pre-nuptial trip to the Grand Canyon—and after that dealt with such minor details as meeting with the minister, purchasing the wedding rings, and inviting guests to our outdoor ceremony.

By the time Mary was born four years later, Gary and I were a bona fide backpacking couple, and we knew we would include Mary in the backcountry outings that were our chief form of recreation. She was only two months old on the first trip, to Manzanita Point in Henry Coe State Park, southeast of San Jose. It was a sunny January day, and I carried Mary in a sling, while Gary heaved about 90 pounds—including Mary's infant car seat—the few miles from park headquarters to our campsite. Except for Gary's enormous load, it was an easy trip with mild weather, only a few miles to walk, and a spacious campsite with a picnic table. I was breast-feeding and we used disposable diapers, so feeding and diapering were simple. We divided tasks so that Gary took care of our camping chores, setting up the tent, arranging the bedding, and making dinner, while I looked after Mary's needs.

Nonetheless, I was nervous those first few trips taking our baby into the wilderness. I couldn't sleep because I was so worried about how Mary would fare on those chilly nights in the tent. Infants can't regulate their body temperatures as well as adults, and they don't wake up and cry when they get cold, as older children will. They can quietly slip into hypothermia. I arranged Mary as warmly and comfortably as possible in the car seat, inside our four-person dome tent. Then I crawled into my own sleeping bag next to her. I would check her every few minutes to make sure she was warm enough. If I didn't think she was, I'd take her into my bag to warm up. I didn't dare fall asleep, for fear of rolling over on her. Every couple hours, she would cry and I would nurse her.

Some of the adjustments we made for family backpacking trips would occur to any experienced parent: Allow extra time for camp chores, and venture out only during good weather. But I quickly learned other tricks, like trying to schedule our trips during a full moon, which made it easier to discern the outlines of baby, blankets, and diaper bag in our dark tent. Some things we learned the hard way. During a particularly inconvenient phase in our backpacking history, Mary was throwing up—a lot—and it was then that we discovered the importance of sealing everything that is wet, or could possibly get wet, inside two Ziploc bags. I even got the hang of breast-feeding while walking. This was an invention born of necessity: We were hiking near our home to a backpackers' site in the Sunol Regional Wilderness, and a steep hill lay ahead of us, when Mary made it clear she needed to be fed. But if I stopped for 20 or 30 minutes, darkness would overtake us before we reached the top. I stopped long enough to let her latch on, arranged the sling around her securely, and carefully resumed walking. To my surprise, the motion didn't bother her, and we reached our destination in plenty of time, with a happy, well-fed baby to boot.

At six months, Mary moved into a Tough Traveler "Stallion" model baby backpack, with all the options: a rain hood with a clear plastic window, side pockets, and an extra clip-on pouch. Mary frequently fell asleep in the backpack. Her little head would rest against the pack's coarsely textured fabric, and she would develop a rash there. So we padded those parts with flannel from an old nightgown. We also made a two-part rain cover out of waterproof, ripstop nylon, with Velcro to hold the two parts together. On clear days, we used diaper pins to clip together receiving blankets or old crib sheets to ward off the sun. I also bought a little round rearview mirror from an auto-supply store that I used to check on Mary when she was on my back. You wouldn't think a small child could get into trouble in a baby backpack, but during a trip to northern California's Lost Coast, she managed to pull some leaves off a tree and stuff them in her mouth. Another time, while we were returning from the summit of Utah's highest mountain, 13,528-foot King's Peak, she somehow managed to squirm around until she was riding sidesaddle.

By the time Mary was 1 year old, we had taken her backpacking six times, and to celebrate her first birthday, we took her on a trip down the New Hance Trail off the South Rim of the Grand Canyon. Each year, we kept hiking and backpacking as a family, tailoring the trips to Mary's needs and abilities, but always challenging ourselves to do more. Back then, there were few books on backpacking with children, and the few in print suggested that it just couldn't be done at certain ages. We never found that age. If Mary couldn't walk the entire distance, I would carry her part of the way. If she wanted to walk but was getting tired, I would entertain her with endless stories to keep her mind off her problems. On our trip to the Grand Canyon, we hit bad weather as we were hiking out. We had swathed the pack with our home-sewn rain cover, but this meant Mary couldn't see out the plastic window in the hood. And she got bored. I sang. I told stories. And then Gary hit on the perfect boredom reliever: raspberry sounds. One of us would make a loud noise, blowing out with our lips flapping, holding it as long as we could, and then the next would try to top it. This got us all laughing, and eventually we made it back to the trailhead.

As Mary got older, we discovered that dehydration was the surest source of trouble, and that crankiness was the surest sign of dehydration. Whenever Mary complained about the heat or the distance, or sat down in the trail and refused to move, we'd have her drink a cup of water. If it was late in the day and Mary was getting too cold or sleepy, we'd start looking for a place to set up camp. Just knowing she wouldn't be forced beyond her limits, or criticized for weakness, helped Mary enjoy backpacking when she was small. By the time Mary was in kindergarten, she could easily hike 10 or 12 miles at a stretch, climb Mission Peak (the 2,517-foot hill that dominates the skyline around our home in Sunol), and help with camp chores.

Although Mary, Gary, and I don't remember exactly whose idea it was to hike the Pacific Crest Trail as a family, I can trace the genesis of the plan to 1999, when we hiked the 76-mile portion of the PCT that runs from Tuolumne Meadows in Yosemite National Park to Sonora Pass. That ambitious expedition was the watershed trip for everything that followed. Mary was five-and-a-half years old when we began planning. Initially, we decided we would take her out of first grade for a week in October and hike what is known as Section J of the Pacific Crest Trail in the central Sierra Nevada. (The PCT is divided into sections of 38 miles to 176 miles, labeled alphabetically from south to north. All of California is divided into sections A through R, and then the alphabet starts over again. Oregon and Washington are divided into sections A through L.) On the map, the 60-mile stretch from Sonora Pass north to Carson Pass looked rugged but not too challenging. Two weeks before our start date, however, I suddenly remembered something I had almost forgotten after 10 years of living in the heavily populated San Francisco Bay Area: hunting season. Gary and I might have risked it anyway, with the help of matching Day-Glo orange vests, but we weren't about to put Mary in harm's way. She was a strong hiker, but hardly bulletproof. We hastily rewrote our plans so that we would go south from Sonora Pass instead of north, thus spending most of our trip on National Park Service land, where hunting is prohibited. This change from Section J to Section I also meant a longer and more difficult trip. Gary arranged to change our permit, and I talked my older sister, Carol, into picking us up in Yosemite.

When we reached Smedberg Lake in the Yosemite backcountry's perfect alpine setting of granite and evergreens, we had been out five days and were 50 miles into the trip. That day, we had walked 12 miles with a total elevation gain of 3,500 feet. Mary was happy as a lark. While Gary filtered water and I set up the tent, she took my bandanna down to the edge of the water and "washed" it over and over. Mary had been in particularly fine form that day, leading us up the initial 1,000-foot hill to Seavey Pass, down 1,590 feet to Benson Lake, and then up 2,500 feet before dropping down to Smedberg Lake.

That's when we realized that Mary had it in her to tackle a really long hike. This particular section of the PCT is one of the most remote parts of the entire route. The trail doesn't cross any roads, paved or dirt, for the entire distance. If one of us had suffered sickness, injury, or snakebite, we could have been as many as 38 miles from a road. Most of the eight days we were on the trail, we saw nobody, so we were completely on our own. As it turned out, the Section I trip was a tremendous experience, but not a perfect one. In fact, several things went wrong. What was so encouraging was that we were able to deal with them.

The problems started on our first day. Leaving Sonora Pass in late morning, we ran into trouble after a few miles when the trail headed straight into a steep snowfield that looked too dangerous to climb. We followed footsteps off to the right, marked by rock cairns, but we still ended up on a precarious, unstable slope. We spent a lot of time working our way down through the shattered rock. Mary took a fall and Gary caught her just in time to avoid injury. This delayed us to the point that we were 3 miles away from our intended campsite as darkness fell. We were all very tired, and we had enough water to get through the night, so we set up the tent on the first flat space we found. The next day, we easily made up the 3 miles and got to Lake Harriet by dusk.

Second day, second problem. About half of the rechargeable batteries that should have been enough for the entire trip turned out to be duds. Most backpackers are early risers, but not us. We like to get up in full daylight, hike until dusk, and then set up camp by headlamp. But now we had to change our habits, getting up at the icy crack of dawn each morning and hiking quickly to take advantage of all the light that an October day holds. We wanted to be in bed, not just in camp, by full dark each evening.

Third day, third problem. When we left our campsite at Lake Harriet, we headed up the obvious trail, only to arrive at Cora Lake, most definitely not where we wanted to be. I was tempted to try to cut cross-country at this point, rather than backtracking and wasting all that time and effort. I stared off across the trees, in the general direction of where we should have been, and asked Gary if we could go that way. His response: Definitely not. Cutting cross-country, he explained, sounds simple but is usually a mistake. Unless we could see our goal, plus an easy route to it, we'd be better off going back to our campsite and starting over. Otherwise, we'd probably get off course, or find our route blocked by a drop-off or impassable thickets.

Gary and I are devoted readers of news articles about people who come to grief in the backcountry. Trying to make up for a mistake by cutting cross-country instead of backtracking ranks high on the list of how hikers get into serious—and sometimes fatal—trouble. A few years after our Section I trip, an experienced outdoorsman decided to take a shortcut through California's Big Sur wilderness in order to shorten his planned two-week, solo backpacking trip. He ended up stranded at the top of a 100-foot waterfall. Fortunately for him, campers below heard him yelling and got help. He had to be plucked from the inaccessible terrain by helicopter. A year earlier, another experienced hiker found himself off the trail in the Sierra Nevada's Stanislaus National Forest. Rather than retrace his steps, he looked on the map for a shortcut, and thought he had found one in the shape of a dry streambed. The streambed was so rugged and steep, he eventually fell, ending up too badly injured to walk away. He staggered out days later. Gary had a simple rule to follow whenever we were unsure of where we were, whether on trail or off: Go back to where we were certain of our location, and then decide what to do. So it was back to Lake Harriet.

The fourth and fifth days brought only minor problems, like snow and cold. But on one particular day after we were halfway through, we couldn't seem to get along with each other. At home, we simply would have avoided each other for a while. Unfortunately, this is not a solution in the backcountry. The interactions among groups of people who tackle stressful activities such as long backpacking trips, big wall climbs, and mountaineering expeditions are pretty intense. The stresses can bring people closer together as they learn to value each other's strengths while becoming more tolerant of each other's weaknesses. But it's just as likely—probably more so—that the stresses will tear a group apart, or weaken it to the point that it doesn't function adequately. We heard tales about couples who broke up on the trail, or even after finishing.

On our seventh day, when we left our frosty campsite at Miller Lake (at 9,550 feet above sea level) and headed for Glen Aulin High Camp, Mary and I were heading down a hill in thick woods a couple hundred feet ahead of Gary. Instead of focusing on the route, I had my mind on my grievances with my husband. I followed what I thought was the main trail, heading off to the right into a meadow. Gary spotted the correct trail, heard our voices, and realized we had gone the wrong way. He shouted for us to stop and to head back toward him. If we had been much farther apart, we might have gone our separate ways for an hour before realizing our mistake. As it was, we all stayed together (however unhappily) until we reached Glen Aulin.

Perhaps what truly foreshadowed our future PCT expedition was the particular stuffed animal Mary had set aside for this trip. We always allowed Mary to bring one stuffed animal on backpacking expeditions, and making the choice was a big deal for her. For this trip, Mary had originally selected a little stuffed porcupine. However, when we arrived at my father's house in Minden, Nevada, to spend the night before starting, she discovered that my cousin's son, Andrew, had left her a little stuffed Chihuahua that he had won a few days earlier at the Santa Cruz Beach Boardwalk. Mary named it "Puffy" and immediately fell madly in love with it. When Carol dropped us off at Sonora Pass next morning, we learned that Mary had brought Puffy along, and wanted to bring both stuffed animals on the trip. At this age, she didn't carry anything on backpacking trips, and Gary and I refused to add any more weight or bulk to our well-stuffed packs. This nearly precipitated a major argument just as we were ready to begin walking. At the last minute, Mary agreed to leave the porcupine behind and take only the Chihuahua.

Eight days later, we met my sister, Carol, and her husband, George, in Tuolumne Meadows at the end of our trip. As they walked down the trail to greet us, Carol whispered to George, "Get it out of your pocket." George pulled out the porcupine and, with a shriek of joy, Mary rushed down the trail to retrieve her little friend. Two years later, it was again Puffy who got to accompany Mary on a big trip, the 165-mile Tahoe Rim Trail (by this point, Mary carried a full pack, including her "animal friend"). But in 2004, the little porcupine finally got his chance. Mary gave him his own trail name, "Cactus," and carried him on the PCT.

With Section I successfully completed, we began seriously considering a PCT thru-hike. Both Gary and Mary insist it was my idea. (I was willing to take the credit during good days on the trail; on bad days, I was convinced one of them must have come up with such a crazy scheme.) Despite my supposed status as originator of the family thru-hike goal, I had many doubts about whether I could actually do it. When a friend who has known us for several years asked me at a book club dinner, "What will you do when Mary caves?" I assured her I was the weak link in this particular chain. I have always felt somewhat of an impostor among hardcore backpackers. Gary is the most competent person I know in backpacking, rock climbing, and mountaineering. He's totally at home in the woods. And Mary is well on her way down the path trod by her father's boots.

Even before she set out to conquer the PCT, Mary was the youngest person to summit Mt. Shasta and to thru-hike the 165-mile Tahoe Rim Trail.

But I look at thru-hikers, especially the women who are strong enough and brave enough to hike long trails alone, and I think, "I could never do that." I have to remind myself that I am strong and brave and skillful. I lived a full and occasionally adventuresome life on my own before Gary and I married. But sometimes I feel the way I did when I first joined Mensa, the high IQ society. For several weeks after I received the letter announcing I had qualified to join, I was convinced another letter would follow with an apology for their mistake. Months went by before I lost that nervous apprehension every time I checked the mailbox. Eventually, I attended a few Mensa gatherings and discovered I was as brainy as any other member. The same has been true of backpacking. I'll read a trail journal by some woman who set out by herself when she was 60, or some man who went through the Sierra when every trail marker was buried under 15 feet of snow, and feel totally intimidated. And then I'll meet those people at the Pacific Crest Trail kickoff or an American Long-Distance Hiking Association conference and realize that, hey, we have a lot in common.

Despite our ambitions, none of us was immune from worrying about whether we could—or should—try to thru-hike the PCT. I fretted about our ability to handle the physical challenges and, like many parents, nervously imagined how I would feel if Mary were to be seriously injured from a fall, bear attack, or lightning strike. Gary worried about the danger of one of us drowning during a stream crossing. He also worried how an independent-minded 10-year-old would behave when faced with day after day of discomfort, hard work, and enforced togetherness, aggravated by inadequate food and rest. Mary, aware of her father's concern, mostly worried that the trip would be called off at the last minute. Gary was tempted several times to cancel it, but about six months before our projected start date, he made a commitment to go for it, no matter what.

Once we decided to do the trip, computer technology was a huge help in our preparations. Thanks to the internet, we could connect with experienced thru-hikers eager to weigh in on every aspect of the trail experience. Some long-trail veterans have journals online, and many of them are surprisingly personal. Many backpackers and trail fans participate in the PCT-L, an online forum that regularly hosts heated debates on everything from the best type of stove and fuel for long-distance hiking, to whether dogs should be taken on the trail. I conversed via email with a married couple in Pleasanton, California, near our home in Sunol, who completed the PCT in 2000. They were in their early 50s, just like Gary and me when we began. Marcia and Ken Powers went on to complete the Triple Crown: the PCT, the Continental Divide Trail (in 2002), and the Appalachian Trail (in 2003). And in 2005, they achieved the grand slam of long-trail backpacking when they finished the coast-to-coast, 4,900-mile American Discovery Trail. In the same way, I got in touch with a young man in Berkeley who completed the PCT in 1999. I read his online trail journal while he was hiking. After he finished, we exchanged emails with practical discussions about gear. Along with these seasoned backpackers, several trail publications provided essential guidance, most notably the three Pacific Crest Trail guides published by Wilderness Press, plus the accompanying *Data Book*; the *Town Guide*, published by the Pacific Crest Trail Association; *A Hiker's Companion*, by Karen Berger and Daniel R. Smith, from Countryman Press; and *Yogi's PCT Handbook*.

One of the questions they helped to answer was why more people don't hike in groups. Why do so many start out alone? There are obvious benefits to hiking with at least one other person—safety, companionship, a second opinion on trail options, or a potentially cooler head in a pinch. And some thru-hikers are lucky enough to walk the entire distance with one or two others, usually spouses, sweethearts, or very close friends. But many have to plan for a solo experience. Why? Because hardly anyone wants to do it. In the years leading up to our trip, between 200 and 250 people attempted to hike the PCT each year, according to Greg Hummel, who keeps track of such things as part of his involvement with the American Long-Distance Hiking Association. He estimates that 50 percent of those people had the ability to finish, but only 30 percent to 35 percent actually did. So, something like 65 or 75 people might walk from one border to the other in a typical year. About 300 wannabe thru-hikers began the trail in our year; about 75 finished. The completion rate ranges from 60 percent in an exceptionally good year to about 10 percent for a bad one. Those are guesses, to be sure. No one knows for certain how many people start, how many finish, and how many are completely honest about having hiked the entire distance. By the time they reach Oregon and Washington, many former purists find themselves willing to skip small portions. A hiker might have to spend a few days in a motel room recovering from illness and want to catch up with his trail companions with a little hitchhiking. Or a thru-hiker might get a ride into a town stop, and then the next day someone offers to drop her off a little farther along, perhaps avoiding one of the more unpleasant stretches of trail.

The solo nature of the long-trail experience comes as a surprise to many people. They'll ask, "You hiked with a group, right?" What they expect to hear is that we signed up with some sort of guided tour, like a Sierra Club outing or an expedition on Mt. Rainier. But the Pacific Crest Trail, just like its sister long trails, the Appalachian Trail and the Continental Divide Trail, provides one of the few major outdoor experiences that is devoid of professional guides. This is a completely amateur undertaking. Now, to be sure, few people hike alone *all* the time. Those who don't start out with a partner or spouse tend to form casual groups on the trail, as three or four hikers discover that they move at about the same pace and enjoy each other's company. These groups are small and fluid, dissolving at town stops, re-forming a few days up the trail. The speed with which thru-hikers find themselves part of a community stems from this lack of hierarchy. There is no one whose job it is to look out for the rest, so we all look out for each other. But in the end, most thru-hikers have to be ready to be completely on their own for at least part of the trail.

During our research, we realized that every year, many experienced backpackers begin the trail with every expectation of success, only to fail. What makes the difference? Training? Motivation? Luck? Nope. It's a simple matter of weather, and not even the weather during the hiking season. Rather, the biggest factor in completion rates is the snowpack in the Sierra Nevada. Since much of the Sierra's snow falls in March, April, and even May, most thru-hikers have made the decision to hike in a particular year long before the size of the snowpack is known. Just the fact that we chose 2004, a pretty "normal" year for snowpack and for weather in general, was a stroke of good fortune for us. Subsequent years have been anything but.

Considering the time and expense involved in beginning a thru-hike, and the small chance of finishing, it's not surprising so few people attempt to walk the entire PCT. The challenges are enormous, and the commitment is even bigger. All thru-hikers must train, buy gear, arrange to resupply along the trail, study guidebooks, and generally set aside their ordinary lives for five or six months. And for many thru-hikers (including us), there are additional headaches. We had to find reliable people to take care of our house, two cats, and a dozen or so indoor plants. I had to set up payment plans for the mortgage and other bills, and arrange time off from work. Mary had to finish all of her fifth grade class work 10 weeks ahead of schedule, which meant that as soon as she finished fourth grade, she began her fifth grade math, literature, and social studies at home. Luckily, the teachers and superintendent at Sunol Glen School were eager to help us in this regard, but what it meant for Mary was that she got no real summer vacation in 2003. Gary figured out what we would need in each resupply box, planned our town stops, and ordered all the gear. The financial hit can be substantial: By the time Gary replaced most of our old gear with the lightest, strongest, and warmest he could find, we were out thousands of dollars. That's a big deal when your annual income is about to be cut in half.

By the time April 2004 rolled around, we were about as prepared as it was possible to be. We were probably the most prepared newcomers to the trail that year, mainly because we had to do so much extra to safely include a 10-year-old on an undertaking on the scale of a PCT thru-hike. Every possible safety issue had to be taken into consideration, and a child's differing point of view had to be accommodated. We could never rely on luck. Thankfully, after all those years of hiking together, we knew what to expect. For example, a 10-year-old's energy levels rise and fall differently than an adult's, and rely more on her state of mind. At the beginning, Gary and I frequently took extra weight from Mary on steep uphill sections, especially in the desert heat. But Mary grew stronger as we headed north, while Gary and I developed a long list of ailments. By the time we reached

Washington, Mary was carrying more weight, as a percentage of her body weight, than I was. But in April, of course, all we cared about was that the apparently endless preparations were finally over and all we had to do was put one foot in front of the other. Or so we hoped.

Once we started training, we discovered which bits of the avalanche of advice we'd received were the most important. One nugget that proved extremely important in guiding both my training and my actual experience on the trail was a chance quip by a longtime backpacker, Lipa, a retired park ranger and an experienced outdoorswoman. We ran into her on a training hike in Sunol Regional Wilderness, just a few miles from our home. She was planning to climb Mt. Whitney, California's highest mountain and the highest point in the lower 48 states, for her 65th birthday. We told her about our plans. She listened approvingly, and then remarked: "Once you get to a certain level of physical fitness, the rest is all mental." I took her words very much to heart and focused equally on physical fitness and mental preparation. I've met too many people who thought they could get by with just one or the other. Mary and Gary could train together frequently—Gary was a stay-at-home Dad, and Mary didn't have all that much homework in fifth grade—but I worked full time and had to force myself to find opportunities for strenuous hikes with a heavy pack, or to work out on our one piece of home exercise equipment, a stepper.

Gary took charge of guiding the mental preparations for all three of us. I tend to rely too much on him to do the thinking, and also to provide the determination and motivation, for backpacking trips. Gary encouraged me to push myself beyond my comfort level, to hike in the rain (which I hate), to think ahead, to be more aware of my surroundings. During off-trail trips in the Sierra, he taught Mary and me to use the compass and topographical maps, watch for landmarks, figure out which drainages go where—in other words, to be prepared to save ourselves if he were hurt. Intellectually, I agreed that this was a terrific idea. But on the ground, breathing hard and going rapidly insane from mosquito assaults, it was all too easy to just turn the whole thing over to Gary. Gradually, however, I began to develop the right combination of determination, caution, and creativity. I learned when I could push myself to go farther—at the base of a 1,000-foot hill, for example, on a hot day, when what I really wanted to do was lie down on the fire road, put my cap over my face, and not move. I also learned when I should stop even before I really wanted to. This happened rarely, and usually only above 10,000 feet, where the thin air brought on a euphoric feeling that, like Julie Andrews, I could climb every mountain. Gary also pushed me to think in terms of solving typical backpacking problems, such as broken buckles or misleading instructions, by myself. (He didn't entirely succeed. To this day, when something breaks or doesn't make sense, Mary and I tend to turn to Gary first.)

The second bit of advice that helped me so much is a cliché I've heard so often that I had come to ignore it: Take one day at a time. It's so common that a Google

Day 1

Today we left the border. Sara dropped us off in her rental car. Soon after we got there, Amy, a B.P. lady drove up and talked to us and made sure we were thru-hikers, not aliens. We walked 17 miles, 2 being a deture to sign the official register.

Then we intrepidly hiked on. We hiked on to a dirt road, where we camped in a little turn out.

search brings up millions of hits. That is so trite, I had always thought. So banal. But it came to mean a great deal to me in the first few weeks on the PCT. As we struggled through the heat and rough terrain of our first 700 miles, I often asked myself, "Can I possibly keep doing this for another month? Another week?" The answer was often, "No way!" But if I asked myself, "Can I just make it to tonight's campsite?" the answer was always yes.

As our departure date neared, we had one more major chore to confront: choosing our trail names. The use of special nicknames is a long-trail tradition, generally considered to have begun on the Appalachian Trail. Some people choose their own, some have them assigned by other hikers, and some don't use trail names at all.

Mary acquired her trail name, Scrambler, in the time-honored way of having it given to her by other hikers—her parents. This happened on our second thru-hike of the 165-mile Tahoe Rim Trail in 2003, when we knew that we would be tackling the PCT the following year. We were heading down a very rocky section of trail near Aloha Lake, heading into Echo Lake. While Gary and I were making heavy weather of the bad tread, Mary was just skimming over the rocks, almost as though she were skating over the tops of them while her parents followed laboriously behind. "Look at her, just scrambling over the rocks," Gary remarked enviously. And thus a trail name was born. We ran it past Mary, who liked it and promptly adopted it as her own.

Gary acquired his trail name from his daughter one evening a few weeks before we had to leave, while they were packing food, toilet paper, and other essentials into resupply boxes. He was, in her words, "bossing me around too much," and she told him, "You're just like Captain Bligh," referring to the tyrannical captain in *Mutiny on the Bounty*. When I learned of the exchange, I endorsed the nickname because the real 18th century Captain Bligh was most famous as a navigator, and Gary's wilderness navigational skills are superb.

I chose my own trail name, which is something many people do, sometimes as a pre-emptive strike against being stuck with something they don't like. Nellie Bly, a name from American folk tradition, was the pen name used by the first American woman to be a true investigative journalist, back in the 19th century. She was an early hero of mine when I was growing up, and the children's biography of her that I read probably had some influence on my decision to make journalism my career.

As a family, we became known on the trail as "the Blighs."

Finally, we were ready to go—more than ready, in fact. Coping with the months of preparation, advance bill-paying, and arrangements to take off from work and school and to have the house and pets and cars taken care of left us with one burning desire: to start walking. So on April 8, 2004, a friend dropped us off at the border. We shouldered our packs, faced north, and began putting one foot in front of the other, on our way to Canada.

CHAPTER 2

TOGETHERNESS

Day 132: *South Matthieu Lake. Today we spent the whole day cooped up in the rain. It was horrid to have so much togetherness.*

—from Scrambler's journal

IT FELT SO GOOD TO GET AWAY from the daily distractions and irritations of ordinary life. On the trail, we escaped from telephones, televisions, and computers; from bills, advertisements, and junk mail; from teachers and bosses; from paid work, housework, and homework. But we couldn't escape from each other. We hiked together, ate together, slept together. Sometimes we even "went to the bathroom" together, our backs carefully turned toward each other to preserve an illusion of privacy, when there weren't enough bushes to provide the real thing.

As much as we love each other, Gary, Mary, and I appreciate the ability to occasionally get away from each other at home. But on the trail 24/7, there was no escape. We saw each other all day. We listened to each other talk, eat, snore, and burp. We smelled each other as the days stretched out since our last showers. And sometimes, believe it or not, we got on each other's nerves.

Adult hikers who travel as a pair or a group generally learn to respect each other's hiking speed and style and often spread out along the trail during the day. One couple we knew left camp a couple hours apart to accommodate their differing abilities. They would wake up at the same time, but she would devour breakfast, dress, pack, and get walking as quickly as possible. He would get ready in more leisurely fashion, taking down the tent and doing most of the camp chores. Once he finally started walking, he usually caught up with his wife within a few hours. This approach worked well for them, although she had to make sure she marked her route carefully at trail intersections.

132

Today we spent the whole day cooped up in the rain. It was horrid to have so much togetherness. We wrote one verse in our song and practiced it. I read a lot.

Some couples and even threesomes intend to stay together, only to discover early on how difficult it is for one person to match his hiking style to another's. Standard advice: Don't even try. If you want to hike with someone else, be content to share campsites and break stops, but don't worry if you get separated in between. People hiking or doing any other task for hours at a time naturally settle into a speed that's most efficient for them. Trying to adjust to someone else's level isn't just frustrating—it's exhausting. Two people can start out the best of friends, but imagine how they'll feel toward each other after a few weeks if their hiking styles don't mesh.

Consider this scenario for two hikers—call them Eagle and Badger. Eagle gets up at the crack of dawn, packs up within half an hour, and puts in 3 or 4 miles on the trail before he stops to eat breakfast. Badger doesn't wake up until the sun is high, cooks and eats a hot breakfast, then packs up at a leisurely pace. He might take 90 minutes to get out of camp—on a good day. Eagle moves fast but takes frequent breaks. With military precision, he sits down, eats a granola bar, drinks half a liter of water, and is on the move within 20 minutes. Badger walks for two or three hours between breaks, but then spends 45 minutes or so eating, filtering water, and treating his blisters. Eagle moves like lightning on the flats, slows on the upgrades, and crawls down the hills with aching knees. Badger moves at the exact same 2.5 miles per hour regardless of the terrain. Eagle stops only to take photographs, but then he might spend 15 minutes getting just the right frame. Badger doesn't even carry a camera, but he'll spend 30 minutes chatting with anyone he meets along the way. Force these two guys to stay together on the trail for more than a day, and watch out for the fireworks. But let them hike at their own pace, and when they meet in the evening to camp, they'll get along great. Badger and Eagle will tell everyone later how lucky they were to find the perfect backpacking companion.

Gary, Mary, and I have different hiking styles, too, but we had fewer options than most hiking trios. Our rule was that Mary must be with an adult at all times. Frequently, we all three hiked together. I was a good pace-setter on moderate terrain, and often I would lead, with Mary (whom I generally addressed by her trail name of Scrambler) in the middle and Gary bringing up the rear. But if we split up, I was usually the adult who stayed with Mary. If Gary (a.k.a Captain Bligh) got ahead, he would wait occasionally for us to catch up, and he'd stop at any confusing trail intersections. But because of the size of his load, he couldn't just stop and stand there; he had to find a suitable boulder on which to prop his heavy pack, which sometimes took a while. If the Captain fell behind, he usually caught up with us easily because of our frequent stops to take jackets off, put jackets on, adjust packs, or go behind a tree. Sometimes I became impatient with Scrambler, who initiated the majority of these pauses, but most of the time I was grateful that she and I moved at more or less the same speed. We chose 2004, when Mary was 10, to attempt our PCT thru-hike, partly because Scrambler's speed and strength had increased to the point that she could keep up with Nellie Bly (that's me) most of the time, and I hadn't yet become too old and decrepit to keep up with her. Our joke was that we wanted to hike the PCT at just that magic point when Scrambler's upward strength line crossed my downward one.

When she was younger, Mary needed a lot of cajoling to keep her moving. On the PCT, she just needed a lot of what Gary called "mindless chatter." Mary loves to talk: It helps her keep going and takes her mind off the weight of the pack and the heat of the day. Gary does better without distractions. Listening to Mary and me talk endlessly about how we would design fancy costumes or plan a 15-course meal or redecorate our home if money were no object drove him insane. Sometimes we had to agree to let Gary stay a couple hundred yards in front or behind just so he'd be out of earshot. I'm somewhere in the middle on the talk vs. no-talk scale, but I did find that a half-hour quiet time each afternoon did me a world of good.

A typical conversation on a hot day on the trail went something like this:

Scrambler: Mommy, can we talk about the restaurant we're going to open when we get home? Just pretend.

Nellie Bly: Sure, honey. Where shall we start?

Captain Bligh: Wow, did you see that hummingbird that just flew by?!

Scrambler: Yeah, Daddy, it was beautiful! Hey, Mommy, how about we call it the Hummingbird Restaurant and serve all-vegetarian food?

Nellie Bly: Sounds like a plan. Tell me more.

Scrambler: We'll have pancakes and waffles and scones and muffins on the breakfast menu, and people could have them made to order while they wait, and you could bake them and I could be the waitress and Daddy could meet them at the door ...

Captain Bligh: Wait a min—

Nellie Bly: Great idea, Scrambler. We could spend whole days dreaming up exotic kinds of food to serve, and if we stick with vegetarian, our ingredients won't be all that expensive. And then we could offer lunch with all kinds of soups and breads and quiches. And we could hang hummingbird feeders outside all the windows for diners to watch.

Scrambler: Yeah, that's a good idea! And we can have hummingbird-embroidered placemats and napkins and ...

Captain Bligh: Hey, look at that lake down there! That's the bluest blue I've ever seen!

Scrambler: Wow! Take a picture, Daddy! Hey, Mommy, we could have special desserts named after all our favorite places on the trail. Like Purple Lake blueberry pie. And Mt. Whitney chocolate cake.

Nellie Bly: Yes, and Golden Staircase ice cream sundaes. How about Mojave Desert broiled custard?

Scrambler: Yes, and Burney Falls blackberry shakes!

Captain Bligh: Don't you two ever notice the scenery anymore? Here we are in one of the world's most beautiful places, and all you can talk about is food!

Scrambler: We notice the scenery, *Daaaad*! We can talk and see at the same time! We're *giiiiirls*.

Captain Bligh: Aaaaggghhh!

Before we left home for the trail, Gary's friends at the rock-climbing gym he visits every week teased him that his real goal was to drive me to divorce him after six months on the trail, so he could spend even more time climbing. I thought that was pretty funny. We did drive each other crazy once in a while, but we'd learned on previous trips how to get along in the woods. That's not the case with every thru-hiking duo or trio. We heard of one couple who had completed the trail a year earlier, put together a slideshow, presented it—and then got divorced. Romantic bonds less binding than matrimony have also become unraveled on long trails.

Trail journals provide a window into the relationships between people who find themselves hiking together, not always by choice. One online journal I read revealed a hiker's resentment at being forced (in his opinion) to take responsibility for another who began walking with him in the southern desert. At first he enjoyed her company, but eventually he came to fantasize about ditching her. Another journal contained a backpacker's bitter words about getting into a town stop with another hiker, who pulled a vanishing act at the first opportunity. More common, however, are reports of deep friendships formed along the trail.

The social aspect of thru-hiking is very important to some hikers—so important, in fact, that when we chatted with a bunch of Appalachian Trail thru-hikers in 2005 in Maryland, they mentioned one solitude-averse hiker who had quit the PCT because he met only a dozen people in a week on the trail. He returned East to hike the AT again, where it's common to see a dozen people in just one day. Millions of people walk on the Appalachian Trail every year, most for dayhikes or weekend outings. But somewhere between 2,000 and 3,000 attempt thru-hikes each year, 10 times the number who start the PCT. And thousands more are doing section hikes on the AT. Most backpackers plan their days around the 250 shelters along the trail, so the AT during the day can be almost as well-used as a city sidewalk, and the shelters at night can be as crowded as a Yellowstone campground on Labor Day. This scene isn't for me. I loved going for days on the PCT without meeting any strangers, and I would go crazy if I had to share an AT shelter every night with eight or 10 other people.

Partnerships formed on the trail can become a wonderful source of companionship, but they can also become the cause of deep irritation. Gary insisted before we start that we all agree on one thing: We wouldn't let anyone glom onto us. If someone occasionally opted to hike or camp with us, he said, that would be fine, but under no circumstances should we let anyone join our group to the extent that we would be expected to alter our schedule for him or her, or in any way take responsibility for another person. I thought at the time Gary was overly insistent on this point: What would be the harm? And how long could someone possibly stick around?

I realized how smart he was to insist on this policy later when we ran into one backpacker near Lake Tahoe who gave us cause for concern. He seemed friendly at first, but soon we noticed he was subtly trying to boss us around and take charge of our decisions. When we arrived at a popular backcountry campground that evening, he tried to tell us where we should set up our tent and hang our food. We chose our own site and stashed our food in our usual way. (Later, a bear tried to get his food, but ignored ours.) The following day, we drew ahead of him when we chose to tackle a 1,000-foot elevation gain at the end of the day, and he chose not to. We didn't see him again. We did hear about another backpacker, however, who didn't find it so easy to ditch this guy. The desperate hiker finally got up very early one morning, snuck out of camp, and walked 30 miles to escape the pest.

We were not strong hikers by PCT standards—we never reached the 30-mile-a-day pace many backpackers achieve—so we wouldn't have been able to outrace a strong hiker really determined to keep up with us. And time-wise, we couldn't afford to take unscheduled zero days to let an unwanted companion get well ahead of us. Luckily, the few people we met whom we disliked either fell behind or dropped out, sparing us any unpleasant confrontations.

For the most part, it was just each other we had to deal with, on and off the trail, which was good sometimes and not so good at other times. Niceness and politeness in particular took a severe beating during the last few weeks we spent preparing for the trail. It wasn't easy for friends and relatives to be around us during this period, especially one friend who stayed with us the last few days and then drove us all the way to the border. Gary and I were up past midnight every night counting supplies, putting precise numbers of vitamin pills in Ziploc bags, estimating toilet paper use, and so on. Then we'd get up after only a few hours of sleep to get Mary off to school. What with the stress and lack of rest, we became the classic Mr. and Mrs. Bicker, snapping at each other and generally leaving behind all pretense of a respectful relationship. The stress didn't end when we thought we were ready to leave the house. Our friend, Mary, and I were in our cars and actually had our seat belts fastened when Gary decided we couldn't leave. He didn't feel confident that every last little item had been adequately and redundantly and obsessively counted and packed and checked. We got out of the cars and I called my sister, Carol, in Carson City to let her know our arrival would be delayed by one day (we were going to leave one car at her house). I ordered Chinese takeout, and then we spent another night in Sunol. The next day we finally did get going.

Thru-hikers sometimes have to be brutally honest with each other. As the leader of our little group, Ol' Cap'n Bligh had, on occasion, to lay out some unpleasant truths. Gary had been involved in two expeditions to Denali in Alaska—one successful, one not—and he knew from those and other experiences that an expedition is doomed if it has the kind of group dynamics that value niceness and politeness at the expense of honesty and attention to detail. He frequently challenged us, and his remarks sometimes seemed hypercritical. But hurt feelings are a small price to pay for safety.

Nine years earlier, when he was preparing for his first expedition up 20,320-foot Denali, Gary was anxious, short-tempered, and frequently frustrated with everything that had to be done. This climb was fulfilling a dream Gary had pursued for many years, and I naively assumed that the last few months would be a time of happy anticipation, rather like a child's run-up to Christmas. Silly me. About two months before he was due to fly to Anchorage, I came down with a cough bad enough to send me to the doctor. He diagnosed bronchitis, and put me on antibiotics. Then Mary, just 16 months old, acquired a deep, racking cough unlike anything she'd ever suffered. This time, the pediatrician took a nasal swab, and the next day she gave us the shocking diagnosis: whooping cough. We'd all been immunized and, furthermore, we thought whooping cough had gone the way of smallpox and polio, no more to be found in the developed world. We were wrong. The next thing I knew, Mary and I were spending the night in an isolation ward at the Kaiser Permanente hospital in Walnut Creek. There, she had a little gizmo shining a light through her finger so her blood oxygen could be measured, and every few hours she coughed so badly that she would throw up. Gary got sick, too, and he and Mary were quarantined for a week at home while the antibiotics took effect. And in the middle of all this, our beloved elderly cat died. With Gary's training schedule in disarray and his health in question, he seemed to me both insensitive and selfish. I really hadn't grasped that with a major mountaineering effort in his near future, he had to look out for himself more than for us. He had to be picky and self-centered if he wanted to survive. But I didn't know that. By the time I took him to the airport, I was ready to tear up the return half of his ticket.

So in 2004, it came as no surprise to me that we were at our worst during those frantic last days. But we were hardly unique in that regard. Many thru-hikers also start the trail in something less than an ideal frame of mind. There are others whose leave-takings with spouses are tense, whose parents are reluctant to let them go, who wonder if relationships will survive or erode during the next six months. Those people are out there, but they don't talk about it on the trail.

Once people start hiking, they generally shake off all those doubts and stresses, at least for the first few weeks. All that really matters is that they're finally walking. Everything lies ahead, and only Mexico lies behind.

●　●　●　●　●

WITH THE STRESS OF PREPARATIONS finally over, we began our hike as a family. And, of course, as a family, the dynamics of how we behaved at home continued on the trail. A complete change of surroundings didn't change the fact that Mary and Gary share many personality characteristics, including stubbornness. This made for more than one tense day in the backcountry. As for getting out of camp in the morning—well! Any parent who has ever shouted at a dilatory child to "for heaven's sake, find your shoes and put them on before the school bus gets here" can understand perfectly well what it was like for us. (How Mary could misplace so many personal items in the confines of a 6-by-8-foot tent is a mystery to this day.) We accomplished many goals during our six months of hiking together, but achieving quick starts in the morning wasn't one of them.

Nonetheless, backpacking as a trio was wonderful. We were never lonely, on the trail or off. The longed-for but sometimes disturbing phone calls home that thru-hikers make during town stops, with their reminders that loved ones are far away and relationships and responsibilities are being neglected, didn't trouble us. Our most important relationships were moving up the trail right along with us. The PCT became a shared experience we can draw on for context the rest of our lives. A day featuring particularly heavy rainfall will always be "an Olallie day," and an unexpected treat will be "like that Gatorade near Bear Valley." If I want to warn Mary that a new acquaintance strikes me as untrustworthy, I need only say, "He reminds me of Zeke."

Having Mary along set us apart from the multitude of what some people refer to as "hiker trash." Her presence guaranteed us a warm welcome and often an admiring audience at many of our stops. As a pre-teen attempting to walk from Mexico to Canada in one year, Mary inspired scores of parents to reconsider their own children's outdoor experiences and ambitions. As trail celebrities, in a minor way, we occasionally enjoyed greetings such as, "Are you the famous 10-year-old?" (from a teacher hiking near Kennedy Meadows in the southern Sierra) and, "So you're the famous family!" (from the postmistress at Belden in northern California). When everything from our feet to our feelings was hurting, the open admiration we encountered gave us a tremendous boost.

When we returned home, adjusting to routine life was made infinitely easier because of the shared nature of the experience. Solo thru-hikers in particular often find it terribly difficult to make that transition, because there is no one who can hold up the other end of the conversation. True, everyone asks questions, but they're invariably the same questions. Once the returning hiker has explained

Day 13 today was Mom's Birthday. I drew a heart.

Then we all sang Happy Birthday to her. She liked it alot! We hiked early to a cash, where

we got water. Then we hiked up a steep hill, and I ran down to carry my water bottle.

Then we had a damp camp on a hill.

how boxes of supplies are mailed to post offices and how food is protected from bears, conversations usually revert to the latest news about jobs and politics and vacation trips to Disneyland. As Triple Crowner Jackie McDonnell put it in *Yogi's PCT Handbook*, her guide to all things PCT, "They'll never understand."

In our self-assumed role as crusaders for childhood exercise, Gary and I spent a fair amount of time talking to people we met along the PCT and explaining how it was that two 50-somethings and a 10-year-old could tackle a 2,650-mile trail. We told them all about our family values of exercise, good nutrition, and healthy living.

But as we worked our way up the trail, many of our other family values fell by the wayside or had to be adapted for the trail. I spent a lot of time thinking about these as we progressed on the trail:

EQUALITY: At home, I am the breadwinner, while Gary is a stay-at-home father. We spend most holidays with my family, but we fly East every year to visit his friends and relatives. I do the cooking, Gary does the laundry. I pay the bills, he keeps the cars running. We both wash the dishes. Sounds like the very model of a modern-day marriage based on equality between the sexes, but put us on the trail and it all disappears. I told Gary before we even started, "There are going to be times when I am too cold, wet, hungry, and miserable to even think. At those times, you will have to take charge, tell me what to do, and tell me in words of one syllable. Don't worry about hurting my feelings." Several times, I stood alongside the trail, cold, wet, and hungry, and moaned to Gary, "What shall I do?" Groan, whine, whimper. And Gary, who was also cold, wet, and hungry, would tell me what to do.

Now, I'm not totally insensitive. There were plenty of times when I resented Gary's commands. I'd think to myself, just you wait until we get home! I'm going to tell you just where to put the dishes and just how to wash the clothes and just how to vacuum the living room rug! And I'll use that same snarky, sarcastic tone of yours, you jerk. There were times when I thoroughly understood the homicidal feelings some people hold toward the leader of an expedition. Several years ago, I read the book *Shadows on the Wasteland*, by an Englishman who skied across the Antarctic with another explorer. The author, Mike Stroud, described his feelings on an earlier expedition—an effort to reach the North Pole unsupported by dogs, machines, or air drops—toward his partner, Ranulph Fiennes. Each pulled a heavy sled, and they had a gun to use against polar bears. It was clear from the start that Fiennes was the stronger of the two, and he was usually way ahead. This bothered Stroud. A lot. In fact, it bothered him so much that one day he concocted an elaborate plot by which he would catch up with his partner, pull out the rifle, and *kapow*! Death to the evil one. He would throw the body into the ocean, and make up a story about a polar bear and a frozen gun. He could call off the trip and still go home a hero. I never got quite to that point of resentment on the many days when I had trouble keeping up with Gary, either because I had to stay back with Mary or because I just couldn't move that fast. On the other hand, I didn't carry a weapon, either.

There were times when Gary reminded me of the tyrannical Captain Bligh in the movie version of *Mutiny on the Bounty*. But Gary didn't want to be a trail dictator. Rather, he put considerable effort into teaching us how to be more independent.

It was a hard job. Take our packs. I thought because I had been carrying a backpack on our vacation trips for more than 10 years that I knew how to assemble one. Nope. I didn't know squat. Gary had shown me how to pack, but somehow I hadn't absorbed the reasoning behind the lesson. Finally, he had to line up Mary and me and give us a demonstration: light, bulky things like sleeping bags and down jackets in the bottom. Then the heavier things higher up, and close to the body. He repeatedly emphasized that point: Everything heavy should be packed so that it's in the top half of the pack, and as close to the hiker's body as possible. Water bottles should be arranged so they won't slosh—and on hot days, they should be insulated with clothing to retain their morning coolness. Gary is a slow, meticulous packer, much to the irritation of more slapdash packers—me, for example. But once Gary gets moving, he doesn't have to stop to adjust the contents of his pack. I started each day determined to emulate him, but it never seemed to work out. When Gary distributed items of mutual use among us, I ended up carrying each day's food bag and the trowel bag, which contained the trowel, toilet paper, baby wipes, and Ziploc bags for used toilet paper. (We carried out all of our toilet paper so that it wouldn't be dug up by animals or uncovered by wind and water. Too many popular backpacking routes nowadays are lined with used toilet paper, and we didn't want to contribute to the unsightly result.) Every time we stopped, I had to pull out at least the food bag, probably the trowel bag, and frequently smaller items such as the foot-treatment kit, sunscreen, and insect repellent. I never could seem to get everything back in quite the same order as when I'd started. As a result, my pack would gradually become unbalanced and tilt to one side, adding to any other resentments I had picked up during the day.

A few weeks later, Gary gave us another lecture, this time about toilet paper. We had been on the trail more than a week since Kennedy Meadows and still had several days to go before reaching Vermilion Valley Resort, our next resupply point. I was suffering from a bit of diarrhea, so I was using more toilet paper than planned. Gary was shocked to discover we were getting low on the precious stuff, and even more shocked to learn that Mary and I fell into the category of people who wad up their t.p. before using it (a wasteful habit, in Gary's opinion), rather than tidily and frugally folding it. Fifteen years of marriage, and he'd just now figured this out. This time, Gary lined us up and proceeded to give a drill sergeant's rendition of Personal Hygiene 101. "You don't have to use more than eight sheets of paper per day!" he exclaimed. "You don't wad it up! You fold it in half, and use it, and then fold it in half again. And then you use it again, and fold it up and use it one more time!" All of this was accompanied by appropriate hand gestures and body posture to indicate how to accomplish the goal. Gary was dead serious about this. Running out of toilet paper is no laughing matter. But Mary and I couldn't help ourselves. We kept seeing him through the eyes of a possible stranger traipsing down the trail and coming across our little tableau. We just couldn't keep from giggling. However, we did take the lesson to heart, and rationed our cherished toilet paper carefully until we got to Vermilion Valley.

Stream crossings brought out the worst in me. Gary has good balance and can cross rushing streams on slippery rocks or teetering logs. Mary can, too. I take one look at anything less sturdy than an Army Corps of Engineers bridge and freak out.

Usually, our stream crossings went like this:

Captain Bligh: Well, don't just stand there, look for a good way across.

Nellie Bly: Hmm ...

Scrambler: I'll just wade across.

Captain Bligh: No, you won't. You'll hurt your feet on those sharp rocks. And it takes forever to get your boots and socks back on. Here, look, this log goes halfway across, and then you just step on that boulder, jump over there, and you're done.

Scrambler: Hmph.

Nellie Bly: Looks impossible to me.

Captain Bligh: Just watch. ... See? All done.

Nellie Bly: Hmph.

Scrambler: Hey, look at me!

Captain Bligh and Nellie Bly: Be careful!

Captain Bligh: Very good, Scrambler. Now you, Nellie.

Nellie Bly: I'm sure there's a better place downstream ...

Captain Bligh: No, there's not. Now just come across or we'll be here all day!

Nellie Bly: I'll try ... Oh! ... Ouch! ... Oof! ... Aaaaggghhh!

Stream: Splashhhh!

THRIFT: Frugality was another family value that disappeared. It vanished long before we even got on the trail. On the "You might be a thru-hiker ..." list posted at one trail angel's home in southern California, an item reads, "If your REI dividend last year was over $150." REI, or Recreational Equipment, Inc., is the giant co-op based in Washington state. (I think of the Seattle store as the REI mother ship.) It returns to each member a dividend of about 10 percent of what that person spent the previous year. For a family of three determined to replace every last piece of heavy, outdated gear with the lightest and most modern stuff possible, $150 is chicken feed. Our dividend from REI for 2003 was $318.18, and REI was only one of the many places we shopped. When it arrived in the mail, I just stared at it. I couldn't imagine how we could have spent more than $3,000 at REI alone.

Gary and I dislike spending money. He buys his jeans from Goodwill, just like fashion-conscious high school students, although not for the same reason. I'm still wearing outfits to work that date from the Carter administration. (The trick is to change jobs every time the White House switches parties. That way, co-workers don't notice how your wardrobe never changes, year after year.) But when it came to equipping ourselves for the PCT, money was no object. I had to stifle my objections every few days when I'd come home from work and Gary would tell me he had tracked down just the right jacket, or the world's lightest ice ax, or that he had finally found a tent that would hold the three of us but still weigh less than 6 pounds. The credit card bills began mounting. And that was nothing compared to our on-the-trail expenditures. I'm famous for tracking down inexpensive motels—I once wrote a newspaper article about the techniques involved in finding cheap but comfortable lodging—and I've been trained since childhood to scrutinize the prices on a restaurant menu a whole lot more carefully than the menu items themselves. But those habits of a lifetime soon disappeared.

We started out well. Our town stop plans called for lodging at Motel 6-type establishments and eating at diners or fast-food places. But, oh, how that changed as we worked our way north. As most of the other thru-hikers fell by the wayside, so did our sales resistance. In Mojave, in southern California, we paid about $60 for a night at White's Motel, and ate at McDonald's. At Echo Lake, we bought sandwiches and fruit smoothies at the lodge, but eschewed the temptations of a motel night in South Lake Tahoe, camping at Aloha Lake, instead. At Belden, we cheerfully paid $85 for a cabin, ate any hot food the bar had to offer, and scoured the little store for extras. And by the time we'd suffered the rains of Oregon, we were ready for the Timberline Lodge on the slopes of Mt. Hood. I'm glad we slept and ate at Timberline, because we'll probably never do it again. We could never afford it. Pay $125 for one small room? Fork over $25 for a plate of fish and veggies? Granted, fish at the Timberline isn't anything like the stuff Long John Silver's calls fish. Oh, no. Fish at the Timberline is baked Alaskan halibut in chipotle apricot glaze, with lobster risotto, pickled onions, and organic asparagus on the side. Or it might be Pacific ahi, crusted with toasted coriander and ginger, paired with a crispy macadamia nut sushi roll, Chinese snow cabbage slaw, and sweet orange soy reduction over more of that organic asparagus. And it's not served by a pimply teenager stabbing a finger at the food symbols on a cash register, but by a waitress who's pursuing a Ph.D. at Oregon State University in her spare time. On the other hand, we probably came out ahead by the time we finished breakfast the next morning. For $12.50 apiece, we got the all-you-can-eat breakfast buffet, and by the time we finished, all we could do was lie on our comfortable beds and groan. While we were eating, other lodgers came in, ate, and left, then more came in, ate, and left, then more. In all, we gobbled our way through the equivalent of three shifts of diners, and even got free beignets.

MANNERS: I tried. I really tried to develop a salty vocabulary on the trail. But my good Lutheran upbringing wouldn't let me do it. I managed an occasional "hell" if I not only slipped on a boulder but banged both shins while crossing an ice-cold Sierra stream. And I managed to squeeze out a few "damns" here and there when the mosquitoes per square inch of skin exceeded a dozen, or when I stubbed a blistered toe for the tenth time in one day, or when I realized that the road crossing we'd just reached still left us 10 miles short of the campsite I had confidently anticipated seeing in just half an hour. But I never became any good at it. Gary, on the other hand, swore like the proverbial sailor, and used up the entire family's quota of cuss words in an average morning. Mary, being 10, was the manners police officer for all of us. Ask the parents of most any grade-school child, and they'll tell you how that works. Little Miss Enforcer never missed a chance to remind us that good manners could and should continue on the trail. And Gary never missed a chance to push her buttons.

Somehow, I always found myself in the middle of these discussions, which usually went something like this:

Captain Bligh: Burrrrpppppp!

Scrambler *(after waiting for a good three seconds)*: Daddy, say, "Excuse me."

Captain Bligh: Daddy say excuse me.

Scrambler: Daddy! Say, "Excuse me"!

Captain Bligh: Say excuse me!

Scrambler *(louder and more agitated)*: Daddy! Excuse yourself!

Captain Bligh: Excu—

Nellie Bly: Oh, shut up, both of you!

Captain Bligh and Scrambler *(in unison)*: We don't use that language in this family!

Nellie Bly: Well, *excuuuuuuse* me!

CLEANLINESS: Hah! Normally the kind of people who obsess over showers and clean clothes, we were the trail's dirtiest hikers. Others somehow found time to take dips in lakes and streams, but slowpokes that we were, we always seemed to have barely enough daylight to get from tent site to tent site, eat, and sleep.

It got to the point that Mary found clean people objectionable because the fragrance of their soap, shampoo, and deodorant was too strong. We have photos of our legs as black as obsidian from shorts-level to socks-line. We did wash our hands after every "bathroom break," which is more than many backpackers can say. But without soap, our hands always looked grimy. And our fingernails were just filthy.

I hadn't always felt so comfortable with dirt. When Gary and I first started backpacking, I insisted on taking along enough clean socks and underwear to put on fresh pairs every day, and enough T-shirts to change every other day. I would bathe in cold streams if nothing better was available. Gradually, I learned that I didn't need clean clothes to survive, and that just because I smelled as bad as a three-day-old corpse, I wouldn't automatically become one. On the PCT, we each carried two sets of clothing—shirt, underwear, and pants—and wore one set between each pair of town stops, saving the clean set to put on after our showers while the dirty clothes were being laundered. The one thing we carried an ample supply of was socks. We realized early on that dirty, gritty socks contributed to foot problems, and on many days in northern California, I spent my snack breaks washing socks in the dwindling creeks, downstream from where Gary was filtering water. We would dry the wet socks by hanging them over the horizontal straps on the outsides of our packs, cinched tight so nothing would fall off. In case there was any doubt, this clearly identified us as thru-hikers. After Captain Bligh spilled a bit of macaroni and cheese on his trousers during dinner, Mary wrote a brief journal entry that summed up the state of our personal hygiene: "Dad spilled food on himself. He thinks he'll smell like sour milk. What's the difference?"

Our hygiene was a little better when it came to food, although we occasionally ate something that had touched the ground briefly, as long as it didn't look dirty, and there were no cows around. I forget who told us the M&M riddle, but it came to express my views pretty accurately:

Question: How can you tell different kinds of hikers apart?

Answer: Put a red M&M on the ground. A dayhiker will step on it. A section hiker will step over it. A thru-hiker will pick it up and eat it.

PRIVACY: In a tiny tent? Gimme a break. We did have our customs that provided a little privacy. I would wake up first, get into my clothes, and then wake the others. Mary, being so small, figured out how to dress inside her sleeping bag. Once we were both out, Gary would dress. But there were plenty of times when we all had to change clothes at once, and just ignore each other. Bathroom breaks were no problem during the first several weeks—we were among the first on the trail, and during April and May, we often went for days without seeing a soul. When nature called, I would just step a few feet off the trail and squat while Gary and Mary traveled on. (When it was Mary's turn, I stayed with her.) But on the more popular sections, I got caught a couple times. Luckily, the two men near the San Joaquin River in southern California pretended they hadn't seen me. The seven or so hikers near Thielsen Creek made believe that being mooned on the trail was just another part of the Oregon outdoor experience.

FOLLOWING THE RULES: For backpackers, Gary and I are on the obsessive side of the ledger when it comes to obeying regulations. We get permits to hike, we get permits to camp, we fill out all the forms, we follow the rules about fires, and we stuff our dollar bills in those little "iron rangers" if no live rangers are there to collect our money. We're that way in private life, too. We pay our bills on time, drive the speed limit (OK, I go 5 miles per hour over), and never miss a vehicle registration deadline. We started out on the PCT with every intention of continuing our straight-arrow ways. Gary wrote in for our trail permits and paid for the Whitney stamps so we could climb the highest peak in the lower 48 states without worrying about hassles at the top. (Only a few thru-hikers skip the permit stage, but many don't bother getting the Whitney stamp.) We generally camped where we were supposed to, never built a fire, disturbed no archaeological treasures, and harassed no endangered species.

But as we moved north, we discovered that you can't do the trail and still follow all the rules. In serious bear country, we were really careful about food storage, but there were rainy nights in Oregon when we slept with our food in the tent. As for campsites—there were places where we just couldn't obey every last regulation. I particularly remember a long section of trail approaching Castle Crags State Park in northern California. The guidebook noted that camping was illegal for several miles before the park border, because the trail ran through private property. And it was also illegal to put up a tent once inside the state park, where camping was allowed only in established campgrounds, and the trail didn't go through them. Thanks to water concerns and other logistics, there wasn't a way we could avoid camping somewhere in that stretch. Imagine my complete lack of surprise when, just before the park border, we found a spot where people obviously camped quite often, sometimes in large numbers. We stayed there, too. We bent the rules as little as possible, but without some bending, it would have been very difficult to finish.

We also went from purists to pragmatists when it came to staying on the official Pacific Crest Trail. We all agreed on our definition of a thru-hike: Walk all the way from Mexico to Canada in one calendar year, with all sections linked together on foot. (For example, if we had to skip a section due to a forest fire, which often happens to PCT thru-hikers, we would have to go back and walk it after finishing the rest of the trail.) We also started out determined to stick with the trail as much as possible. During our town stop in Idyllwild, we engaged in a long discussion of whether we did wrong to take an alternate route, the Little Tahquitz Valley Trail, when we couldn't stay on the official route because it was buried under snow and I kept falling down. My feeling was that the detour was perfectly OK. Bolstering my opinion was the fact that another hiker, Walks Alone, had to drop out because he broke his collarbone falling on the slippery official route. That could have easily happened to me. As we moved north, we kept it official as much as possible, but when the weather began to worsen, we took occasional alternate routes, especially if they were recommended in the guidebook. Taking an alternate route sometimes was safer, but not always. The closest we came to risking death was in September when we decided to walk around Russell and Milk creeks because of their reputation for danger during rainy weather, which—this being Oregon—we had seen a lot of. From Pamelia Lake, we hiked down to a highway, and the next day had to walk through a construction area that put us right smack in the path of high-speed traffic. I still shiver, thinking about those huge vehicles hurtling down on Mary as we rushed along the road.

PUNCTUALITY: When Mary was born, the reputation for punctuality that Gary and I had built up took a severe hit. As new parents, we had an excuse. But on the PCT, there was no excuse for our inability to get out of camp more quickly each morning. Three hours to break camp and get walking, without even cooking a hot breakfast? Good grief. The most humiliating day was the time we camped with a thru-hiker with the trail name of Pineneedle at Spanish Needle Creek two days before Kennedy Meadows, which marks the end of the southern California section of the trail. We had a 25-mile day ahead of us with significant altitude gain and loss, so we got up at 4:30 a.m. We did cook breakfast that morning, probably because we had more freeze-dried food left than any other kind. We really pushed hard and managed to get out of camp at 7:10. Meanwhile, Pineneedle woke up at 6:30 a.m. and left at 7. He just got up, packed up his tent and so on, put on his boots, and hit the trail. Amazing. We weren't any better at sticking to our original schedule, which called for us to finish the PCT in early October. We lost a day or two in the first seven weeks through the desert, then lost another four days because it took us so long to complete our resupply work while we were at home after our June trip to Maryland. We took unplanned zero days at Vermilion Valley, Carson City, and again at Cascade Locks, Oregon, when I realized I would have to leave the trail temporarily for dental and medical treatment. We had to spend a day at the Portland REI buying a two-person tent for Gary and Mary to continue with, plus some cold-weather gear. We lost so many days that when we finally headed into a late-October snowstorm in hopes of completing the final stretch of Washington state, we were the last people on the trail.

SIMPLICITY: We're not Luddites, honest. We decided, years ago, for perfectly logical reasons, against having a television set at home (and thus no VCR, no video games, and no video cameras). Same goes for cordless phones and cell phones. So it was ironic that when we headed out on the trail to spend time outside of civilization, we were lugging a video camera, a cell phone, and a new digital camera that we didn't even figure out how to use properly until halfway through California. The digital camera replaced the film cameras we had used and abused over the years to the point of unreliability. The video camera was for shooting film for a documentary that died stillborn but that seemed like a good idea at the time. And the cell phone was for calling motels and arranging rides along the way. Many backpackers whose houses are loaded with the latest technological wizardry deliberately eschew all gadgets on the trail. Some don't even carry a camera or a wristwatch. We felt as though we were the last people in the English-speaking world to acquire a cell phone, but once we had it, we were glad we had brought it along. It's no good for emergencies—there's hardly any cell phone coverage in the backcountry—but it was very useful for calling for a ride from the trailhead and for calling friends and relatives when motels lacked working telephones.

We didn't carry a TV with us, of course, but we watched more television while we were thru-hikers than we ordinarily see in an entire year. At almost every town stop, we'd check into a motel. And before long, Gary and Mary would be glued to the screen. Channel surfing drives me into a homicidal rage, so I generally retreated to a corner of the room with the newspaper and tried to ignore the monster truck pulls, cooking programs, historical re-enactments, and ancient cartoons they were watching. I couldn't help noticing that at one town stop in Oregon, Mary watched *The Matrix*, which struck me as not entirely suitable for a 10-year-old. But I decided to let Gary be the adult that night, as far as monitoring the TV went.

Living without television at home is a major plus for anyone who wants to have a family that's seriously involved in outdoor adventure. That wasn't why we got rid of ours before Mary was born (we did that because we feel television is the biggest time-waster ever invented), but it turned out to be a big help. Without spoon-fed electronic entertainment, children grow up learning how to create their own entertainment, indoors and out. They learn to be content with a lightweight paperback book for relaxation, and to focus on the real world long enough to watch a hummingbird visit a feeder or a deer climb a hill. In the wilderness, Mary likes to braid pine needles while walking, and in camp she depends on her imagination to create stories around the towns she builds with rocks, twigs, and pinecones. Kids who grow up with TV are attuned to fast-moving, all-engrossing entertainment, and it's hard for them to make the transition to the slow-moving natural world. But for Mary, no TV and no VCR meant she grew up without knowing quite all the characters on the Cartoon Network, without memorizing all the lyrics to *The Little Mermaid*, and without playing video games. And thus, she didn't miss them on the trail.

ENVIRONMENTALISM: I should have felt really good about this one. We followed Leave No Trace standards as much as possible, including packing out our toilet paper, which is more than most hikers do. And, of course, we weren't burning any gasoline on the trail. But although we didn't drive a car for most of the time, I made up for it during the last month, driving about 5,000 miles to get home, get back up to Washington, play trail angel all over the state—including side trips to Yakima and Seattle—and then finally go home again. In the end, I probably drove as many miles as if I'd never set foot on the PCT that year.

* * * * *

IN SPITE OF THE CHANGES we made to our family values on the trail, the one we did retain, without compromise, was togetherness. It may have been horrid, as Mary suggested in her journal entry at the beginning of this chapter. Sometimes we were so much on the outs with each other, I thought we'd never be on speaking terms again. But we've always been a close family, and it was that willingness to stay close, no matter how badly we wanted to divorce and disown each other, that formed us into a group capable of taking on almost any challenge. The hardest thing for all of us was when we split up in September, when I had to return home briefly for medical treatment, and Gary and Mary had to continue without me. And the happiest day for me was when we teamed up again in Mazama, Washington, to take on the frozen barrier of the North Cascades. We were worried, we were stressed, we were in some degree of danger. But we were together again.

CHaPTeR 3

BacKPacKeRs A To z

Day 123: *It was cold, windy, and foggy. We almost got lost around Grouse Hill. The high point was definitely meeting Scott Williamson. He told us a lot, like how people often got sick around Crater Lake, and the South Brown Mountain Shelter well water was highly suspect. He carried a little rubber ducky! Got to camp, dark and damp.*

—from Scrambler's journal

BACKPACKERS ARE MY KIND OF PEOPLE. When Gary, Mary, and I attended our first Annual Day Zero Pacific Crest Trail Kick Off (ADZPCTKO) at Lake Morena County Campground, I looked at the collection of long-haired hippie types, the talkative, gregarious types, and the shy, hopeful, and helpful types all exchanging tips on gear, sharing sunscreen, looking out for each other's dogs and children, and volunteering in droves for kitchen duty, and felt right at home. To some extent, they reminded me of the people I got to know during my year as a member of the Lutheran Volunteer Corps, when I lived in Baltimore with five other volunteers and worked for an inner-city health clinic writing newsletters, raising money, and lobbying at the Statehouse. Members of both groups are, for the most part, young or young-at-heart, well-read, and college-educated or self-educated. Both groups include significant numbers of vegetarians, amateur musicians, and pacifists. They're comfortable with eccentrics, uncomfortable with ideologues, and generally opposed to litterbugs, war, and the destruction of the environment. Most of all, they're smart, healthy, and determined to achieve their goals.

Roughly 200 to 300 people make it their goal to thru-hike the 2,650 miles of the Pacific Crest Trail every year. There aren't any official demographic numbers on PCT thru-hikers, but judging from our observations, young men with middle-class backgrounds and college educations make up a slight majority. It would be misleading to envision a "typical" PCT thru-hiker. More women are hiking than ever before, as well as more senior citizens and more people from other countries. We met people who worked in construction or waited tables for a living, along with a sprinkling of Ph.Ds.

Our encounters with backpackers run counter to the picture some news accounts try to draw of thru-hikers, painting them as tortured souls and social misfits. Even professional journalists, whose job it is to explain unusual people and events to their readers and to demolish stereotypes rather than reinforce them, seem to have trouble getting past their preconceptions. All too often, they portray thru-hikers as freaks or lonely losers, people trying (usually without success) to escape the past or find the future, to prove something, or to discover the meaning of life.

During our six months on the PCT, we met 45 or 50 people who were attempting a thru-hike, plus many more who were walking shorter sections. On the whole, these folks were so healthy and normal that I often forgot that they were attempting to do something extraordinary. Typically, these people were taking advantage of a natural pause in life to fit in some adventure. Many had just graduated from college, or were between college and graduate school. Others had been laid off or bought out, and hit the PCT before their next serious job searches. Many ordinary Americans do the same thing, although their "adventures" are more likely to involve a few months of sightseeing or maybe volunteer work. I'm not trying to suggest that thru-hikers are ordinary—they're not. And while we often urged parents we met along the way to take their kids backpacking, we would never suggest they tackle something on the order of the PCT without working up to it. That would be like suggesting that anyone with an ordinary level of physical fitness and a spare $60,000 can safely climb Mt. Everest. But neither are backpackers very different from the mainstream.

One of the characteristics that does set thru-hikers apart from the mainstream is their use of nicknames during their time on the trail, and even afterward. For some backpackers, acquiring a trail name is a matter of great consequence. Others use them but don't attach much importance to them. And some very serious and even famous thru-hikers never do acquire trail names. The trail name tradition is generally considered to have begun on the Appalachian Trail. But the custom of assuming, or assigning, nicknames related to an intense experience goes back much further. The military in particular seems to generate nicknames that are based on experiences only other members of the unit can appreciate.

Trail names also serve a practical purpose. They are an easy way for thru-hikers to establish an identity within the group. Since there are no professional guides on the long trails, and no one individual is responsible for looking out for us, we learn to watch out for each other. If someone named Jim or Karen doesn't show up as expected at a trail angel's house or at a road crossing, it's going to be pretty hard to track down that particular Jim or Karen because they are such common names. But if word goes out that Sandpiper is overdue, or that Chocoholic left his camera and his passport at the Summit Inn, the trail community can focus on the right person and solve the mystery, sometimes with amazing speed.

A couple years after our PCT trek, I mentioned to Mary that a columnist in a southern California newspaper made fun of people who use trail names, suggesting it's pretentious and immature. Mary thought seriously for a while, and then opined that while people's "real" names are important, sometimes the trail names they choose, or which are chosen for them, become their "true" names. (Other times, of course, they're meant to be a joke and are taken as such.)

· · · · ·

WHEN WE BEGAN THE PCT, like all prospective thru-hikers, we looked forward to awesome scenery and unforgettable trail experiences. By the time we finished, like all successful thru-hikers, we realized that many of our best memories were of the people we met along the way, and of the relationships we formed with them. That's why our fellow backpackers deserve a chapter of their own. That's also why I've chosen to present real people, rather than the composite characters found in many books about outdoor adventures. And rather than pseudonyms, I'm sticking with people's actual names—first, or first and last, whichever they tend to use—or their chosen trail names. Some were thru-hikers, others section hikers, and some were just out for a long weekend. They're arranged alphabetically by the names they prefer or by the names for which they are best known in the thru-hiking community.

ALICE AND PAUL were heading north from Muir Pass on a cool, rainy July 3, when they spotted us taking a break among some junipers. They swung by to say hello and offer us their extra food. From then on, we saw them almost every day until they left the PCT eight days later at Tuolumne Meadows to complete their south-to-north journey on the John Muir Trail. (The 211-mile JMT coincides with the PCT along most of its length, but splits off at the north end to drop down to Yosemite Village, and at the south end to summit Mt. Whitney.) Each time we parted, we'd say a final goodbye—only to see them again the next day. One day, Gary, Mary, and I topped a pass south of Yosemite to discover someone had spelled out a message in rocks. As soon as I stopped tripping over the rocks and figured out what it said—HI SCRAMBLER—I knew who had left it.

Paul and Alice had met through a mutual interest in organic chemistry at the University of California-Irvine. After they married, they went to work for a big pharmaceutical company, only to be laid off after it merged with an even bigger company. Paul had thru-hiked the PCT several years earlier, but the John Muir

Trail was Alice's first major backpacking trip. An attractive couple in their early 30s, they were among the finest people we met, not to mention the smartest. They were excellent conversationalists and took a strong liking to Mary. A year after we met them, they moved to California from the Midwest, eventually settling in Berkeley, where Alice attended the University of California's Boalt Hall School of Law, and Paul launched a career in forensics and criminology research.

BRIAN AND CARYL, whom we first met at the Kennedy Meadows campground in June, were long-distance bicyclists and strong hikers. Brian is only a few years younger than Gary and me, and Caryl is a few years younger than Brian, so they were among the older people on the trail. But they have the strong, youthful look of people who keep in top physical condition all the time. We ran into them again on Glen Pass and at Vermilion Valley Resort, and expected they would finish the PCT without difficulty. But on July 15, we met them again at Sonora Pass—and this time, Caryl was on crutches. They had taken an alternate route through Section I, in hopes of avoiding the notorious elevation losses and gains in Yosemite National Park's high country. At their third crossing of Matterhorn Creek, Caryl tossed her boots onto the opposite bank while she crossed in her spare shoes. Unfortunately, one boot didn't make it all the way across and began floating downstream. While scrambling after it, Caryl slipped and cracked her kneecap. They had to hike out several miles before the Mono County Volunteer Search and Rescue team met them and took them to a hospital. Several weeks after we saw them at Sonora Pass, the fracture had mostly healed and they resumed the trail, but by now it was mid-September. A month later, with a winter storm threatening, they called it quits at Castle Crags State Park, and made plans to resume their PCT journey from that point the following summer.

Unlike many in the outdoor recreation community who can only dream about such a life, Caryl and Brian quit working to spend all their time bicycling, hiking, and traveling the world. They gave up their engineering careers in the aerospace industry several years before we met them, sold their home, and determined that by careful budgeting, they could turn their passion for bicycle touring and outdoor recreation into a full-time experience. Since then, they've covered most of North America on two wheels or two feet and have seen much of South America by bus as well as bicycle. Another bicycle trip took them through Portugal, Spain, France, and the Alps. After that, they began planning a unique approach to the Continental Divide Trail: hiking the southern half of the CDT and bicycling the northern half of the more-or-less parallel Great Divide Mountain Bike Route one year, and then the next year, hiking the northern CDT and bicycling the southern half of the bike route. Caryl calls it their "thru-hike-bike."

CHACOMAN was standing on the bank of Whitney Creek, a few miles from Mt. Whitney itself, on June 26 when a clumsy female hiker slipped on the rocks and fell into the water directly in front of him, with a tremendous splash. That was me. As I scrambled out of the stream, my first sight was of a pair of sandals, next a pair of thin legs, and finally all of a very slender thru-hiker. "Sorry about that," Chacoman said, as though thru-hikers were always falling at his feet into rushing mountain streams. I felt like an idiot, but my embarrassment soon disappeared. Chacoman turned out to be one of our favorite trail people. A young computer programmer between jobs in Ohio, he was fun to talk to, made friends with Mary by treating her as an adult, and was unfailingly calm and polite. That ability to remain tranquil served him well at the end of the trail, when he tackled the notorious reroute around Glacier Peak in Washington state, and then had to wade through waist-deep snow in the North Cascades. And all this in his namesake pair of Chaco sandals.

Chacoman had a trail name without even realizing it at first. Another hiker named Kat recognized the tracks left in the trail by the distinctive tread of his Chaco Z1 sandals. After seeing the tracks for a while, she declared, to the disbelief of her hiking partners, that someone was hiking in Chacos. From then on, they referred to the unknown hiker ahead of them as Chacoman. Later, they caught up with him at Pioneer Mail in southern California, where Kat immediately looked down at his feet and declared, "Look, it's Chacoman."

Like us, Chacoman hiked the PCT three years after the events of September 11, 2001, which made Americans more aware of the porous U.S. border with Canada. Although the rules hadn't officially changed yet, word on the trail that year was that hikers should have a birth certificate in addition to their driver's license in order to get across the border. But by the time most of us heard about that, it was way too late. For Chacoman, serendipity eased his journey from Canada back across the border.

"I took the bus back to Seattle," he recalls. "When we approached the border, I moved to the front of the bus so I would be the first one in. That way, if I got pulled aside, there might be a chance they would finish with me before the bus was ready to leave. When I got to the immigration official, I put down my driver's license and told him I had just found out I was supposed to have my birth certificate."

This is how their conversation ensued:

Official: Where were you born?

Chacoman: Ohio.

Official: Where in Ohio?

Chacoman: Marietta.

Official: I've been there.

Chacoman: Really? That's a small town.

Official: I'm originally from Youngstown.

Chacoman: Really? Cool!

Official: Now just step up to have your pack checked, and welcome back to the U.S.

Chacoman: Thanks!

"Then I just put my pack through the machine, and I wasn't even asked to take anything out of my pockets," Chacoman says. A fine end to the trail.

CROW was named for her habit of picking up litter the way a crow will gather shiny items. Her partner, SHERPA, was named for her willingness to carry extra weight to help Crow while she recovered from the broken wrist she suffered a few weeks into the trail. They met Gary at Horseshoe Meadows, a popular entry and exit point for the High Sierra. Gary had walked down to a bear box at the campground there to retrieve a nine-day supply of food we had cached three days earlier on our way back to the trail after our three-week break. Crow and Sherpa had decided to skip part of the Sierra because Sherpa's knees were bothering her a lot. Much of the southern Sierra resembles a series of giant, rock-strewn staircases—very hard on the knees. We hooked up with them again in northern California. Crow and Sherpa, despite their youthful appearance, had raised five daughters between them, and Mary immediately recognized a pair of surrogate mothers. She and Crow, especially, took a liking to each other and enjoyed hiking together. When I checked in with Crow and Sherpa a couple years later, they had moved from Colorado to Washington state. They were studying and working at Evergreen State College, Crow in a tree canopy lab and Sherpa studying climate change and its effects on the marine environment. They, too, have the long trails bug, periodically leaving behind the comforts of home for another adventure.

GREEN BEAN AND WOOLY MAMMOTH (a.k.a. Jeremy and Courtney) are a young married couple from Decatur, Georgia, whom we met at Aloha Lake near Lake Tahoe. I admired Green Bean because he continued hiking despite an injured foot. He was wearing a walking cast, and was experimenting with variously textured substances on the bottom to keep it from slipping. At that point, he was trying a piece of old bicycle tire. He gained his trail name on the Appalachian Trail in 1999, thanks to his green T-shirt and shorts and generally tall, skinny physique. "His hiking partner told him he looked like a green bean," Courtney told me. "The name stuck—perhaps because he was afraid of ending up with a worse trail name like the one he gave his partner: Numbnut." Good decision, Jeremy.

Ironically, Courtney acquired her trail name in the desert, an unusual place for her namesake animal. "My trail name almost became 'Juicy' due to the three layers of blisters on the bottom of my feet, but I didn't really like that name; it just seemed a little gross," she says. Jeremy already had his name, but Courtney was still looking for a name when they hiked out of Pioneer Mail. Because they started out early and a chilly wind was blowing, she forgot to put on sunscreen. By the time they took a break to put sunscreen on at 10 a.m., it was too late. "By 3 p.m., my hands and thighs were covered with big red blisters that just burned like mad when the sun shone on them," Courtney recalls. She covered her hands with bandannas, but she was wearing a skirt and had no cover for her legs. She tried duct-taping Green Bean's pants legs to her skirt, but they didn't stay on. "I was never so relieved to see a big ugly tank of water (yes! water!) in the middle of some chaparral that signaled the end of our day," she says. "Well, the next day was just as sunny, but we had to hike on. My only choice was to wear my long wool underwear and gloves to cover the burned spots on my thighs and hands." For two days, Courtney hiked in this get-up in 100-plus-degree heat. (They registered 108°F in the sun at Scissors Crossing.) Luckily, it worked, and with the help of some Neosporin, the burns healed quickly.

"The next day, I was hiking along (finally sans long underwear!) and listening to some tunes, and up comes a song by Widespread Panic called 'Big Wooly Mammoth' that just seemed to exemplify my plight," Courtney says. "The song is really about evolution, but the chorus is about the big wooly mammoth having to wear his coat in the desert in the middle of the summertime. It is a great hiking song with a quick rhythm that makes you want to boogie and puts a little spring in your step." At lunchtime, Courtney told Green Bean she had found a trail name. "He didn't like it at first, but when I played the song for him, he laughed and agreed that it was appropriate," Courtney says.

Courtney's decision to do the trail with Green Bean reflects the philosophy of many thru-hikers. "There is just something wonderful about seeing nature close up and personal, and about getting a better understanding of ecosystems and how everything in nature is connected," she says. She also appreciates what she calls the juxtaposition of the reality check and the escape from reality. "The reality check is that you really don't need much to live a happy and fulfilled life—no car, no designer labels, no gourmet meals. All you really need are a few essentials and the knowledge that you can rely on yourself," Courtney explains. The escape from reality? "No cell phones ringing, no bills to pay, no blaring TV commercials, no telemarketers, no job, no schedule to keep. Your time is yours to use how you want. You don't even have your mom calling, telling you what to do (unless you're Scrambler). It's hard for non-hikers to understand how such grueling exercise is actually relaxing," she adds.

A couple years after we met Wooly Mammoth and Green Bean, they had a baby girl who was immediately christened with her own trail name, Pollywog. Within a couple months, she experienced her first backpacking trip, just as Mary did at that age. I foresee great things for little Pollywog.

HIKER 816, a.k.a. Chris, was a section hiker finishing up the trail after completing law school. We met at the end of a cold, wet, miserable day at Olallie Lake Resort, where we shared a cabin for a couple days.

Chris was another one of those backpackers whose trail name was imposed on him, rather than chosen by him. He had been hiking with a woman named Veronica and a man who went by the trail name Beaker. When they went to resupply at Echo Lake, someone had written Chris's date of arrival on his package—8/6. But the "/" looked more like a "1," and when Veronica saw it, she asked, "Why does it say 'Hiker 816'?" Then Beaker arrived, looked at the box, and said, "Hiker 816?" He was followed by a dayhiker Veronica had met about an hour earlier, and that man also asked the meaning of Hiker 816. "From that instant forward, Beaker started calling me Hiker 816," Chris says. "When I sat down by a stream to get water he would say, 'Hiker 816 obtaining H2O,' etc. The name stuck."

Chris returned to Washington, D.C., to finish up law school, and then took a clerkship with a federal district court judge in Los Angeles.

JOHN, a weekend backpacker, became part of our trail experience for only a few minutes, but he definitely made our day brighter. And it was a day that needed some brightening. Here is Mary's succinct description:

Day 30: *Today, Ma took a wrong turn and WASTED 2.5 miles. Then we met John who gave us chicken bouillon and noodles. Then we hiked to ratty Glenwood and camped there.*

Yes, I had indeed taken a wrong turn, and we had wasted time and energy going clear out to Mt. Williamson's summit on a spur trail. Also, we were running low on the snack foods we ate all day. Our appetites had increased even more than we expected after four weeks on the trail, and we were looking at the very unpleasant prospect of rationing our food. When we stopped at Cooper Canyon Trail Camp to filter water, we met John, who was walking out from a four-day backpacking trip and offered us his leftover pasta, raisins, and bouillon cubes. With the extra food on board, we were able to eat normally until our next resupply.

K-Too of Massachusetts was one of the older hikers we met, having just turned 50. He gained his name on the Appalachian Trail, where he was huddled in a shelter with several other hikers during a storm. He was one of three Kens, and to tell them apart, the other hikers named them K-1, K-2, and K-3. He altered his to K-Too.

Friendly and gentlemanly, and with a striking white beard, K-Too had a natural dignity that I found calming. Calming is a good thing on the trail as the weather worsens, which helps explain why I was so delighted to see him in the

Mazama Country Store on a cold October day with snow threatening Washington state's North Cascades. I was surprised, too. We thought he (and everyone else) had either finished the trail weeks earlier or given up. But like us, he and a few others were determined to give it one last try despite the bad odds.

LEPRECHAUN deserves that old-fashioned description: tall, dark, and handsome. He caught up with us at Hiker Heaven, a camping spot run by trail angels Jeff and Donna Saufley, in Agua Dulce. At first, the young man seemed standoffish, but soon we got to know him better. He took a particular liking to Mary. At 6-foot-7, he towered over little Scrambler, but conversationally, she was his match. When she asked him why he chose his trail name, he told her with apparent sincerity that it was because he was "small, green, and could hide easily." We last saw him striding away from us at Mojave, where he had just realized that he'd better make tracks if he wanted to get to the next water source before dark. We kept track of his progress by reading his wry remarks in trail registers at post offices and resort stores, all the way north.

MOUNTAIN TRIPPER was the first thru-hiker we met along the trail. We ran into him on a terribly hot afternoon when we reached Scissors Crossing, on Day 5. It was late afternoon, and I was totally trashed. Some trail angels had left a couple wooden chairs next to a water cache, screened from the road by tall brush. I grabbed one of the chairs, shed my pack, plunked myself down, and promptly put my head between my knees, because I was feeling so faint. But I sat up straight a moment later when a voice said, "You must be Scrambler." A tall, muscular backpacker carrying an ice ax along with the rest of his gear, stood there, smiling at us. He'd heard about us from trail angel Laurence. We saw Mountain Tripper again a couple days later when we camped near a large water cache, the "third gate cache," and again the next day when we reached Warner Springs Resort. He was going on ahead, while we were staying at the resort one night. We didn't see him again that season, although we did find a hat he had left behind.

A friendly, cheerful, but inexperienced backpacker, Mountain Tripper's name soon stopped showing up on trail registers, and we realized he had dropped out. He tried again the next year, which happened to be one of the Sierra Nevada's heaviest snow years in decades. Like many of that year's backpackers, he attempted a "flip flop" by hiking sections out of sequence in order to avoid impassable snow, forest fires, or other major inconveniences. He didn't get very far, so he tried again a third year. That time, he made it as far as northern California when an early winter storm walloped the Northwest. He emailed us for advice on snowshoes, which Gary gave him, along with advice not to risk his life. Mountain Tripper decided snow conditions were rapidly making the risk too high, and he called off his trip in November. Mountain Tripper had no particular job or home to get back to—years ago, he had quit a factory job and then spent three years helping

Day 2

We saw Mountain Tripper once again. He was heading down the trail as we were packing up and he stopped to talk. Then he went on and we left before. lol! Then we hiked through flowers until we saw to TRT thruhikers

and their in number 8 dog, cloudy. When we got to Barrel Spring, Lawrence was there. He showered us with cold drinks, fresh fruit, and pastries. There was Water Mellon and Pizza! He's great. Then we had a great

Campsite (Close to Mountain Tripper, who was at the spring) On some sand at San Esedro. When my Dad filtered water with Mountain Tripper, I shepherded a leaf all the way down the stream!

yellow

care for a bedridden uncle suffering from multiple sclerosis—and the little California town of Etna seemed like a friendly place, so he stayed. The town adopted him, and he made a living doing odd jobs and construction work, sometimes for money, sometimes for meals. That spring, he moved to Skykomish, Washington, and became part of the construction crew for the hiker dormitory being built by trail angels Andrea and Jerry Dinsmore. No doubt, he'll show up at Campo again some year soon for another try.

Wife and husband NOCONA AND BALD EAGLE, engineers from Dallas, were a little harder to get to know initially, but by the time we reached Oregon, we had become very fond of them. Not yet parents themselves, they seemed to enjoy Mary as an occasional surrogate daughter. Dark-haired and apple-cheeked Bald Eagle, whose real name is Andy, got his name before he began his Appalachian Trail thru-hike several years earlier. Prior to his AT hike, Andy's friends in Huntsville, Alabama, threw him a big going-away party, during which they took turns running an electric razor over his head. As a result, he began the AT bald, hence "Bald Eagle."

Nocona's real name is Karen, but she's gone by "Nocona" for so many years that many people who have met her on the AT or PCT only think of her that way. Karen, easily spotted in a crowd with her blond hair and beaming smile, carefully chose her name from a story from the frontier history of her native state of Texas. Years earlier, she had read a book about Cynthia Ann Parker, a child in the 1830s who was taken from her settler family's home near Fort Parker, Texas, and raised by Comanches, who at that time still ranged the Texas plains. Cynthia Parker's tribe was called "Nocona," which means "the wanderer" in their language, and the tribe member whom she eventually married also took that name.

Karen was fascinated by the tribe's lifestyle, but she was especially moved by Cynthia's story. "After her abduction, she actually identified more with the Comanche way of life than she had with her pioneer family, marrying into the Indian tribe, then dying a sad death after she was 'recaptured' by her white relatives as an older woman," Karen says. "I suppose because the story was true, I was more moved by it than I would've been by fiction."

Karen was torn between her affinity for "Nocona" as a trail name and the tradition of choosing or being given a trail name during the actual hiking experience. During the first few weeks of her Appalachian Trail hike, she waited to see if an appropriate trail name would make itself known, but nothing that was suggested seemed just right. Enlightenment arrived in Hot Springs, North Carolina, in the person of a thru-hiker with the trail name "Nyamazoola." If someone could hike the AT with a trail name like that, then certainly she could choose something equally unique. So Nocona it was.

Nocona and Bald Eagle definitely have the outdoor adventure infection. A year after we met them, they bicycled across the country, and then hiked the 300 miles of the PCT they had missed the year we met them. Somehow, Bald Eagle also managed to fit in a climb of Mt. Rainier in Washington state. A year later, Nocona and friends hiked the Wonderland Trail, the rigorous 93-mile path that winds around the same mountain. Their ambition to hike the Continental Divide Trail was postponed when they discovered they were going to become parents, but it's only a matter of time until they add that to their list of accomplishments.

PATTI HASKINS caught up with us on May 6. It had been an unusually brutal day in southern California's San Gabriel Mountains as we started our fifth week on the trail with the ascent of Mt. Baden Powell, named after the founder of the Boy Scouts. It's a magnet for Scouts from southern California, who include its summit on their conquest of the 53-mile Silver Moccasin Trail. Ice and snow made route-finding difficult. I fell enough times that when we reached the side trail to the summit, I told Gary and Mary to go ahead, I was going to sit and rest. Gary's feet were killing him and I wasn't much better off. Route-finding continued to be difficult for the rest of the day, and our doubts were strong enough that when I finally saw a PCT symbol some distance past the summit, I kissed it. Just before full dark, we were at Little Jimmy Campground, all of us complaining about our problems, when we saw a headlamp. It was Patti, a deaf athlete and big-wall climber from Yosemite, out to break the 81-day record from Mexico to Canada. We had managed only 13 miles that day; she was averaging 35. We felt like such wimps! She and Mary conversed via notebook, and then in a snap she had her tent up and her food cooked. She warned us she would be getting up at 5:30 a.m., but we didn't hear a thing. Patti finished the PCT in 105 days, but, unfortunately, she didn't set a record.

PINENEEDLE is a friendly pharmacist in his 30s from Memphis, Tennessee. Two years before we met him in the town of Mojave, he had hiked frequently with the Witchers, a Virginia family who completed the Appalachian Trail with two children about Mary's age. Although he was a very strong hiker, we managed to catch up with him every few days because at each road crossing, he would hitchhike into the nearest town to get a cup of coffee and a real meal, then he'd get a ride back to the trailhead and easily catch up with us. Tall, dark-haired Pineneedle, whose green garb matched his trail name, is the good kind of talkative thru-hiker—he likes to engage people in conversation, not just force them to be an audience. He carried a Bible, and he and I discussed church music and related topics. But he never proselytized, unlike another hiker we met in southern California. (At each water cache, this other guy was in the habit of leaving pamphlets that featured cartoon characters wearing 1940s-style clothing and hairdos. The characters are always discussing the Book of Revelation while carpooling to work, and they suddenly find themselves driverless when the rapture strikes.)

I remember Pineneedle's brief hesitation when I asked him what he did for a living. After a short pause, he admitted to me that he's a pharmacist—almost as though he were actually saying, "I'm a hit man." Pharmacy is, of course, a perfectly reputable profession, but I understood the hesitation immediately. I do the same before telling anyone I'm a journalist. All too often, the moment people discover someone works in a pharmacy, they pester him with questions about which medications to use for which ailment, or they complain endlessly of the evils of the pharmaceutical industry. As soon as some people find out my line of work, they either pepper me with demands that I persuade my editors to assign a story about their particular obsession, or they bore me to distraction with their endless complaints about the failings of "the media." By unspoken assent, we asked Pineneedle nothing about the relative inflammation-reducing merits of ibuprofen vs. acetaminophen, and he avoided telling me his opinion, good or bad, of Tennessee media outlets.

A few months after finishing the PCT, Pineneedle reported good memories of "following Scrambler's small footprints, your family dynamics revolving around her, and the mini-concert in camp" when Mary serenaded him with her recorder. (The recorder is a musical wind instrument, dating back to the Middle Ages. Gary and Mary carried lightweight, nearly indestructible plastic versions.) Back at work as a pharmacist, he acknowledged the transition from trail to town was difficult and that he missed "the simplicity, adventure, and challenge of the trail." He also admitted to an ailment most successful thru-hikers face when they return to "civilized" society: The adventure of the trail makes it difficult to be content with the boredom of everyday life.

Six months later, while I was still recovering from the trail (and hoping someday I'd be able to sit cross-legged again), he reported an undying urge to do more: "I will never feel completely comfortable in society after two thru-hikes. I can function adequately but long for new adventures and experiences." So it came as no surprise when, a year later, he hiked the Continental Divide Trail, from north to south. The CDT is harder than the PCT by several degrees of magnitude. It's not so much a trail as a route, and backpackers spend much of their time hunting for a path, any path, that goes from point A to point B. Often, according to his journal, Pineneedle had to give up on trails and strike out cross-country, trusting to a compass heading to get him to that night's destination. Dunkings in cold streams, scratches and bruises from tangled vegetation and barbed wire, and miles of backtracking were sometimes his fate.

When I asked him to compare the three trails based on his own experience, he offered this analogy:

Appalachian Trail: Painting by numbers. A social experience.

Pacific Crest Trail: Painting with known colors and most of the picture. Equally social and solitary.

Continental Divide Trail: A blank canvas. Solitary.

His brief explanation of why he hikes and the rewards of the long trail reflect my own family's experience: "The excitement and adventure of not knowing exactly what's coming next is what drew me and drove me to complete the Triple Crown. It becomes a passion and way of life. The people, places, and things you meet and see along the way change you and your perspective on every level."

SCOTT WILLIAMSON, who was making his fourth attempt to yo-yo the PCT—hiking the PCT in both directions in one calendar year—made our day the first time we met him, in Big Bear City, in southern California. We were having one of those days when we all just seemed to be in a bad mood. Scott immediately elevated us several levels of happiness. We were eating lunch at BJ's, a hiker-friendly little restaurant with good food. A tall man with a pack walked in, ordered lunch, and sat down at a table nearby. Gary greeted him by saying, "Hi, you look like a thru-hiker," and then introduced us. Scott introduced himself and soon we were deep in a discussion of pack weights and daily mileages. Mary described it this way:

Day 23: *We had lunch at BJ's, and met a guy named Scott. He said we were awesome, and everyone was saying good things about us (this cheered us greatly), and I was the youngest.*

Scott, who at the time was living in Santa Cruz County, not far from our home in Sunol, had heard about Scrambler from other hikers, and he was eager to meet her. The tall, handsome athlete in his 30s was frankly admiring of our effort to hike the trail as a family, and assured us we were doing well time-wise—which surprised us, considering that it had taken us 21 days to get as far as it had taken him to hike in nine days.

This year, Scott was making exceptionally good time. He'd been thwarted before by snow in the Sierra on the return trip, but this year he was hopeful he could reach Canada and get back to Kennedy Meadows before winter settled in. If he could just reach Kennedy Meadows on the way south, he told us, he'd be home free. Ironically, he did exactly that, only to be stopped in his tracks by the deep snow left by a highly unusual, early autumn storm in the southern California desert. But he persevered, and did indeed attain his goal of being the first person to succeed in a PCT yo-yo. We thought Scott was awesome, and to have him admiring us made us feel just wonderful. A modest man, he even made fun of himself: He told us he set a record for equipment failure one year when his water container failed even before he started—on the way to the monument on the Mexican border.

Exactly 100 days after our first meeting, we saw Scott again as he headed south. We had covered more than 1,800 miles by that day in September. Scott, on the other hand, had walked 3,500 miles—and he'd done that in less time than we'd been on the trail, even though he started later than we did. Gary was in bad shape. He had come down with an undiagnosed illness four days earlier, and was

Day 23

We had lunch at BJ's and met a guy named Scott. This is his 5th PCT hike. He said we were awesome, and everyone was saying good things about us (this cheered us greatly) and I

was the youngest. We hiked to Little Bear Spring, where Dad found water.

still suffering severe muscle and joint pains. Fellow backpackers who had seen us a few days earlier doubted we would be able to finish. As we stood on the trail in Oregon, talking in a light drizzle, Scott remarked on the many hikers who had given up, and the many people who had told him he couldn't finish, either. He had learned to ignore them. "Your hike isn't over until you say it's over," he told us emphatically. By this time, many people had hinted, or even told us outright, that we couldn't possibly reach the end of the trail before winter set in. Scott's remark reminded Gary that we were the only ones who could call off the trip.

Patti Haskins and Scott Williamson joined forces at Vermilion Valley and pretty much hiked together until the Canadian border. We eagerly scanned every trail register for their signatures and for Scott's motto, "Onward to Canada." (Mary speculated that he would change it to "Backward to Mexico" on the way south, but he only changed it to "Onward to Mexico.")

STEVE AND SARA were the only father-daughter duo we've ever met on long trails. Both Canadians, they were friendly, intelligent, well-informed about both Canadian and American culture, funny, and inspirational. Sara, who was in her late 20s, had cut off her long hair—all of it—before beginning the trip, and donated her tresses to make wigs for children who had lost their hair during chemotherapy. Even without her hair, she was a pretty woman, and well-spoken, whether in English with the other hikers, or in French with a batch of foreign tourists. Steve, whose short beard showed some gray, was a lawyer specializing in securities. We were delighted to catch up with them at Kennedy Meadows, where we spent a rainy afternoon chatting with them, Pineneedle, and another hiker named Hoosier on the porch of the store there, a well-known gathering site for thru-hikers getting ready to tackle the Sierra.

VICE and his boyhood friends and backpacking companions, SPREADSHEET and DUMPTRUCK, had the greatest affinity for water of anyone we met on the trail. Every chance they got, they'd get into a stream or lake, clean up, and even wash their clothes when possible. We, on the other hand, were probably the filthiest hikers on the trail; our relatively slow pace didn't allow time for bathing, a time-consuming chore in the wilderness.

As it happened, we were very clean when we met Vice the first time in late July. We had just returned to the trail from my sister Carol's home, and my father had dropped us off where the PCT crosses Highway 49 near Sierra City, California. After he drove away, while we were adjusting our packs, Chacoman stepped out of the woods, and we sat down to talk a while. Chacoman was in no hurry, since he had to hitchhike into Sierra City on what turned out to be a fruitless quest to pick up new Chaco sandals. He kept having them mailed to him, and they kept not being there. He finished the hike in the same raggedy pair he had started out with. Anyway, as Chacoman headed down the highway to find a more visible place for putting out his thumb, two young men—Vice and Spreadsheet—emerged from the woods, looking freshly scrubbed from their dip in the North Yuba River. We all ended up camping at Summit Lake. We saw them off and on through Belden (where they showered and laundered, despite not staying there), Bear Creek (the only place where Mary was able to get into the water for any length of time), and Humboldt Summit, where we all ended up taking the wrong trail and having to backtrack. They got ahead of us on the correct route later that day, and very considerately left a note for us with directions to a tiny stream along the Carter Meadow Trail, the only water source for miles around. The next time we caught up with them was at Old Station, California, where Dumptruck joined them after having taken time off to allow shin splints to heal. Again, they were clean and shiny, while we were hot and sweaty.

At Burney Falls State Park in northern California, "the Guys" (our trail name for them) dipped their shirts in the pool at the base of the falls, much to the amusement of the crowd of tourists at the popular site. We caught up with them the next day while they waited for Dumptruck's trekking poles to arrive. At that point, Gary and I were so crippled up that we didn't even bother to visit the base of the falls (which we had toured extensively just two years earlier), contenting ourselves with the view from the top. Later that very hot day, we stopped to filter water at Rock Creek. When the Guys arrived, they provided the entertainment with their plunge into its chilly waters. Mary waded in the stream; Gary and I just sat in the shade. Although they hiked faster than we did, we caught up with them fairly often because they would take long breaks at water sources, such as Moosehead Spring in Section O, or hitchhike into towns for resupplies (and showers). We saw them last at Seiad Valley, where they arrived in blistering heat and left—of course—in a downpour.

The Guys, all in their early 20s, had attended the same San Francisco schools since kindergarten. After high school, they went to different colleges, and now were back together on the trail. As a group, they had been christened the Stupid White Men, which was especially funny considering they were highly intelligent and attended top-notch universities. Vice, whose real name was Willie, was the organizer and informal leader of the Guys. He based his trail name on the number of vices he'd had to give up. Good-looking and gregarious, the last I heard of him, he had joined the Peace Corps and shipped out to Africa.

Spreadsheet (a.k.a. Jon) was the quartermaster for the Guys. He spent so much time planning (and charting) every last detail of their trip, that he got his name even before they started hiking. "My trail name came from the admittedly dorky Excel spreadsheet I created for our trip and carried around in my journal," he explains. The chart listed the number of miles and the elevation gain between resupply points. He programmed the spreadsheet to determine a target pace in miles per day based on the average grade of a section (a slower pace for steeper sections, of course). "Then—and here is the dorky part—I had the spreadsheet calculate the amount of food, in pounds, we would need for each section," he says. "The number was based on (a) the number of days the section would take to complete at the target pace, (b) the number of calories three 22-year-old men of our heights and weights were expected to burn daily, given nine hours of backpacking (around 6,000 calories per person per day), and (c) the assumption that we could pack an average of 125 calories per ounce of food, a number I had determined in a separate spreadsheet that listed the calorie efficiencies and relative amounts of the types of food we would be eating." Spreadsheet's affinity for details and numbers will serve him well in the profession of architecture, which he hopes to pursue.

Dumptruck (a.k.a. Austin) acquired his trail name after the Guys' worst morning on the trail. The night before, they had feasted on macaroni and cheese, followed by an indulgent dessert of candy and Oreo cookies. By the time they finished eating, it was dark and cold, and they were so exhausted, they elected not to hang their food. Instead, they stuffed it into Austin's backpack, which they wedged into the crook of a tree. Then they went to bed.

They awoke early to a chilly morning and unzipped their tent door to get started on their day. "Spread before us was a scene of total carnage," Austin recalls. "Wrappers and bags and crumbs and jars covered the ground. My backpack lay slumped and torn off to the side. It's hard to say exactly how long we sat in the doorway in shock, but it was long enough to take stock of the entire situation: Our food was gone, we were stranded in the middle of a five-day section, my pack was destroyed, we had a huge cleanup operation to complete, and our stomachs were growling."

You might be inclined to think, as I did, that Austin earned the trail name "Dumptruck" because of all the trash he had to carry out of the woods that morning. But, as he put it, "To brand me with a name to remind me of that moment of shock would have been cruel, especially for a community of people that understood the importance of food." Instead, "Dumptruck" came to be because of the one detail of that episode that made him laugh—and helped him and his growling stomach hike the 38 miles to resupply in Vermilion Valley. "In the center of the carnage was a gift from our visitor that could only be understood as a final, taunting gesture," he says. "Clearly the result of digesting the very food it had stolen, the bear had left a present for me that was, by the estimate of our peers, so big we would have needed a dump truck to move it."

Dumptruck has a philosophical perspective on the role his name eventually played in their travels. "Faced with two days without food, something about that steaming pile cracked me up and made everything seem less traumatic," he muses. "I laughed every time I told the story of my trail name, which is what a hiker needs to get through the tough times. More important, though, was that my name emerged when we overcame hunger and distance and pain—and our own stupidity—by relying on each other, our humor, and the thru-hiker community."

WALKS ALONE spotted us one morning as we were breaking camp in Nance Canyon in southern California. He stopped briefly to be friendly and to read our copy of the water report. We caught up with him in Idyllwild, where we had adjoining rooms in the Tahquitz Inn. When he departed early the next morning, he left a couple pears for us, which we appreciated greatly, and then he dropped off a bag of pretzels at the top of Devil's Slide. Unfortunately, he didn't stay on the trail for much longer. On the way into Idyllwild, a few hours ahead of us, he had faced the same choice we did when he found the trail was covered with snow. He chose to stay on the official route, whereas we opted for an alternative after I fell several times trying to stay on the PCT. It was a bad choice for Walks Alone: He fell on the icy snow, broke his collarbone—which he didn't realize for several days—and had to drop out.

I admired his choice of trail name: Without rudeness, it expressed his preference for solitude. I have since wondered if his Appalachian Trail experience influenced his choice. It's fairly easy to walk alone on the PCT, especially if you start in early April, as he did. But on the AT, there's such a crowd of aspiring thru-hikers (upwards of 2,500 each year) and so many others hiking smaller sections that solitude is difficult to come by, except during the most difficult and remote parts of the trail. Or perhaps he was a fan of Henry David Thoreau: "He who walks alone, waits for no-one."

WOMEN ON TOP is a group of friends who gather annually for a weekend hiking trip. When we met them, they had kept the tradition going for 14 years. There are six or eight core members, mostly living in the Sacramento area, plus a fluid collection of friends who join outings occasionally. About eight of them were sitting in the Sierra Club's Peter Grubb hut near Truckee, California, one warm evening in July, sipping wine and speculating about the people who had signed the trail register. Who are these thru-hikers, they mused, and what kind of people would spend five or six months carrying heavy packs up and down mountains, while fighting snow drifts, heat stroke and hungry bears? At that very moment, the door opened and in walked my family, right on cue. We were the grungiest hikers they had ever met, and they were just delighted. They treated us like celebrities, gave us food and drink, asked lots of questions, let us cook in the hut, and persuaded us to sleep in the loft (they had tents set up outside). In the morning, there was more conversation, hike-related and otherwise, and we separated with great feelings of amicability, as they departed for a morning hike and afternoon swim, and we started out on an 18-mile day in the intense heat of the northern California summer.

ZEKE told us a lot about himself after we met him in mid-May. The problem was, we didn't know if we could believe any of it. Zeke is one of those trail names that shows up every now and then, so don't assume our Zeke is your Zeke. Anyway, our Zeke was staying at a supposedly hiker-friendly establishment on Highway 138, where the business owner was reportedly trying to provide water and a place to sleep for thru-hikers. But the place felt strange, and the people working there even stranger. In fact, it appeared to us that thru-hikers were welcome only if they were willing to provide free labor on the half-finished building where Zeke had been sleeping. We left quickly, not even taking advantage of the water in a garden hose by the fence, and took a 1-mile detour to the country store.

After that, we stretched our legs along the California aqueduct for several miles, finally making a dry camp among the Joshua trees alongside the buried waterway. Zeke caught up with us the next morning, having decided he'd spent enough time off the trail. He walked with us for only a few miles, to the Los Angeles Department of Water and Power spigot in Cottonwood Creek, but during that time he just about talked Gary's ear off. If he had really done all those important things for the government and the military, then Zeke was quite a guy. So why did we get the feeling that he was making most of it up, and that if we stuck around with him long enough, he'd hit us up for a loan? And if he were such an accomplished hiker, why couldn't he keep up with a 10-year-old going uphill? We were glad when he decided to camp for the day in the shade of a bridge near the spigot, while we continued on. The next time we saw Zeke was at Kennedy Meadows, where he got my brother to give him a ride to Lone Pine, since George was taking the rest of us to Carson City anyway. We've always wondered how he managed to catch up, speculating that he engaged in more than a little hitchhiking to do so.

Despite our misgivings, I feel a certain fondness for Zeke. He fit a particular stereotype of the long-distance backpacker popularly known as "hiker trash" and, as such, filled an important role in our trail experience. "Hiker trash" is a phrase that's used rather loosely, but generally describes people who have made long-distance backpacking their lifestyle of choice, and who only take jobs (or arrange slightly bogus "fund-raisers") when it's time to earn the money to return to their preferred free-ranging existence. Philosophically, they're cousins of the ski bums hanging out at Sierra resorts and the rock rats who spend their summers bending the rules at Yosemite's Camp 4. But, as is the case with those other targets of ordinary civilization's scorn, "hiker trash" is too broad a description for people who discover that their psyches are more suitable to the freedom, dangers, and privations of the long trail than to the comforts, restrictions, and constant petty hassles of the civilized life that the rest of us pursue.

Perhaps "hiker trash" as a personal description should be put to rest. Or maybe a new definition is in order, such as the one trail angel Jeff Saufley came up with when he looked at the dumpster he'd put next to his house in Agua Dulce in expectation of the late-spring onslaught of thru-hikers. Scanning the contents of the bin—the empty food wrappers, used Pringles containers, and worn-out socks—he remarked, "It gives a whole new meaning to the words 'hiker trash.'"

CHaPTeR 4

TRaiL ANGeLS aND DeMONS

Day 95: *We walked 10 miles. We went to the Heitmans'. Georgi and Dennis Heitman were very nice. I learned how to spin. I played with their new kitten, Scamper, and soaked in their hot tub.*

—from Scrambler's journal

ANDREA DINSMORE AND I couldn't have less in common. She's a retired truck driver; I'm a newspaper copy editor. She's outgoing and enthusiastic; I'm introverted and restrained, like one of Garrison Keillor's Norwegian bachelor farmers. She was a heavy smoker when we first met, and swore like a character in a Carl Hiaasen novel; I've never smoked and, as I've mentioned, strong language doesn't come easily to me. We hit it off immediately.

Andrea, who is a couple years older than me, and her husband, Jerry, a few years older than her, are widely known as the trail angels of the far north. In the backpacking community, trail angels are the people who make a hobby of helping hikers by providing water caches, letting people stay with them, giving rides, cooking meals, accepting resupply boxes, and otherwise making backpackers' lives easier. But the angelic circle is much larger than that. We were helped by an entire host of trail angels, before and during our PCT experience, from the on-trail angels, like the Dinsmores; to the off-trail angels, like my little sister, who mailed all our resupply boxes; to the accidental angels who were in just the right place at the right time to help us in some way. We also met a handful of memorable characters—and just a few demons.

The Dinsmores' activities during the hiking season exemplify how the serious on-trail angels do their thing. Jerry and Andrea live west of Stevens Pass, where the PCT crosses Washington's Highway 2. A typical hiker might arrive after dark and, having been provided with Andrea's phone number at an earlier town stop, pause at the pay phone in front of the highway maintenance shed and call that number. Since this is Washington in autumn, it's not only dark, but cold and drizzly as well. While daytime arrivals hitchhike to Skykomish and call from town, backpackers who arrive at the pass after dark can call and ask for a ride from there. The voice on the other end of the line is so cheerful, it's downright surreal. In a few minutes, a pickup truck arrives, with Andrea and a tiny dog in the front seat, and room under the camper shell for a backpack and trekking poles. And in a few minutes, the hiker, his faith in human nature restored, has been whisked away to Dinsmores' River Haven on the banks of the Tye River, where the Cokes are always cold and the showers hot, and where Andrea's parrot, a Congo African grey named Topper, swears like President Nixon on a particularly bad day.

I stayed with the Dinsmores nearly a week, first plotting an alternate course around the storm damage through Section K's Glacier Peak Wilderness, and then shuttling Gary and Mary back and forth for three days between the alternate route and the travel trailer we three slept in. At this time, I was off the trail recovering from injuries and was acting as a mobile trail angel myself, so that my husband and daughter would have a better chance of finishing. I arrived at the Dinsmores a day or two before Scrambler and Captain Bligh did and was sitting at the little kitchen table one evening reading a Seattle newspaper when I heard someone upstairs cussing vigorously. "Blanketty-blank-blank you, you blanking blank-blank, Jerry!" Omigod, I thought, they're having a fight and I'm an unwilling eavesdropper. And then I remembered I had just seen Jerry in the living room, smoking a cigar, and watching television. I crept up the spiral staircase for a look-see. It was the parrot, Andrea explained from her second-floor desk. A couple weeks earlier, she had stepped a little too close to the bird's spacious cage, and the feathered ingrate had bitten her on the lip. Andrea had reached through the bars, grabbed the offensive fowl by the throat, and hissed, "You (fill in the blanks with a long string of epithets culled from a 25-year truck-driving career) bird, I'll throttle you!" The parrot wasn't particularly good at memorizing phrases, but it picked this one up perfectly, just as when a parent lets slip an unfortunate remark in front of a small child. Over the next several days, Topper gradually shortened the string, but improved upon it by adding "Jerry" to the end of it. And the result is what I overheard from the Dinsmores' kitchen.

Topper could memorize more than just cuss words. He also learned a phrase that struck fear into our hearts as we headed into the North Cascades. "Snow, snow, snow," he would recite in a rising tone, and then add with great emphasis, "Scary! Scary!" Andrea monitored the TV weather reports as well as the National Weather Service website, and her avian Cassandra must have picked up on the emotion in our voices when we discussed the forecast.

We learned about the Dinsmores by lucky happenstance. While hiking north through Washington state without me, Captain Bligh and Scrambler met a couple heading south who gave them Andrea's contact information, which they passed on to me. I then phoned Andrea from Snoqualmie when it was time for me to move my base of operations northward. But it's no accident that they take in thru-hikers. The quiet life of retirement isn't for them, not when there are hikers out there to share their adventures and tell their life stories. Andrea gave me the most concise explanation I've ever heard as to why so many people, who will themselves never walk a long trail, are so eager to help. "They need us!" she exclaimed, opening her arms wide as though to enfold all those hapless hikers who, having experienced Washington's bad weather, voracious mosquitoes, and difficult resupply logistics, needed a warm heart and a warm room off the trail. A couple years after we stayed with the Dinsmores, an electrical short caused a fire that severely damaged their home during March. A house fire is a traumatic event, but Andrea's primary concern even then was the welfare of the thru-hikers. In her messages, it seemed her biggest regret was the loss of her hiker boxes with food and spare gear. And one of her happiest moments came in June when the first thru-hiker resupply box arrived in the mail, proof that she was again in the business of being a trail angel, even if she and Jerry were still living in their motorhome next to the damaged house.

Contrary to how it might seem, given how well the trail angel network runs, there is no official system. People become trail angels by chance. There's no individual or organization that oversees their activities or keeps track of who's doing what in any particular year. The trail angels who regularly let people stay with them advertise their charitableness in various ways, from word of mouth to sophisticated websites. There are so few of them that there is no typical level of involvement. They became interested in different ways, they participate in the trail community at various levels, and they discover individual solutions to the problems of incorporating their trail angeling into their personal, professional, and financial lives.

The Dinsmores became trail angels in 2003. Jerry had dropped by the Skykomish post office after meeting friends for coffee one morning. The four men he talked to at the post office looked like homeless people at first, but when he realized they were thru-hikers looking for a place to clean up and sleep, Jerry brought them home. Andrea remembers meeting them for the first time. "All it took was chatting with them for a bit to figure out that what they looked like, and who they really were, was night and day," she recalls. Andrea and Jerry took in six or eight more hikers that year who found their way to Skykomish, about 15 miles off the trail, in search of shelter and laundry facilities.

The next year, Gary, Mary, and I were among the swarm that suddenly discovered the River Haven. "Had no idea what we were getting into," Andrea says, recalling their start. "But, we love it." The Dinsmores now ask thru-hikers to contribute a small amount toward their lodging, which must be pretty special in the new hiker dormitory that was being constructed in 2007 just for backpackers, complete with bunk beds, TV, phone, internet connection, movies, microwave, and a coffee pot. How to host a couple hundred backpackers over a three- to four-month period without losing all control over one's own personal life is a problem trail angels solve in a variety of ways. The Dinsmores' hiker hut is the approach they've chosen to have their visitors close, but not constantly underfoot.

As with the Dinsmores, an encounter at the post office led to Georgi and Dennis Heitman becoming trail angels. In 1998, a young lady whom they had known for many years through Georgi's work with the San Francisco Bay Girl Scout Council asked if she and her new husband could stay overnight at the home the Heitmans had built at Old Station, in northern California's Shasta County. Melody and Darren were planning to hike the PCT on their honeymoon and knew roughly when they would reach the tiny resort town a few months later. The Heitmans said, sure, come on by. But then Georgi's mother suffered a massive stroke, and what with the stress of driving several hours to Oakland, California, every other week to help her mother, she forgot about the visit. Luckily, as Georgi was returning home from one of those trips, she stopped by the post office, and, she says, "There they were, waiting for me to pick them up." They stayed two nights, and before leaving, Melody asked that fateful question: Could they put the Heitmans' name and phone number in the PCT trail register at the Old Station post office, in case other backpackers needed a trail angel?

They said yes, but for the next several years, only a few hikers called for help. The most they hosted at a time was five. Everything changed in 2004, when, for some unknown reason, more than three dozen hikers stopped by. Now the Heitmans are known well enough that they can expect to host dozens of thru-hikers and section hikers every summer, all based on that one visit. Looking back, Georgi says, "We were clueless, but it's all right, we love this uproar. It keeps us young, and how else could you get the world to come to you, here in the back of beyond?"

Our visit with the Heitmans was a high point for all of us, but especially for Mary. Dennis had just acquired a new kitten, and Mary got to play with it. Georgi showed Mary how to spin wool on one of the spinning wheels she collects. This extra kindness that many people showed Mary was one of the things that made our trip special. Many people we met seemed to consider it a privilege to do little extras for the little girl on the trail. And Mary responded by eagerly participating in whatever activity arose, from playing with a tiny puppy at the Seiad Valley post office to enjoying an impromptu early birthday party at the Dinsmores, complete with Andrea's gift of a Barbie doll in an outfit as extravagantly removed from a thru-hiker's travel-worn garments as it's possible to get. As word spread ahead of us that we were on the way, we discovered, trail angels would actually look forward to meeting us—and if logistics didn't allow a visit, they seemed genuinely disappointed. One of these much-anticipated meetings occurred in the southern California town of Agua Dulce.

When PCT hikers hear the words "trail angels," the names that most often come to mind are Jeff and Donna Saufley. At first, I thought this couple was too good to be true: At their ranch-style home in the desert near Palmdale, they welcome thru-hikers, let them camp, cook, and shower there, and even let them sleep in their mobile home. As if that weren't enough, the Saufleys also do their laundry, accept their packages, and loan out their car. Too good to be true? For once, I was wrong. The Saufleys live a few days' hike from a particularly hot and dry section of trail that backpackers dread. Every year, they welcome hundreds of thru-hikers and section hikers to their home. They do indeed perform an amazing variety of services, while working full time and caring for their two draft horses and half-dozen or so dogs. Most any online trail journal or PCT-linked website tells backpackers everything they need to know about finding and staying at Hiker Heaven. The amazing thing is, everyone who stays there comes to feel in a short time that he or she has formed a personal friendship with the Saufleys. We were fortunate to be ahead of the main wave of hikers when we arrived in early May, and we were among just a handful of people staying there. Donna had heard we were coming and was very eager to meet Scrambler. The two of them became instant friends. But I've talked to many other backpackers, and read their journals, and each one felt while staying with the Saufleys that he or she was made to feel special. Jeff and Donna are just plain amazing.

Among the stories trail angels tell about how they came to embrace thru-hikers as a vocation, Jeff and Donna's is my favorite. Donna starts the story with the exact date: Saturday, May 31, 1997. "What was extremely unusual about that evening was that I was going to be home alone, presumably all night, for the first time in the five years Jeff and I had been married," she remembers. "My son was with his father, and Jeff was going to an all-night bachelor party." Donna wasn't one to sit around alone on a beautiful evening, so she called all her girlfriends. "But it had been some time since I'd talked to them, and they all had husbands or kids or some other reason they couldn't go out," she says. "So I struck out. I was bummed, but I figured I'd find something else to do." She remembered seeing a sign advertising a powwow down at Vasquez Rocks, a large county park characterized by huge sandstone slabs tilted up at an angle of about 50 degrees. The park is named for Tiburcio Vasquez, a 19th century bandit who built up a Robin Hood-type reputation while robbing stagecoaches and rustling livestock. (Scrambler describes the rocks as resembling giant pancakes, made from different recipes—thus the varying colors—and flipped up into the air. By the time we reached the rocks, we were seeing reminders of food almost everywhere.) Other people must see something alien in the rocks, which have provided the backdrop for TV episodes of *The Outer Limits* and *Star Trek*, as well as *Blazing Saddles* and many other movies.

The only problem was, Donna didn't have a car. "After all these years, Jeff and I still can't figure out why we had only one operating vehicle at the time," she

Day 34

This morning, we had bredafast at the Surfleys. Then we got finsh aid stuff and 2 books for me- Anne of Avonlea and Rasco and the Rats of NIMH. Then we had pizza at Vincenzo's with Leprechaun. When we drove "home" Donna was riding on Rick. And she ASKED ME to RIDE WITH HER! I did, of coarse. It was one of the best things ever! (No saddle or pad, so riding this Giant! was my introduction to riding bareback) I'm glad I rode bareback. He was warm and velvety. We rode around the yard 3 times, and then I got off. Instead of just watching, this time I actually helped feed them, I love horses! (and Donna) says. "Jeff had taken the Taurus to go to the bachelor party in Sierra Madre." So Donna walked the short distance to Vasquez Rocks for the celebration. Donna always laughs at the memory of her pride in walking a few miles, when soon she would be hosting people who regarded 20 miles with a full pack as no big deal. When she reached the park, she was disappointed to discover that the event was going to end much earlier than advertised. She attended anyway, and enjoyed the beauty of the dancing and costumes among the spectacular rocks. But afterward, the rest of the evening still stretched out in front of her.

"I walked out from there and thought, well, I've gotta eat, and I didn't want to go home and heat up a pathetic frozen TV dinner, so I decided to go to the pizza place," she says. "I went in and ordered chicken and sat down by myself for this very exciting Saturday night.

"So, in walks this couple. They were absolutely, disgustingly dirty. I mean, it was awful. I thought, I know what they're doing! Now, when Jeff and I first moved here, we didn't know anything about the PCT. We had seen hikers, not knowing what they were. I thought they were homeless people, or dayhikers who had somehow gotten absolutely dirty. We were mountain biking one day, and Jeff sees this blaze. We weren't on the PCT, just near it." (Donna always points out that she and Jeff weren't riding on the actual PCT. Bicycles—indeed, all wheeled vehicles—are forbidden on the PCT for safety reasons, and the number of mountain bikers who ignore this rule is a sore subject with thru-hikers.)

Jeff had read a *Los Angeles Times* article about thru-hikers, and they had both been impressed by the story about people who hiked the equivalent of a marathon on some days, carrying everything they needed with them. Donna had helped at a local marathon, handing out water, and she remembered the excitement of watching the runners. "It fascinated me how people would line the streets and cheer for strangers—they don't know who you are, but they cheer for the effort," she says. She and Jeff discussed the hikers and agreed they wanted to help them in some way. "Here they are doing this every day, they not only look like homeless people, they are being treated like homeless people," she says. "They're just invisible. We saw no sign of people helping them in any way. We wanted to do something, but we didn't know what."

All of this was going through Donna's mind as she watched the couple walk up to the counter. "They were very dirty but also very wholesome," she remembers. "Her legs were a real mess. It looked like she had fallen into a patch of poison oak. She had the raised blisters and the dirt and all. Down here, in the heat, the dirt just clings to you." At the counter, the hikers asked the workers if they had seen their friends, three guys with backpacks. The counter workers replied that they hadn't seen the other backpackers. "They were so extremely disappointed at not seeing these guys," Donna says. She watched as the backpackers ordered a pizza and then went into the tiny bathroom, where they proceeded to do their best to wash up before eating. Donna was between jobs in what she calls "corporate America," where people are always clean. "These people were putting entire limbs into the sink!" she marvels. "And then they took paper towels and were sort of smearing the dirt around. And I kept thinking about her and how she really needed a bath. As they came out of the bathroom, they were facing the window, and the three guys they were looking for (they'd been in the Mexican restaurant) walked by and they saw them. They were so thrilled."

The three came in, and one said to the other, "We knew you were ahead of us. We saw your tracks."

"They 'saw their tracks'?" Donna thought. "I'm into mountain biking, and you do look at tracks—you see if there are many riders and where they've gone—but they knew exactly who it was by the tracks. What do these people do, sit around the fire and show off their boot soles to each other?"

Then they said, "We were camped over here, you must have been over there." Donna was amazed. Not only did they recognize each other's tread, they had figured out the way they had leapfrogged each other.

Pretty soon, their conversation turned to where to camp for the night, and one of them informed the others that a permit was required for camping at Vasquez Rocks. "Little did I know, I was about to start on years of trail angeling," Donna says. "The next thing I know, one of them says, 'Miss? Miss? Do you know where we could stay tonight?'"

Donna, who had no idea what was happening, was the subject of a "yogi," a technique thru-hikers use for getting help from strangers who might not realize at first that it's their turn to provide a little trail magic. It's not outright asking, nor is it begging like a hungry chipmunk for part of someone's picnic lunch. It's more a matter of insinuating oneself into the good graces of someone who happens to have a barbecue dinner spread out with more food than he really needs, or who happens to have a car handy and may not have been planning to run into town, but could if she thought of it. Gary and I didn't have to develop a yogi technique. Thanks to having Mary along, people frequently offered us water, food, rides, and so on, without us doing anything. But for many hikers, it's a useful talent. The origin of the word is no mystery to those of us old enough to remember the Yogi Bear cartoons of 1960s television. Yogi thought he was smarter than the average bear and was constantly teaching his sidekick, little Boo Boo, how to separate the tourists of Jellystone National Park from their picnic baskets, while outsmarting the rangers who tried to stop him. (Yogi Bear's clever schemes often boomeranged, to the amusement of the misnamed Boo Boo.)

In response to the yogi, Donna mentioned a little motel on the Sierra Highway. "Their faces just lit up like Christmas," she recalls. "I didn't know this at the time, but it had been 11 days since they'd had showers, since Big Bear." But when they found out the motel was several miles away, and that Donna didn't have a car to give them a ride, their faces melted.

"Then I thought, you know, Jeff would probably be OK with this," she says. "He'll call me, and besides which, I don't need his permission. I'm a big girl and I can do this by myself. So I resolved: I can have these people over to my house without his permission. I turned to them and said, 'I think I know where you can stay. It's not much, but I have this little single-wide trailer.' If gratitude were terminal, they would all have died right there." At this point, the pizza the couple had ordered was ready, and the group decided to bring it along, so some of them could be showering and laundering while the others ate. Even in her enthusiasm, Donna was a wee bit cautious. While asking the owner for a hot bag to carry the pizza in, she leaned over the counter and whispered, "If I don't bring this hot bag back by 5 p.m. tomorrow, could you just remember who you saw me with last?" It was the female hiker who broke through Donna's reservations about the group. Her heart went out to the girl, Sarah, with her poison oak rash.

So off they went on the 1-mile walk to Donna's place, and soon the five happy hikers were taking showers, washing clothes, eating pizza, listening to the stereo, and generally having a great time. Donna sat outside with them, "grilling them with every stupid question," until about 11:30 p.m., when she decided to turn in. She said goodnight, encouraged her guests to carry on, and headed inside her house, still wondering if she'd done the right thing. "I didn't want to offend them, but I was still very nervous," she explains. "They seemed real nice, but I locked every door and window in the house—very quietly. Then I went to bed. I was very nervous, but I did finally fall asleep."

Jeff's story begins at about 2 a.m. The bachelor party was winding down, and he realized he really didn't want to spend the night with that bunch, so he decided to drive the short distance home. "I remember going up to the front door to walk in, and the door was locked," he recalls. His first thought was that Donna was just being cautious, since they didn't normally lock their doors. But Jeff didn't have a key. After he checked all the doors into the house and the garage, he decided that rather than waking Donna, he would sleep in the trailer for the night.

"There's a little porch light that illuminates the steps. I saw these black lumps against the trailer and thought, 'Wow, Donna has been doing some late spring cleaning. She's been busy while I've been gone, that's good.'" Jeff says. The lumps that Jeff saw, of course, were five backpacks leaning against the trailer.

"I walked into the trailer and looked at the couch and there was a big black lump on the couch," Jeff remembers. "I didn't know what to think—and then it moved! My first verbal reaction was, 'Who in the hell are you?'" After a brief moment, the response came back: "Well, who in the hell are you?"

"I said, 'I'm Jeff, and I live here!'" Jeff remembers. Then there was a more timid response: "I'm Jeremy, and didn't Donna tell you? She said we could sleep here tonight."

"Once he said that, it dawned on me what she had done because we had talked about the hikers, what they were doing, wouldn't it be nice to invite them up for lunch," Jeff says. "So I said, 'Sorry to wake you up. Go ahead and get some sleep, and I'll see you in the morning.'"

Jeff walked back out to the soft, warm darkness of the desert night in late spring, looked around, and thought, "I have nowhere to sleep tonight." His need for rest finally overcame his reluctance to awaken—and possibly frighten—his wife. He rapped on the bedroom window and stage-whispered that it was him and he needed to be let in. As expected, Donna was momentarily frightened. "All I could think was, why don't they come to the door like normal people?" she says. But she eventually let Jeff in the house and told him the story of her evening.

The next morning, they peeked out a window to see if the hikers were up. From there, they spied one hiker, Todd, sitting on the steps preparing his breakfast. "He's got this little teeny stove and this little teeny pot," says Donna. "This great big guy is hunched over this little teeny thing, and he's stirring it, and we say, 'My God, is that how they eat?'" Jeff leaped into action, and soon had prepared a procession of pancakes, tortillas, salsa, and fresh orange juice ready to be taken outside. "Their eyes were just as big as saucers when they saw all that food," says Donna. "We had a lovely time. They said, 'This is trail magic.' We'd never heard the term before. And then they cinched the deal for all time: 'And you guys are trail angels.'

"Something happened at that moment. I had a personal epiphany: That's what I am, I'm a trail angel! This is the thing I had been looking for, what I was meant to do. We just looked at each other. I don't know what was going through Jeff's mind, but we just knew without words, this is what we could do."

That was 1997. The Saufleys hosted a few dozen thru-hikers that first year. "I used to seriously go out and troll for hikers," Donna says. "I'd go up and down the road looking for them." Soon the word got out, and thru-hikers began showing up at Hiker Heaven in significant numbers. The Saufleys took on more chores: accepting resupply boxes, maintaining water caches in the desert, working with the Pacific Crest Trail Association to promote the trail. Through it all, Donna says, they've had a wonderful time. "We've hosted over 1,700 hikers since we started in 1997, and we've never had one problem," she says. "We haven't had to ask anyone to leave. There have been no serious issues—a few things—but nothing unmanageable. It's a real testimony to who the hikers are. You couldn't pick 1,700 random people and have this experience. It's been an absolutely marvelous experience."

A long day's hike north of Hiker Heaven is Casa de Luna, the home of Joe and Terrie Anderson. They knew about the Pacific Crest Trail before they moved to Green Valley because Joe had thought about hiking it, and they had seen occasional hikers in town. Their fateful day was a Monday—they know that because the town's restaurant was closed on Mondays. "We saw this elderly couple from

Maine walking down the road," Terrie recalls. "They went to the restaurant, but it was closed. Joe had spent all day making this vegetable soup, for no reason, so we see these hikers and start talking and we invited them over. The woman said, 'My husband has been craving vegetable soup,' and we said, 'You're not going to believe this, but come on in, it's ready.' So they came in. They were the first people we had over. They had dinner and spent the night."

The next year, the Andersons began reading trail journals online. "We saw Nocona and Bald Eagle's trail journal, and we got hooked on it," says Terrie. "Every night we'd call it up, and it was like, where are they now? Where are they now?"

Terrie thought it would be wonderful to meet the couple whose journal was so interesting, but how? Joe pointed out that their online itinerary indicated a stop was coming up in Wrightwood, so Terrie wrote a letter to be delivered to them at the post office. Thru-hikers have many of their resupply boxes mailed general delivery to post offices near the trail, so a letter addressed to them, also general delivery, would be picked up at the same time. Joe recalled it was a little awkward explaining why they were so eager to meet people whom they only knew from the internet, and they were a little concerned the backpackers might think they were more like stalkers than fans. Roughly paraphrased, they remember their letter said something like this: "We're Terrie and Joe Anderson, and we're, like, 38, we have kids and we're not weirdoes, and we'd like to meet you because we feel like we know you, and you're, like, celebrities." Next thing, Joe says, "They called, and they were a little concerned, but evidently Terrie passed the test on the phone and they said they'd be there in a week." The week stretched out and then some, and the Andersons were beginning to think the meeting wasn't going to happen after all. Finally, they got a call from the Saufleys' place. It was Nocona. She told Joe they would be there the next day, but that there was a problem. They had four people with them. "They didn't want to just show up with six people on our door-step, but they didn't want to bail on their friends, either," Joe explains. "So we said, 'Bring them all, after all, it's a party.'" Since they were already inviting over six hikers, Terrie figured there might be other people who needed a place to stay. So she drove up to the ranger station and started soliciting hikers. "She found one and brought him back, and he spent the night and we had a great time," Joe says. "And then she just started picking people up."

That year, 2000, the Andersons hosted 40 backpackers. The next year it was 80, and 170 the year after that. "Now we run about 225 a year, plus southbound-ers," Joe told us at the 2006 Annual Day Zero Pacific Crest Trail Kick Off. "This will be our seventh year, and it just keeps getting better every year."

Not every trail angel is as established and well-known as the Saufleys, Ander-sons, Heitmans, and Dinsmores. Our first angel encounter began in an atmo-sphere of apprehension. It was Easter Sunday, our fourth day on the PCT, and we were very aware that we hadn't traveled far from the border. That morning, a

U.S. Forest Service employee happened to see us from his truck while we took a lunch break in a woods. He walked over with the sort of deliberate steps people use when they're not sure what they're getting into. He asked us a few questions, and after it became obvious we really were innocent backpackers from the San Francisco Bay Area, he relaxed enough to ask whether we had seen any illegal immigrants. We hiked on to Chariot Canyon, a big, dry wash with a few wildflowers to attest to the fact that water had been there at one time, although not recently. We didn't see any water, but that didn't really matter, as we had expected a dry camp and were carrying plenty with us. We established a pleasant camp on a sandy bench above the dry streambed, and let Mary explore while Gary and I set up the tent and cooked dinner.

About 9 p.m., it was just getting to be full dark. The night was warm, the stars were out, and I had walked a little ways from the tent for a final pit stop before crawling into the tent. So I was crouched there, hidden by the darkness rather than by vegetation (of which there was hardly any), when I heard—to my horror—the sound of a vehicle approaching. I quickly zipped up and hurried back to the tent, where we all froze in place as we saw headlights winding down the dirt road into the canyon. We knew that the pickup truck that eventually came into view couldn't go much farther—the road was eroded to the point of being impassable just beyond our campsite. The truck went past us a ways, and then stopped. We looked, we listened. But without using our headlamps or getting closer, we couldn't tell what was happening. We whispered back and forth our fears: Could this be a "coyote," a smuggler of human beings, come to pick up the undocumented immigrants who might, at this moment, be slipping through the dusk toward the canyon? Could it be a drug smuggler, waiting for another vehicle or even a plane to drop off a load of pot or cocaine from south of the border? Or mightn't it be a local yahoo, looking for a private spot to get drunk, get stoned, or get laid? Whoever he was, he showed no signs of leaving, or of approaching us, either. In the end, we all got in the tent and eventually fell asleep, after Mary wrote this journal entry:

> **Day 4:** *Today my dad got water from the Shriners and we walked through more burned area and we saw a rusted old car that had rolled off the road. We also saw the Lucky Five cache. We then went down in Chariot Canyon and found a great site, but then a white truck came up. We don't know who he is. He's parked by a big hole in the road. He might even be a 'coyote.' I'm kind of scared.*

In the morning, as soon as we were all out of the tent, a tall man with wild gray hair approached us from the truck. We drew together like a flock of sheep confronting a stray dog. The man in the old shirt and ragged straw hat, carrying a gallon jug, came closer. The irrepressible Mary said cheerily, "Hello!" And he said, "Hello, I'm Laurence. Would you like some water?"

Laurence turned out to be a gentleman from Warner Springs who had unofficially taken over a section of trail and made its maintenance his chief preoccupation. He restored springs, trimmed vegetation, and saved hikers who had gone astray. He had driven out to Chariot Canyon the night before so that he could get an early start on trail repairs that morning. Laurence took us under his wing, meeting us at various points along the trail with extra food and water and pointing out ways to find springs in the backcountry. Several days later, he gave us a ride all the way down Van Dusen Canyon to Big Bear City, the northernmost point of his circuit. Laurence is in many ways a typical old coot of the desert, but he helped us out a lot, while making us his particular hobby for those few days.

Many people who run businesses in towns near the trail make a special effort to help thru-hikers. Mary Ellen, at the Redwood Motel in Bridgeport, California, provided extra towels as soon as she knew we were backpackers, and also gave us an old sheet to spread out on the bed before sorting our gear, thus sparing the clean bedspread. She described the town's eateries, let Scrambler help her fold the laundry, and made us feel that we were interesting people in our own right, not just another set of backpackers with dirty hands and faces. Not everyone who makes that special effort finds that it's always appreciated. Some motel owners have described encounters with what amounted to "a pack of spoiled brats" who made a mess of their rooms, left trash lying around, and treated the hosts rudely. Some business owners and volunteer trail angels alike have encountered unpleasantly demanding thru-hikers who take their help for granted. These instances are rare, but they are a source of worry to the trail community. Help from trail angels and others is so important on the PCT, the hiker community does not want a few bad seeds discouraging these random acts of kindness.

Through most of southern and central California, trail magic consisted of chance encounters or planned acts of kindness from "the Trail Ratz" (Dave, John, and another Dave), who provided water caches and even chairs where they were most needed; accidental angels such as Walt, Donald, and Ted, who gave us lifts into town on the rare occasions when we hitchhiked; John, who gave us his extra food on his way out of the woods after a four-day backpacking trip; Todd at Cooper Canyon Trail Camp, who donated energy bars, plus fresh cilantro from his garden; Mary Barcik, who carried water jugs into the desert; and Bruce Osgood, who provided Gatorade.

We encountered fewer trail angels in northern California, probably because so many thru-hikers drop out by then, so we considered ourselves pretty much on our own. And then, one cold, wet day, we discovered the Big Lake Youth Camp run by the Seventh-Day Adventist Church near Sisters, Oregon. Seventh Day Adventists trace their church back to the 1840s, when the end of the world was confidently predicted by one William Miller. Modern-day members have put Armageddon off a little longer, and meanwhile have adopted habits of healthy living that have given them a well-deserved reputation for longevity. A small

Day 5

We hiked to
scisors crossing
cash,@ miles.
    We found that
the guy was
Lawrence, A Trail
ANGEL! He put a
        fire pit in
and made tomales
and corn on the
cob. then we
hiked on to a
fire water tank,
where there were
wonderballs in
oval shapes.
Then we hiked
rockily down
to scisors cro-
ssing, where we
met Mountain
Tripper and
camped.

denomination, Adventists are best known for encouraging a vegetarian diet and abstinence from tobacco and alcohol; running a first-class research hospital in Loma Linda, California; and insisting on a strict observance of the Sabbath, which for them is Saturday. However, it was their reputation for hospitality that mattered most to us.

September 11 that year was a rainy day. So rainy, so cold, and so windy, in fact, that for the first time, we stayed in the tent all day. The next day, we packed up and got going, despite the almost constant rain. We had heard that thru-hikers could stay at the youth camp and possibly get food there, too. We assumed this meant we could pitch our tent on the grounds, get water, use the bathrooms, and maybe visit a camp store. It was getting on toward dusk when we arrived at what was obviously a pretty big operation. There we met Tammy, whose full set of rain slickers let us know that this kind of weather was the norm. When she told us we could borrow a cabin, raid the pantry, and cook in the big kitchen—well, it was that good old died-and-gone-to-heaven feeling I hadn't enjoyed in a month of Sundays. Or Saturdays. First, we moved into a big A-frame cabin with a huge, wall-mounted propane heater, which we turned on full blast. Then we hung up our wet clothes to dry, put on what clothing was left, and headed for the kitchen. There, we were invited to help ourselves to a huge quantity of leftovers in the camp kitchen's walk-in refrigerator, which itself was about the size of our home's kitchen and living room combined. About that time, seven more backpackers, who had arrived earlier, joined us in the kitchen: Nocona and Bald Eagle, Crow and Sherpa, Dirty, Chef, and K-Too. The 10 of us cooked and ate and cleaned up—and talked a lot—and then retreated to our warm, dry, roomy cabins. Gary and I each took a bunk bed downstairs. Mary climbed up to the loft, where I presume the camp counselor slept during the busy season. (Mary told me later that, to her surprise, she felt a little lonely up there. I guess after four months of sleeping inches away from me, that was only natural.) Here's the journal entry she penned that night before drifting off to sleep:

> **Day 133:** *It was either misting or raining the whole time. Finally we got to Big Lake Youth Camp. Paradise! Food and a microwave!*

The next morning, it was back to the kitchen, where I fried up a dozen eggs just for the three of us, to go along with some toast, cereal, milk, and fruit cocktail. I love to cook, and after months of adding boiling water to ramen noodles, the opportunity to engage in actual cooking was gratifying. When we dropped by the home of resident staff members Tim and Brenda to leave a donation, we had a hard time saying goodbye.

Some people who hold special places in our memories were neither trail angels nor demons, just people we happened to encounter and who left a big impression. A fair number of people in this world enjoy predicting disaster, and we ran into a few who let us know they doubted we'd be able to complete the PCT, especially as we brought up the tail end of the hiking herd in Oregon and Washington. Our favorite herald of catastrophe was a man we came to call the "Pig-Tailed Prophet of Doom." To this day, Gary can get a laugh from Mary and me just by dropping his voice, glaring at us, and declaring in a sepulchral tone, "The snow level's dropping to 3,000 feet! Run for your lives! We're all going to die!"

We ran into the prophet in September, the day we returned to the trail after a stopover in the tiny Oregon resort town of Detroit. We had already had a full day: breakfast at the Cedars Restaurant, a lucky offer of a ride back to the Pamelia Lake Trail from a sweet local guy named Jim, and a scary road walk that took us through a construction area with no shoulder and big trucks barreling down on us at 65 miles per hour. We were taking a break in a turnaround where the construction crew had piled several steel beams. A couple drove up in a faded orange Toyota pickup truck and asked us whether the dirt road there led to the trailhead. The man had long hair in braids and wore one of those colorful knit Peruvian "chullo" hats with the long strings hanging down. We started discussing the weather. Gary said he'd heard it was going to be bad. The man turned to the woman and assured her the weather was going to be fine and not to worry. They then drove on up the road, and a few minutes later we followed on foot.

We stopped briefly for a snack at the trailhead, where it started to drizzle, before we walked up the trail that connects with the PCT. We stopped to chat with two women on their way down the trail—one a cancer survivor, the other a rock climber who rhapsodized about Oregon's famous Smith Rock—and soon after that we had our second encounter with the couple we'd met earlier. They had run into yet a third group, which had brought along a weather radio. The forecast was grim, the group had informed the couple. At this point, the previously sanguine male half of the pair experienced a sudden epiphany. The woman was calm when we met them again—they were on their way out after all, after having walked only a mile or so from their car—but the man was agitated and kept exclaiming, "The snow level is dropping! To 3,000 feet! The snow level is dropping!" His manner was reminiscent of Chicken Little's "Sky is Falling" routine. Finally, he rushed down the trail. We could see him on the switchback below us, moving so fast that his braids flapped in the breeze.

He became forever after the "Pig-Tailed Prophet of Doom." He was right about one thing: The weather was lousy. We camped near Whitewater Creek, it rained and snowed all night, and we had to pack up under the tarp the next morning, patting our bent-over backs for having chosen the only tent site of three that didn't fill up with a puddle. But it was nothing like the near-death experience our pig-tailed friend had anticipated.

The employees of the U.S. Border Patrol were memorable, for sheer persistence if nothing else. They were everywhere. We had been at the Mexican border for about 15 minutes when Officer Amy drove up in her official government truck to ask us who we were and where we were going. These were my tax dollars at work, of course, and I had to ask myself just how likely it was that a group of undocumented immigrants, including a little girl, would arrive at the border from the north, driving a rental car with San Francisco Bay Area license plate frames, and stand around the PCT monument taking pictures of each other and arguing about how the digital camera worked—in broad daylight. Illegal aliens are known to try all kinds of inventive, and frequently dangerous, stunts to get into this country, but really now. Us? As we headed north, we became accustomed to the constant scrutiny from cars, helicopters, and airplanes. But I felt somehow relieved once we hiked north of Palm Springs and the surveillance pretty much stopped.

Another memorable law enforcement encounter took place months later, near the end of a scorching day on the infamously hot (and dry and dusty) Hat Creek Rim of northern California. We had spent the night before with Dennis and Georgi Heitman in Old Station. Georgi fixed French toast in the morning, and we ate our second breakfast at the Coyote Cafe. (The concept of a second breakfast, which I first came across in J.R.R. Tolkien's *The Hobbit*, is eagerly embraced by thru-hikers during town stops.) Late that afternoon, the sun was westering, but the air was still hot. We had walked off the trail a hundred yards in order to read the signs at an intersection of dirt roads, and since we were there, we decided to take a sit-down break. Gary and Mary had taken off their boots (smart thru-hikers take off their boots every chance they get in hot weather, to let their feet cool off), and I had set out the food and water. We were sitting on the little dirt berm that had been created by the last road grader that had come through, probably months earlier. I couldn't think of a more desolate, godforsaken spot in northern California. Just then I saw a plume of dust and announced, "There's someone coming!" We hastily got ourselves, our food and water, and the packs off the road, just in time for the arrival of a sheriff's deputy in a four-wheel-drive vehicle.

Deputy B. looked like he'd just spotted a UFO, complete with a family of space aliens. We were quite obviously the last thing he ever expected to see out back of beyond—a middle-aged couple and a little girl, enjoying a picnic as though we were visiting a city park. No vehicle, no nothing. How in the heck had we gotten there? It took a long time to persuade him we had a good reason to be there. I think what finally did the trick was that no matter how bizarre our story seemed—we'd really been toting backpacks for 1,300 miles just so we could take a roadside rest in his jurisdiction?—there wasn't any better explanation. Finally convinced that we weren't space aliens, weren't lost, weren't crazy, and weren't going to die of thirst on his watch, Deputy B. bid us farewell, told his radio dispatcher not to bother sending reinforcements, and went on his way. A nice guy, on the whole, just not accustomed to thru-hikers.

Alas, we also encountered a few demons, of the two-wheeled variety. Gary, Mary, and I believe that if backpackers don't stick up for the trails, no one else will. So when we see mountain bikers using trails where they're clearly banned, we speak up—nicely, of course, until they try to run us down. A few years earlier on the Tahoe Rim Trail, we had encountered a few aggressive bicyclists who seemed to feel that since they were already breaking the rules about where and when they could ride, they might as well wipe out a few backpackers while they were at it. Before all you mountain bikers protest—yes, I know, most of you are considerate and law-abiding and all that. Too bad we've met so few of you. Yogi, a Triple Crown hiker and one of the nicest people I've ever encountered, has had similar experiences and has come to a similar conclusion. She explains her don't-back-down philosophy in *Yogi's PCT Handbook*, her invaluable guide to all things PCT: "There are signs at every trailhead indicating that bikes are not allowed on the PCT. The people on the bikes must see those signs when they get on the trail, but every bike person I've met has denied any knowledge that bikes aren't permitted." Once Yogi explains the rules to the errant bicyclist, she continues on her way—but she doesn't get off the path. She sums up her attitude thusly: "You don't belong here, so I'm not going out of my way to make this easy for you." Yogi admits there is an element of danger to this, but she also notes how many hikers she has heard complain bitterly about bicyclists using the trail—just minutes after passively letting one go by without saying a single word.

The bicyclist we met on the PCT in early May was riding in a popular hiking area that sported "no bicycle" notices about every hundred feet. But we always assume (or at least pretend) that people may have honestly strayed, so when we saw this guy sitting in the middle of the trail next to his bike, Gary informed him politely that he was on the Pacific Crest Trail, where bicyclists are forbidden. Too bad, was the stranger's attitude. We walked around him and were continuing single file along a narrow trail on a steep hillside when he caught up with us from behind, and demanded we let him pass. Gary didn't see why we should have to get out of his way—especially when it would have been really awkward at that point—but the biker didn't want to wait. "I'm bigger than you!" he announced. Gary quickly dropped his pack and got ready for trouble. Mary grabbed the camera, I got out my notebook and pen, and we prepared to report on the impending fisticuffs. Perhaps Gary's stance—he learned to box while working as a roughneck on an oil rig in Louisiana's bayous—made an impression on the aggressive two-wheeler. Or perhaps the trailside press gallery gave him pause. Either way, he abandoned any idea of taking on Gary, grabbed his bike, ran uphill from the trail to get around us, and pedaled madly away.

We met a gang of dirt-bikers riding their noisy little motorcycles along the California aqueduct about 10 days later. All dressed up in their flashy costumes, their faces invisible inside their *Star Wars* helmets, they were merely a nuisance on what was essentially a public dirt road. But as we hiked away from the aqueduct and on toward Mojave, we saw evidence of other dirt-bikers everywhere. The damage was appalling. The dirt-bikers, not content to tear ruts in the PCT by riding on it, had also ridden up and down the steep slopes at right angles to it. Where they crossed the PCT, they tore trenches in the trail and caused erosion that destroyed portions of it, making it difficult and even dangerous to hike. Farther on, in the more level areas, the dirt bikers had created moguls on the trail, humps that forced us to walk in and out of dips constantly. What should have been an easy, pleasant walk through the pine and juniper forest was thus made tedious and tiring.

We discussed what we would do if we saw any more dirt bikers. At first, our intentions were reasonably humane: We would stop them, lecture them, and try to gather enough information in the process that we could call the appropriate land-management agency from the next town with the details. But as the damage continued, we began to fantasize a bit. While Gary was lecturing the bikers, I said, I should accidentally-on-purpose push their dirt bikes off the trail and down the steep hillside. As the destruction continued north of Mojave, however, I eventually decided there was only one fair way to treat dirt-bikers who knowingly travel where they're forbidden and deliberately destroy the desert landscape. I won't say exactly what that fate was, except to mention that the world has too many morons already, and that we were always short of protein.

Chapter 5

Food and Water

Day 32: *Gift Soup*

> *Handful of noodles (from John)*
> *2 large chicken soup cubes (from John)*
> *Cilantro leaves - fresh (from Todd)*
>
> *Boil 3 to 4 cups water. Add noodles and chicken bouillon. Simmer*
> *until cubes dissolve and noodles are floppy and slippery. Turn heat off*
> *and add cilantro leaves. Stir well. Let cool nine minutes. Serve. Do not*
> *drain! Water will boil off, leaving a starchy, delicious sauce.*
>
> —from Scrambler's journal

WE ARE SUCH FOOD SNOBS in California. We've all read Eric Schlosser's *Fast Food Nation: The Dark Side of the All-American Meal* and Greg Critser's *Fat Land: How Americans Became the Fattest People in the World*. We buy boxes of organic fruits and vegetables direct from the farm, and we eat whole-grain everything. Wonder Bread? We wonder what it is. We call ourselves vegetarians, even if we're really beady-eyed vegetarians (eating fish and chicken, but nothing with four legs) or even flexatarians (vegetarian when it suits us). We think of PETA's animal rights activism as mainstream, and the National Cattlemen's Beef Association as a fringe organization. And we feed our kids diets that would gladden the killjoys at the Center for Science in the Public Interest.

That pretty much described my family—until we hit the trail. Breakfast, from one international border to the other, consisted of Pop-Tarts. Why? Because they don't melt in the heat, they don't harden in the cold, and they come in an amazing array of flavors, not to mention startlingly vivid colors. Food during the day was nuts, dried fruit, Pringles potato chips, bags of crackers and pretzels, and many, many bars: granola bars, PowerBars, energy bars, protein bars, and candy, candy, candy bars. Mary wasn't much of a chocolate fan before the PCT. But when we took our three-week hiatus in June, we went to Costco and bought just about every chocolate-coated, chocolate-filled, and chocolate-flavored bar in the store. Evening meals were a little more healthful, consisting of comparatively nutritious freeze-dried dinners. Although they were on the costly side, they included grains, vegetables, and protein. And they were tasty, filling, nutritious, and—best of all, especially in the Northwest—hot. We augmented them with ramen noodles, which gave us extra carbohydrates and broth, also blessedly hot.

Many casual hikers we met along the trail assumed there is some sort of master plan for thru-hikers to reach the optimal daily intake of calories, fat, carbohydrates, protein, and vitamins—sort of like a food pyramid for backpackers. But there are nearly as many menu plans as there are individual hikers. There are a few main themes. Some backpackers—probably more than in the general public—are vegetarian or vegan. Some go without stoves, which means they can't use the dehydrated food most of us eat. Some spend much of their pre-trip time preparing their own food, while others—us, for example—rely almost entirely on store-bought items, supplemented with a daily vitamin pill.

K-Too of Massachusetts is one of the home cooks. He made vast quantities of spaghetti sauce and dehydrated it. He also bought fruit in season during the months leading up to his trip out West and dehydrated that, too. One of his favorite dinners was instant mashed potatoes topped with a packet of tuna fish. K-Too liked variety in his morning meals, so at town stops, he would buy different kinds of dry cereal, mix them together, and top them off with dried fruit and almonds. For breakfast, he would have a serving of the cereal mixture topped with Nido, an instant whole milk product. (Most instant milk is nonfat.) Although he rarely eats meat, K-Too is honest about needing an occasional serving of animal protein—especially after recovering from giardia in northern California. "I skipped up to Ashland (Oregon) and got cured," he recalls. "I hadn't eaten prime rib in 15 years, but after losing so much weight, I had one at Camper's Cove." On one occasion, a stranger presented him with a dozen eggs on the trail. Luckily, two other backpackers found him standing there with this unexpected but impractical bounty, helped him cook the eggs, and then helped eat them.

Bald Eagle and Nocona, the engineers from Texas, typically began their day with Clif bars. "I also liked Carnation instant breakfast with Nido," Bald Eagle says. They drank Emergen-C, a vitamin-packed drink that he describes as "a fizzy cocktail." Their second breakfast typically consisted of Snickers bars and nuts. Lunch was jerky and Pringles. "I love Pringles!" Bald Eagle exclaims. "And after you eat them, you can use the can to hold trash." The day's meals continued with bread and cheese if they had recently made a town stop where they could purchase such perishables. Nocona learned to pack bread without crushing it too much. Also welcome on the trail: tortillas and what Bald Eagle describes as "super-nitrated summer sausage." The evening meal was frequently pasta with dehydrated vegetables and olive oil. Packaged tuna, clams, or oysters went on top. Dessert was more candy or gummy bears. This sounds like an enormous amount of food. Yet, by the time we got to know Nocona and Bald Eagle in northern California, they had each lost about 35 pounds.

We lost weight, too. Gary and I each shed about 20 pounds. Mary lost only 7 pounds, but considering she weighed only 70 pounds and had no body fat when we started hiking, that worried us. We always urged her to eat more. At the beginning of a trail section, when our packs were heavy with the contents of a resupply box, I consumed roughly 3,100 calories a day. Gary probably ate about 3,400. Mary's total per day was around 1,850. Our caloric intake dipped a bit toward the end of each section, as we ran low on the highest-calorie chocolate bars.

Scott Williamson, the first yo-yo finisher, is one of the few backpackers we met who knew precisely how many calories he consumed in an average day on the trail: 3,500. However, he estimated that if he wanted to replenish the calories he expended, he would have to eat 5,000 calories, a nearly impossible task. "If I eat 5,000 calories a day, it slows me down," he explains. "My body uses so much energy to process the food." Also, 5,000 calories would equal about 4 pounds of food, far more than the 2 or 2.5 pounds a day backpackers tend to aim for. There's a point at which the weight of extra food is more than a hiker can carry and still make the miles.

So if he eats 3,500 calories per day but burns up 5,000, how does he make up the difference? "I pig out in town—I'm famous for that," he says. But he doesn't indulge on the trail. Scott goes for the healthy stuff: dried beans, dried fruit, bagels, and cheese. "I don't eat much sugar and candy on the trail. It messes up my rhythm to eat too much sugar," he says. Scott, who at the time of our hike made a living by trimming trees during the off-season, says it takes more than calories to keep going. "Calories are important, but if calories were enough, we could just hike with sticks of butter," he says. "We need nutrient-dense food with vitamins and minerals. The two foods I really craved on the trail were spinach and red meat—two foods with lots of minerals." Scott was a vegan for several years—no meat of any sort and no animal products, such as cheese or eggs. However, he was a carnivore like most of the rest of us when he completed his yo-yo.

Thru-hikers like K-Too who choose to prepare their own dehydrated food at home have to start the process way ahead of time, washing, peeling, and slicing quantities of fresh fruits and vegetables, and cooking up vats of spaghetti sauce, then drying everything and sealing it in plastic. We had no interest in adding another difficult, time-consuming task to our long list of difficult and time-consuming pre-trail chores, so we skipped that route. Others order five-month supplies of protein powder, whole-wheat pasta, powdered soy milk, tofu jerky, and other really healthy foods. We knew they ordered huge amounts because we kept coming across Ziploc bags full of this stuff in hiker boxes all the way north along the trail. Hiker boxes are where backpackers shed the food items they've grown tired of, with the idea that a subsequent backpacker who has become sick of entirely different items will decide to make a switch. Hiker boxes are also useful for people whose supply boxes fail to arrive in the mail, as well as those who try to resupply at stores along the way, only to discover that the previous three days' worth of dayhikers and tourists had bought up everything except canned pears and fishhooks.

Gary and I had been happily eating freeze-dried dinners since he took me on my first backpacking trip in Shenandoah National Park in 1988. I was exhausted and covered in bug bites after a strenuous day in Virginia's typically hot, humid, and mosquito-infested summer weather. Gary set up his tiny stove on a ledge overlooking a forested valley, boiled some water and presented me with my first freeze-dried meal. It was called Spinach Florentine, or something like that, contained rice (or was it noodles?), and while it's no longer manufactured, I still count it among my top 10 favorite flavors. Mary is less enthusiastic about freeze-dried food, but she did develop a taste for the organic dinners from Mary-JanesOutpost, especially the buttery herb pasta.

When it came time to order food for the PCT, we wanted a variety of dinners we could all eat for five or six months without getting too tired of any of them. We came pretty close. Our one mistake was ordering about a dozen packages of a pasta dinner with sun-dried tomatoes. We'd eaten it once, and I thought we all liked it. But the first time I cooked it up on the PCT, we discovered it was too spicy for any of us. For the rest of the trip, any time I came across that dinner in a resupply box, I mailed it back to my sister or left it in a hiker box. To make up for the missing dinner, we'd buy a couple packages of ramen noodles, available at practically every store in the known universe. (Mary never developed a taste for ramen. She loathes every variety, from "roast chicken" to "oriental" flavor.)

"Waste not, want not" certainly applies to long-distance backpackers. After Kennedy Meadows, we realized we needed more protein on the trail, so I bought peanut butter in squeeze tubes and put one in each resupply box. It was a big hit. And after we had squeezed all the peanut butter we could out of the tube, I would take my Swiss Army knife and cut the tube open. Then we would pass around the messy, dissected container to get every last possible molecule out of it. How to get that final bit was one of the few food-related issues Gary and I disagreed on. He insisted the best way was to cut off the top and squeeze from the bottom. But I was the one with the knife, and I insisted on carving up the tube as though I were butterflying a steak. It turned out not to make much difference. We also bought a lot of dried fruit, thinking we needed more vitamins and minerals. This didn't work as well. More than a little bit of it gives me the g.i. trots, and none of us really cares for dried fruit all that much. I ended up sending bags of

155

Today it rained.
at the end of the
day, we had to
ford a stream.
We finally had
our celebration diner.

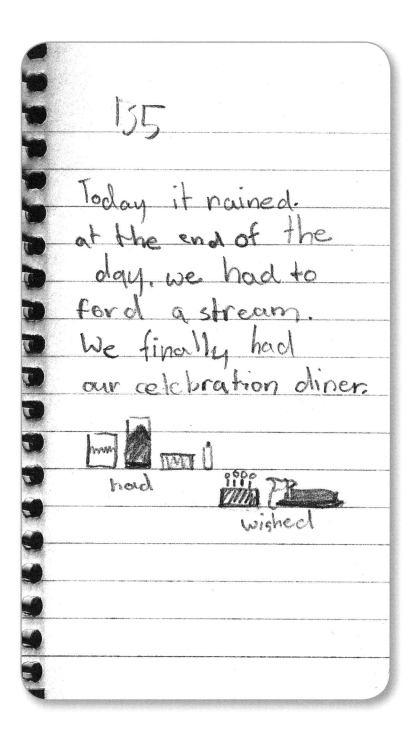

had

wished

dried cranberries, raisins, and "dried plums" (the food industry's new name for prunes) back to my younger sister, who saved most of them for us despite our generous suggestion that she serve them to her family. When we returned home, after trying out various recipes, I ended up mixing most of the fruit into scones. We ate most of the nuts we brought along, generally salted cashews or mixed nuts. And we never wasted a single Pringle. We realized in our first seven weeks how much we liked them. So when we packed our resupply boxes for the second leg of the trip, we bought enough for a tube every day. I tried to organize them in such a way that we never had the same flavor two days in a row. We alternated among original flavor, ranch, pizza, cheddar, sour cream, and barbecue. Gary never got sick of Pringles, and only wished there were more flavors. He saw a can of "ketchup blast" Pringles at a store in Kennedy Meadows, and one of his chief regrets in life is that he didn't buy it. We never saw that flavor again, although I believe it's been on sale in Canada. How that container ended up in a little store in the southern Sierra is one of those mysteries of the market we'll probably never solve.

Once we got to a town, our low trail-food standards dipped even lower. McDonald's, Burger King, or whichever fast-food joint was within the shortest walking distance became our Chez Panisse for the day. Mary in particular dived into burgers, fries, and malts with surprising intensity. Sometimes she even ate more than I did. And this from a child who had to be cajoled into eating when we were at home, and who periodically considered going totally vegetarian.

Our first trip away from the trail to visit relatives in Carson City was an eye-opener for my family. My brother, George, picked us up at Kennedy Meadows after our first seven weeks and 700 miles. Soon, we were speeding north on U.S. Highway 395 along what was literally a moveable feast. At Lone Pine, we stopped at McDonald's and stuffed ourselves. At Bridgeport, we stopped at the Sportsmen's Inn and gorged some more. George had a bite in Lone Pine but just ordered coffee in Bridgeport, sipping it while watching with a bemused smile as his relatives turned into a shoal of great white sharks. And when we reached Carson City, we raided my sister Carol's refrigerator with grim determination.

That thru-hikers are focused on food isn't odd considering the calorie deficits we build up. There is no way—simply no way—most hikers can carry enough food to meet their needs. I say "most hikers" because once in a great while we came across thru-hikers who claimed they couldn't eat all the food they were carrying. (We stole their food and then killed them and ate them, too.) The result of this chronic starvation diet is a fascination with calories that would gratify a Weight Watchers instructor, but with one big difference: Thru-hikers read the nutrition labels to find the *most* calories and the *most* fat. I used to wonder why Snickers bars are the universal favorite lunch among long-distance backpackers. A look at the fine print on the label cleared that up: At 280 calories, Snickers bars pack major calories in a small package, and they're on sale at every dinky little store along the PCT.

Our food obsession came as no surprise, although it was more intense than I expected. We ran into this on our first Tahoe Rim Trail trip in 2001. The Tahoe Rim Trail follows the ridges around Lake Tahoe, which straddles the Nevada-California state line west of Carson City. We were among the first 100 people to backpack its entire 165-mile length in one trip, and Mary was the youngest to complete it. For the first few days of that 13-day outing, our conversations centered on whether we could even keep going, what with my initial weakness, Mary's spell of sickness, and the onset of serious foot problems for both Gary and me. Once we agreed to keep going, our thoughts turned to other topics: the scenery, the people we met, but primarily the food we were going to consume once we got off the trail. Mary and I began a hobby, which we continued on subsequent long hikes, of making up new food items and recipes. You've heard of French silk pie? We invented burlap pie and denim cake. Fruit smoothies are good, but we went one better, inventing new beverages using weird combinations of fruit, ice cream, and even coffee. (We only tried one of them at home: Gary's suggestion for a banana-mint blender drink. We used fresh bananas, mint-chocolate chip ice cream, and fresh mint leaves. Wasn't half bad.)

Our food preoccupation on that trip became more pronounced as we rounded Lake Tahoe's north end and headed down the Nevada side toward our finish line at Kingsbury Grade. We had three or four days to go when I took inventory of our food stocks at Mud Lake. Our appetites had increased remarkably since our resupply at Tahoe City, California, and while we had enough instant cocoa for breakfast and freeze-dried meals for dinner, we were woefully short of everything else. Strict rationing only emphasized our hunger.

Luckily, we enjoyed a little trail magic at Spooner Lake, although we didn't even know the phrase at the time. We made a detour to the lake, near U.S. Highway 50, to get water from the state park's faucets. After filling our bottles, we sat in a sunny spot to rehydrate and eat tiny smidgens of turkey jerky, plus a few M&Ms apiece. As corpulent tourists wandered around, we fantasized about knocking them down and stealing their picnic lunches. Fortunately for them, I went in search of a trash can and came across something even better—a sign promising ice cream at the end of a paved path. Was I hallucinating? There, just a few yards away, was a store run by Max Jones, a member at the time of the Tahoe Rim Trail Association board of directors, catering to the summer mountain bikers and the winter cross-country skiers. I ran back to get Mary, who was soon in ice-cream-sandwich heaven while I ran up a tab of $30 or $40 worth of energy bars and chocolate. Gary had stayed behind with our packs, but he made up for lost time as soon as I returned with the goodies. He has a vivid memory of standing in front of the water fountain, a candy bar in each hand, eating them alternately and voraciously, while a woman picnicking nearby tried to persuade her kids that they needed to eat their carrots and apples so they could grow up to be strong and healthy.

We created a similar scene during the sixth week of our PCT trek. We had spent much of a hot day meandering through the Tejon Ranch, where the trail zigzagged all over creation on its way toward the Tehachapi hills and the southern Sierra, because the ranch owners at that time wouldn't let the PCT run straight across their land. At the next highway crossing, we learned that a 1-mile detour would take us to the aptly named Country Store. After some discussion, we decided to go for it. (It's hard to believe we even had to discuss it, but our feet hurt all the time and extra steps weren't welcome.) Once at the store, we bought scads of cold drinks and ice cream, which we consumed on the shady porch, and left with lots more of the less perishable items in our packs—$40 worth, in all.

One thing we didn't consume on the trail was coffee. We knew we wouldn't have time to make coffee every morning, we didn't want to suffer caffeine withdrawal on the trail, and we didn't want to have to drink extra water to make up for coffee's diuretic effects. Gary and I gave up our daily cup or three before we started the PCT. We both quit cold turkey.

Here's how I sounded the day I gave up coffee:

"Ooooohhhhh, Gary, I'm miserable! Oooohhhh. I've gotta lie down ... oh, please get Mary ready for school. I can't even stand up. Oooohhhh ..."

Fortunately, caffeine withdrawal wasn't responsible for *all* of that misery. On a February weekend, we had gone backpacking in Henry Coe State Park for two days, preparing for the PCT, and I drank instant cocoa instead of coffee. The day after the trip, I got up as usual to help Mary get ready for school, and promptly collapsed on the bedroom floor. I don't know what hit me, but it hit awfully hard—flu, probably. I didn't drink coffee for two more days while I got over the whatever-it-was. And by the time I felt better, I figured I might as well remain coffee-free, since I'd already gone through involuntary withdrawal. It was a relief—I had been dreading the headaches that sometimes accompanied me to work without caffeine. A month later, it was Gary's turn to get sick, and he also took advantage of the opportunity to quit coffee. We also gave up alcohol, but that was easier. Gary rarely had anything to drink, except on social occasions, when he would down a few beers. I had been in the habit of drinking the heart-healthy quota of 3 or 4 ounces of red wine each night. A few weeks after the first of the year, I bought my last bottle. When I ran out of wine, I just didn't buy any more.

During our months of trail-enforced food deprivation, we occasionally experienced the kind of serendipity that made me believe in manna from heaven. One such event occurred in early July on a day of snow and rain showers a few miles north of Muir Pass. We were running short of food and were still a couple days away from our next resupply. We had walked several yards off the trail for a rest break in the shelter provided by a trio of gnarled juniper trees. We usually made

Day 32

We hiked to North-
Fork Ranger station
Todd gave us 6 bars
and fresh cilantro
for gift soup.

GIFT SOUP

handful   2 large   7-8
of noodles chicken   cilantro
            soup   leaves
            cubes   fresh!

boil 3-4 cups water. add
noodles and chicken boullion.
simmer until cubes dissolve →

and noodles are floppy and
slipperry. Turn heat off and add
cilantro leaves. stir well. let
cool 9 min.. serve.

Do not drain! water will boil
off, leaving a starchy delicious sauce.

so much noise no one could miss us, but this day, for some reason, we kept quiet as two people walked on the trail nearby. They spotted us anyway, and came over for a sit-down break to introduce themselves. Paul and Alice were hiking the John Muir Trail and, by some miracle, they had actually packed too much food. They offered it to us. Showing great restraint, we accepted only what they really, really didn't want. Honest, they insisted they didn't want it—cookies, crackers, pretzels, peanuts. Scrambler's journal entry that night reflected our delight:

> **Day 62:** *Today, we climbed our last big pass, Muir Pass. Surprisingly, we had more snow going up than down. At the top we saw Muir Hut, a cold stone hut on top of the pass. Our way was an easy 10 miles. We met Paul and Alice, who gave us food! Whoopee! Yahoo! We had a wonderful campsite by the river.*

Another pleasant surprise occurred farther north, on a very hot day around the end of July when we were hurrying to reach Highway 49, where relatives had promised to pick us up for a zero day in Carson City, Nevada. We were tramping along through undistinguished scenery when we happened upon a big cache of Gatorade. A man from Sparks, Nevada, had left it there, with a note explaining how much a drink of Gatorade had meant to him on his backpacking trips, and how he wanted to provide others with the same enjoyment. We took him at his word, relaxing on aspen logs and guzzling down the wonderful drink. Mary's account read:

> **Day 84:** *Today we found a Gatorade cache! It was very nice!*

Backpackers love to joke about food, but when it comes to water, they're deadly serious. The pursuit of adequate H2O is a necessary compulsion. Much more so than on other long trails, a PCT thru-hike involves a constant search for water. Except in the southern Sierra, where it's the overabundance of snow and water that's the problem, the PCT is amazingly dry. Everyone expects water shortages in the southern desert; that's why the most well-attended meeting at the annual PCT kickoff is the presentation of the water report. That's why God invented trail angels. But Oregon? There is something uniquely unfair about a state in which we were so wet, so much of the time, that we forgot what dry boots felt like—and yet we had to worry about water just as much as we did in the Mojave Desert. The reason is Oregon's volcanic past. Much of the state is coated with several feet of highly porous, volcanic rock. Besides being a pain to walk on, this kind of rock allows the rain to percolate right down to the distant water table, while leaving hardly any on the surface.

It's no secret that water is especially scarce at the very south end of the trail, especially if you can read a little Spanish. The PCT is a popular route for undocumented immigrants trying to get across the Mexican border to return to their jobs washing dishes in Las Vegas and mowing lawns in San Jose, and the U.S.

THE
BLIGHS'
PCT ALBUM

Captain Bligh, Nellie Bly, and Scrambler began their journey at the Pacific Crest Trail's southern border monument on April 8, 2004.

Looking east from the border monument along the wall between the United States and Mexico

"Thanks for the water," Captain Bligh writes in the trail register at the water cache on Chihuahua Valley Road, 127 miles from the Mexico border.

Scrambler surveys the southern California desert in mid-April.

Nellie Bly and Captain Bligh at the water fountain at the mouth of southern California's Snow Canyon; Fuller Ridge is in the background.

Whitewater Canyon with Fuller Ridge in the background

Trail angels Donna and Jeff Saufley at Hiker Heaven in Agua Dulce

Scrambler makes friends with a skeleton at the Hikers Oasis water cache, maintained by trail angels Joe and Terrie Anderson, north of Agua Dulce.

Afternoon thunderstorms move into Scrambler's so-called "Dragon Mountains" in the southern Sierra Nevada near Mt. Whitney in late June.

Scrambler and Captain Bligh perch high on a pile of rocks near Kennedy Meadows in late May, just before leaving the PCT for three weeks.

This marmot greeted Captain Bligh, Nellie Bly, and Scrambler on Forester Pass in late June.

Scrambler crosses a snowfield on the descent from 11,980-foot Glen Pass in the southern Sierra.

Scrambler pauses on Selden Pass in the southern Sierra in early July.

Nellie Bly and Scrambler above the southern Sierra's Thousand Island Lake, with Banner Peak in background

The moon is visible in a cloudless, late-July sky as Scrambler and Nellie Bly pause on a hot day in the Sierra Nevada north of Highway 49.

An arrangement of pinecones marks the PCT halfway point, just north of State Route 36, near Chester in northern California, in early August.

Scrambler and Nellie Bly at Burney Falls State Park in northern California

Scrambler with trail friends Sherpa (on left) and Crow in mid-August near Mt. Shasta

After the third straight morning of waking up at 4:30 a.m., Scrambler grabs a last few seconds of shut-eye before leaving camp in far northern California.

Scrambler wears her poncho on a drizzly 21.5-mile day in late August, the day before reaching Oregon.

Nellie Bly and Captain Bligh sign the trail register at the Oregon state line.

Crater Lake and Wizard Island

Just north of Crater Lake, Scrambler poses with Scott Williamson as he heads south on his yo-yo of the PCT.

Scrambler and Nellie huddle in the tent during a miserable rainy day in early September at South Matthieu Lake in Oregon.

In order to avoid potentially dangerous crossings of Milk Creek and Russell Creek, Scrambler and Nellie Bly walk along a narrow road from Pamelia Lake to Highway 22 in Oregon.

Scrambler thumbs her nose at a school bus sign in Washington, celebrating the fact that she's not in school in late September.

Scrambler with Mt. Rainier in the background, early October

Nellie Bly says goodbye to Scrambler at White Pass, where Scrambler and Captain Bligh continued on without her in early October.

Scrambler walks among the fall colors as clouds threaten a few miles north of Chinook Pass, near Mt. Rainier.

A glorious sunrise in central Washington swiftly gave way to steady rain, south of Snoqualmie Pass in early October.

10/5 Disappointing to still be here, though it's a nice place. Very nice people. Still sick ⌒ (BUMMER)

NOCONA

10/5 Somehow dragged myself in last night, now I'm trying to drag myself back out & onto the trail. Met EAGLE & NACONA → wish them the best of health the rest of the way! Hopefully the 'indian summer' will hold up & we can trek through the rest of way to CA/OR... I see that the Queen is COWBOYED UP, so I gotta go. Peace & Blessings to all, and MANY thanks to Donna & the staff for all you provide. Congrats to all behind us..... – RAINLOCUS –

10/6 10:25 a.m. We are leaving! The flu had us down, but we're ready to try to move on. Scrambler + The Bly's – weather looks good for the next 2 wks. Hope you catch up to us.
⌒ NOCONA

10/8 Got down last night for dinner and decided I wanted breakfast too, so I hiked back up the hill and camped by the lake. Then I got down here to see a double rainbow over the ski hill I had just hiked down. Probably the most perfect and intense rainbows I've ever seen. Picked up my box (Thanks Summit Inn) and heading out to greet the rain.   – Chacoman
P.S. I'm not sure where you are (but maybe heading South) but Hello to
Bly's and Scrambler; Scrambler did you see all the obsidian way back at Obsidian Falls?

At the trail register at Summit Inn at Snoqualmie Pass, there are two notes to Scrambler, one from Nocona, and a long one from Chacoman.

Scrambler pauses on a snowy trail in Washington's Cascades near Suiattle Pass as she and Captain Bligh encounter bad weather in mid-October.

At Buckskin Pass in late October, Nellie Bly and Scrambler get ready for their final push to Canada.

Scrambler celebrates reaching the U.S.-Canada border on October 25, 2004. She's holding her water bottle and Cactus, her stuffed animal; she carried both the entire 2,650 miles.

Border Patrol is no more anxious than the immigrants are to find people dead of thirst in the desert. The warning signs are bright yellow and very insistent that the terrain ahead is hot, dry, and dangerous: *"Cuidado! No exponga su vida a los elementos. No vale la pena!"* These words of caution (which I translated roughly for Mary as: "Careful! Don't expose your life to the elements! It's not worth it!") are surrounded by whimsical symbols of a glowing sun, precipitous mountain slopes, a saguaro cactus, and, oddly, a man swimming. Ironically, this first section of the trail is practically lined with discarded water bottles (as well as worn-out socks and other trash) left behind by immigrants eager to lighten their loads as they head north, and apparently oblivious to the possibility that they might want to refill those bottles if they can find a seasonal spring or perhaps a cattle trough before they reach their destination.

We carried enough water our first day for a dry camp (one without a source of water) and got more the next day at the Lake Morena campground. In subsequent days, we often carried extra water. Sometimes we knew we had to make a dry camp; other times, we knew caches or natural sources of water were coming up but we didn't want to rely on them entirely. Whether to depend on water caches provided by trail angels is a constant source of concern for thru-hikers, and it's a big topic of discussion during the presentation of the water report at the kickoff. Several people in southern California, and a few in Oregon, have taken it upon themselves to provide jugs of water at strategic locations for thru-hikers to use along the driest sections of trail. These vary from three or four bottles left under a shrub to maybe 100 gallon jugs, their handles carefully tied together against the wind, placed where the trail crosses dirt roads. Supplying these caches is a big job, and trail veterans warn that backpackers should take only what they need to get to the next natural source of water, as it may be weeks before the cache is replenished. People at the tail end of a thru-hiker herd may find the supply exhausted. We were ahead of the pack during our seven weeks in the desert, but not so far ahead that trail angels hadn't begun providing water yet. We were fortunate—all the caches mentioned in the water report had plenty of water. And regardless of how long it had been sitting in the sun, getting warm and absorbing a plastic taste from the jugs, that water tasted good!

Besides being lucky, we were also very careful. We never relied completely on a cache. As a result, our packs were often much heavier than those of other thru-hikers because we were intent on keeping Mary, at least, well hydrated. We were so careful, it wasn't until we'd been on the trail for 104 days that we finally succumbed to an unplanned dry camp. But we did get thirsty, just the same. There is a thirst brought on by hours of strenuous exercise in hot weather that is so deep, only several gallons of water can satisfy it. Sometimes it took a couple days of heavy-duty water consumption to get past the body's constant yearning.

How much did we crave water? Let me tell you about the "small stream."

It was Day 26 on the PCT, and it was hot. Really hot. There was no shade, and there hadn't been any for a couple days as we pushed through the Deep Creek area of Section C in southern California. And it was ugly. This part of the state gets burned over frequently, and the brushfires' destruction lasts for years. Earlier, we'd been walking through areas that had been charred a few years ago, but on this day, we were in Silverwood Lake State Recreation Area, which burned in October 2003, the year much of southern California went up in flames. Satellite photos at the time showed so much smoke wafting toward the Pacific Ocean that it was hard to determine what was burning and what was not. Of state parks affected along the PCT, Silverwood was hit especially hard. The 1,000 acres that burned in Silverwood seems small compared to the 25,000 acres blackened at nearby Cuyamaca Rancho State Park, which in turn is dwarfed by that year's total for wildfire destruction in California: nearly a million acres. But Silverwood brought the destruction home to us because it was so intense—and because that's where we saw the fire damage up close and personal.

The fringes of the park were scorched and blackened. Signs were missing or even melted, hunks of plastic frozen, mid-drip, like the clocks in Salvador Dali's *The Persistence of Memory*. We stopped briefly to eat and drink, while some men working on a road stared at us. Park workers stopped to question us. The park was closed to everyone but thru-hikers, so once we explained what we were doing, they drove away. An important trail intersection existed in a picnic area, but those signs were also destroyed. Gary searched the area and discovered the trail on a hillside. According to the *Pacific Crest Trail Data Book*, there was a small, unnamed stream about 4 miles from the picnic area and 10 miles before our next stop at Cajon Pass on Interstate 15. We followed the meandering trail through the burned-over hills, until we reached a point where the trail was too badly eroded to follow. With considerable difficulty, we descended into the ravine, went around the wash-out, and climbed back up. A couple hundred yards farther, we found another wash-out, only worse. Once past that, I checked the book. Where's that small stream? It was past noon and we should have found it by that point. We kept going, contouring in and out through the dry ravines. No water anywhere. By 1:30 p.m., I had given up. Mary would get the rest of our water, I decided; Gary and I would do without. All of a sudden, there it was! It was small, all right, but it *was* a stream, the most beautiful thing I had ever seen. We clambered down to a good filtering spot on a shelf of rock, with room for all three of us. I lined up the water bottles. Gary assembled the filter. Soon, we were laughing and guzzling water. I splashed the wet stuff on my face with sighs of pleasure. Gary and Mary poured water over themselves with more laughing and shrieking. Blackened or not, it was a lovely grotto and we spent a delightful hour and a half there. By the time we reluctantly packed up to leave, I had swallowed two liters, a record for me.

We continued planning our trail days around water sources, as our appreciation of the people who stocked the caches grew and grew. Once in a while, we found naturally occurring water where we didn't expect it: Tyler Horse Canyon, near Mojave, seemed unreliable judging from the water report, so we didn't include it in our plans. But we discovered running water and very nice campsites there on our way to bone-dry Gamble Canyon, which completely lacked decent sites for a three-person tent. Sometimes we expected water but didn't get it: Robin Bird Spring, north of Mojave, was a major disappointment, especially considering it got a good review in the water report. There was no water coming from the pipe; just a tiny trickle from a culvert. Luckily, we had enough water to carry us through to Landers trail camp, where there was plenty of water from a spring on the edge of a campground apparently used mostly by off-road vehicle owners.

These happy surprises and unsatisfied expectations were based primarily on the PCT water report for that year. The water report, issued every spring, describes water sources from the Mexican border north for hundreds of miles. The printed report is handed out at the Annual Day Zero Pacific Crest Trail Kick Off in late April, and it's also available from some trail angels. (Some information is also available online.) For each of the hundred-plus water sources, the report lists the name, map number in the *Pacific Crest Trail: Southern California* guidebook, its location and number of miles north of the border, the latest information available, the date it was reported, and the person who made the report. For example, in the 2006 report, the San Felipe Hills Third Gate Cache was described as 91 miles north of the border, and it could be found on map A12. "Charlie" reported seeing 102 gallons there on April 21, and he made his report April 23. An editor's note underneath the listing pointed out that it takes a lot of work to haul all that water to the Third Gate's remote location, and urged backpackers to take only as much as they needed to get to Barrel Spring, 11 miles away. In the unlikely event that there's no water at Third Gate, alternatives are offered, with an additional note about the importance of respecting private property the hiker may need to cross. At about the same time, "Scout" and "Sprout" reported that Lost Valley Spring, 120 miles north of the border and two tenths of a mile off the trail, provided plentiful water that was good if filtered. A note from "Monty" added that better water could be found 25 yards beyond the trough. Far to the north, at mile 186, Deer Spring on the North Fork of the San Jacinto River was described by "AsABat" as "flowing strong with snowmelt" and surrounded by "much snow."

The reality of any water source is hard to convey with just these basic bits of information. And one individual's experience will be different from another's over the course of the hiking season, as streams and springs dwindle in the summer heat and as trail angels guess—accurately or not—how often each cache needs to be replenished. When we reached Third Gate, there were plenty of water jugs there, but not 102 gallons. Lost Valley Spring, a very small spring near a hilltop campsite, made us wonder what would happen if many more people began hiking the PCT. Gary doubted it would be able to provide water for more than a handful of hikers per night. Deer Spring was surrounded by snow in 2004, just as it was in 2006. We had hiked out of Idyllwild after spending the night at the Tahquitz Inn, and we needed to filter water before looking for a campsite several miles farther on, where no reliable sources were listed. Everything was pretty much covered in snow, the route was hard to follow, and it was cold. Gary found a precarious place where he could dip the water purifier's intake tube into the ice-cold water. Mary held the water bottles for him while perching on an icy boulder, getting the seat of her pants wet in the process. During this remarkable performance, I more or less stood there and voiced my admiration, occasionally unwrapping a candy bar and stuffing it into somebody's mouth.

From Kennedy Meadows at the south end of the Sierra to Sonora Pass in central California, our water worries focused entirely on a super-abundance of it in rivers and creeks. For that distance, we were more worried about drowning than about dehydration. From Sonora Pass up to Lake Tahoe and on to Highway 49 near Sierra City, California, the water situation was just about right: enough streams and lakes to provide reliable water, but few difficult stream crossings. After that, we had to plan more carefully. The heat was broiling, typically approaching and occasionally exceeding 100°F. The *Data Book* began to show longer stretches between water sources, and some of those sources were less than ideal. One particularly unpleasant day in Oregon, we took the alternate Oldenberg Trail, as recommended in the guidebook, because water sources were more frequent on that route. Gary was feeling very badly, aching all over, especially his knees, and he was in a vile temper. The mistakes I made finding the alternate route didn't help any, and when I triumphantly delivered us to Nip and Tuck lakes, we couldn't get water there—there was no place where Gary could sit and filter. The lakes' borders were nothing but mud. Usually, Gary is a genius at finding ways to filter water despite an apparent complete lack of suitable spots, but at both Nip and Tuck, even he couldn't find a way. So more time was wasted. We finally got enough water at Oldenberg Lake to get us to Fish Creek Horse Camp, where good, cold water gushed out of the taps.

The day we made a dry camp without adequate water had occurred a few weeks earlier, in Castella, in northern California. I should have learned my lesson at Belden, in central California's Feather River country, where I foolishly expected we could hike 20 miles on a very hot day, after a late start, and with a total altitude gain of 5,680 feet. We didn't make it, but we got away with it that time because there was a spring after only 13 miles, and we found a marginal campsite nearby. Hiking out of Castella, we got an even later start after picking up our resupply box at the post office, then eating burritos and drinking Gatorade, and re-organizing everything on the patio next to Ammirati's Market. Like an idiot, I thought we could start in the afternoon and hike 20 miles in 95°F heat, with a 3,800-foot altitude gain, and with nine days' worth of food on our backs. Worse, when we did reach a water source late in the day, we didn't stop to filter water. We paused to admire the carnivorous pitcher plants and to talk to a thru-hiker nicknamed "Dirty," who had wisely halted there for the day. But then we kept on, thinking we were going to reach Helen Lake by dark. We didn't get to the lake. We didn't even find a decent campsite. Instead, we set up the tent on a wide spot in the trail, somewhere east of Trinity Divide, ate a few Pop-Tarts, drank a little water, and went to bed. Our luck changed the next morning when we woke up to one of the most beautiful sunrises I've ever seen. A little trail magic must have influenced the way we set up our tent—we could see the dawn right out the tent door, complete with a spectacular view of Mt. Shasta and Castle Crags. We did eventually reach Helen Lake, where Gary was treated to a view of a woman sunbathing nude on a floating air mattress while he filtered the lake water.

One of our worst disappointments in the water department led to some of our best trail magic. On another hot day, we hiked 24 miles to Scott Mountain Campground in northern California's Trinity Alps. The guidebook indicated there would be water, but there wasn't. Not a drop. We found a campsite and then faced the possibility of having to walk or hitchhike several miles to get water. Fortunately, Don and his son, Adrian, of Berkeley, were car-camping there. When we explained our predicament, Don gave us three gallons of water—more than enough for us, plus the four other hikers who arrived after dark. Don and Adrian dropped by our site for some conversation and gave us a couple peaches, our first fresh fruit in a very long time. They were followed by Peggy of Gardnerville, Nevada, who had hiked portions of the Appalachian Trail, and was eager for a little trail chatter. She also gave us a mango and homemade cookies. And in the morning, Patricia from Arcata brought us a heap of fresh organic raspberries from her garden. She even hauled away a couple sacks of trash for us, which was a great help. (Besides lacking water, the campground also lacked trash cans and outhouses.) A visit that began without even water turned into a cornucopia of fresh food and pleasant conversations.

Along with a constant preoccupation with finding water, smart backpackers are fairly compulsive about safe water. Whether to treat drinking water taken from natural sources is a topic of long and heated debates in the backpacking community. I grew up drinking straight from the creeks of eastern Nevada's Schell Creek Range, muttering my family's mantra about water purifying itself every 30 feet or so, and I never got sick. As late as the 1970s, I drank directly from streams in the Sierra, scooping up my drinking water in a little collapsible metal cup. But today, Gary and I purify all water unless it comes from a developed spring or well. Other backpackers use iodine or bottles with built-in filters. The most technologically advanced have a small, battery-operated device that uses salt and an electric current to purify water. Many use nothing at all. And to be honest, giardia—the bane of backpackers, with its diarrhea, gas, stomach cramps, and nausea symptoms—seems to strike more or less randomly. Over the past couple decades, the giardia parasite has spread throughout much of the Sierra, according to some sources. And according to other sources, giardia isn't that common, and people can safely drink from backcountry streams, as long as they're certain there's no contamination from upstream—say, from an animal taking a dump near the water. Problem is, of course, backpackers don't have the time to check out the entire watershed that flows into every source of water. So we purified our water, and escaped giardia—although we certainly had plenty of other problems.

Pacific Crest Cafe: A "Restaurant" Review

As evening falls on the Pacific Crest Trail, hungry diners can't do better than to try out this delightful eatery, with its woodsy ambience and rustic influences. Although not quite up to white tablecloth standards, the Crest still manages to combine friendly and helpful service with a surprisingly robust choice of entrees. The exuberant menu varies depending on the contents of the last resupply box, but diners can always be certain that the ramen noodles will be piping hot and the freeze-dried dinners competently stirred.

On a recent night, a festival atmosphere imbued the cafe, as a party of three celebrated the recent accomplishment of a 25-mile day, with the added excitement occasioned by reaching an adequate campsite before dark. The occurrence of random piles of dried cow dung interfered only slightly with the overall aesthetics, as the fall of night soon enabled visual distractions to disappear into the dusk. National Park Service rules precluded the lighting of campfires, but the hiss of a small but energetic backpacker's stove sufficed to drive away any gloom that the incipient twilight might bring.

This evening's repast began with steaming hot mugs of cocoa. The choice of Nestle's instant over the competing Carnation product may not have been the absolute best one, but the chef's decision to serve the beverage in transparent acrylic cups allowed the diners to ensure that every crystal of sugar, every molecule of alkali-processed cacao bean, and every delectable tidbit of partially hydrogenated tropical oil was appropriately dissolved. The rather undistinguished presentation of the hot chocolate on bare ground was nicely offset by the gradual appearance overhead of the summer sky's constellations.

Next to appear were the two entrees: ramen noodles, served in a titanium pot, and three-cheese lasagna, modestly presented in a waterproof bag. While the chef's choice of an Oriental vegetable flavor of ramen to accompany the decidedly Mediterranean nuances of the lasagna seemed incongruous at first, the two made for a surprisingly good pairing. As all experienced backpackers know, ramen is simple to prepare, while freeze-dried dinners can be more challenging. In this case, my spork was able to turn up only a half teaspoonful at the most of unincorporated powdered mozzarella—a notable accomplishment for a cook lacking all but the most rudimentary of culinary utensils.

I can say nothing but good about the 2004 vintage California snowmelt vin d'tres ordinaire (estate bottled) served with dinner. Despite its humble packaging in re-used Albertsons water bottles, their paper labels in a severe state of disrepair, this spring-fed beverage (appellation Ansel Adams) was served at precisely the correct temperature and in exactly the right amounts.

The dessert, a chocolate mousse, was extravagant by backpacker standards. The triumphantly outrageous concoction of freeze-dried chocolate and paper-thin Yolo County almonds was a suitable confectionary counterpoint to an evening of dining al fresco.

Reservations required.

CHAPTER 6

THE WORLD OF NATURE

Day 56: *Today we started late. We repacked everything for a "formidable" stream crossing. We saw beautifully breathtaking scenery high up and heard coyotes barking. We also saw marmots standing like sentries. We also saw large rabbits, and at our beautiful tent site, wonderfully colored clouds.*

—from Scrambler's journal

WATCH ALL OF THE NATURE PROGRAMS on television, visit zoos and museums, read *Backpacker* and *Outside* and *National Geographic*—and you won't come even close to the experience of actually moving out of the house and living under the conditions of the natural world. Weather is no longer something you shelter from in a house or car or under an umbrella. It's something you walk in, eat in, set up camp in, sleep in. The animals that ordinarily are occasional treats to see, or occasional nuisances to avoid, suddenly become a major part of life, inescapable. Living inside nature, not just observing it, is one of the greatest pleasures of backpacking. It can also be one of the biggest drawbacks. Just ask people who have been struck by lightning, caught in early-season blizzards, mauled by bears, or who otherwise have fallen victim to Mother Nature's darker side. Even experienced outdoorsy types still ask me how we checked on the weather forecast while hiking the Pacific Crest Trail, and they are taken aback to learn that, except during town stops, we had no way to do that. Like the pioneers of old—the Donner Party leaps to mind—we had to put up with whatever came along.

When we left the Mexican border in early April, the creatures we worried about the most were of the two-legged variety: Border Patrol agents who might question our identities and plans, and illegal immigrants who, rumor had it,

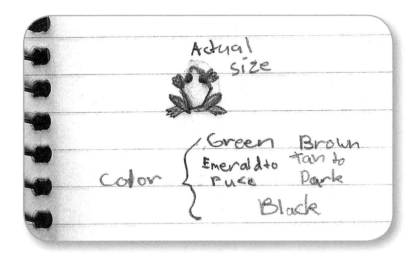

might steal our water. The Border Patrol did take an immediate interest in us, but that didn't last long. As we traveled north, the Forest Service and even sheriff's deputies kept an eye on us. Our worries about being able to prove our citizenship status faded as we continued farther north, while rattlesnakes, bears, mountain lions, and mosquitoes loomed larger on our list of concerns.

The common perception of the desert as a barren place with few animals was disproved right from the beginning. Every day we would see hummingbirds, quail, or crows; rabbits or maybe pika at higher elevations; and lizards and horny toads and boldly patterned king snakes. The list grew longer as we entered the Sierra. We quickly found ourselves growing fond of particular creatures like marmots, the large, furry rodents who live above treeline throughout much of the West. These relatives of woodchucks also symbolized the progress we had made on the trail. When we began seeing marmots, we knew we were truly in the mountains.

Mary named the marmot who greeted us at the top of the highest pass in the southern Sierra "Fed." He looked remarkably like "Teddy," the marmot who had shown up at that morning's campsite. I always got out of the tent first in the morning, and began organizing our food and equipment, but only after a quick bathroom break. That particular morning, taking advantage of the privacy that came with being the first one up, I had chosen a spot just outside the rocks that marked the boundary of our spacious tent site, about 100 yards from Tyndall Creek in the southern Sierra. Later, after Gary and Mary had risen, Teddy the marmot showed up, and seemed obsessed with that particular damp spot. Gary speculated that a previous camper must have deposited food of some sort there—a big no-no in the backcountry, where leftovers are bound to attract vermin and possibly bears. With some embarrassment, I admitted that it was I who had made the deposit in question, and theorized that the marmot had been attracted by the salt in my urine. That didn't leave all prior campers off the hook; Teddy's comfort level around humans made us suspicious that he had received handouts from previous visitors to the well-used site. Mary was able to sit within a few feet of him and draw his portrait while he licked up the salt, although every few minutes he would run off, and then slowly work his way back.

With "Fed," there was no doubt about his affinity for humans. He didn't just tolerate us when we reached Forester Pass at 13,180 feet—he positively welcomed us. Fed hopped around the rocks in excitement, disappearing behind a boulder, then reappearing a little closer to where we sat with our packs, breathing heavily in the thin air at the highest point of the Pacific Crest Trail. We didn't give Fed anything—in fact, we actively discouraged him from approaching the food we were wolfing down—but it was obvious that plenty of previous hikers hadn't been such purists. Marmots are a favorite with many backpackers. They look cuddly, like stuffed animals, with lots of fur and abundant fat for a winter of hibernation. They have heads rather like puppies and they're great fun to watch as they zip between their grassy feeding sites and their rocky hiding places. In 2002, when Mary returned from a trip up Mt. Langley in the southern Sierra with her Dad, she was full of stories about the marmots in the meadows near the campsite: their abundance, their behavior, their cuteness. When I accompanied both of them on another Langley trip a year later, I also became a big fan. (Marmots didn't take the place of our two pet cats in our affections, but some came mighty close.)

Marmots had plenty of competition for favorite animal status. But there was no competition for title of most-hated. Mosquitoes won that contest, big time. Mary, like most girls, has a soft heart for animals. When daddy longlegs climbed into the tent, I had to catch them by the legs and pitch them outside, rather than

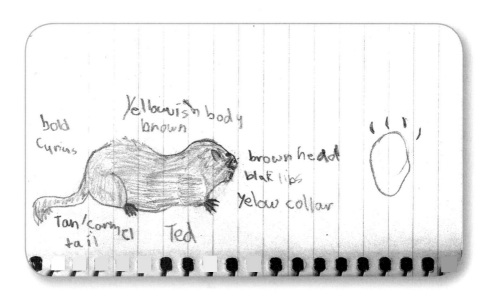

just killing them, which would have been a lot easier. But soon after we entered the Sierra Nevada, Mary was swatting mosquitoes with abandon. A dead skeeter gladdened her bloodthirsty little heart. An evening's entertainment consisted of smashing the nasty little critters that managed to sneak inside the tent, despite our efforts employing what Gary designated "mosquito protocol." That meant that when it was my turn to get into the tent, for example, I would zip open the door just enough to park my fanny inside, while quickly taking off my boots outside. Then I would hastily roll into the tent and close the zipper. This helped, but not even a flamethrower could deter the Sierra's mosquitoes from flying into a tent occupied by anything alive. The tent that had stayed so clean all through the desert rapidly became streaked with little bits of blood—our blood.

The only serious argument Gary and I had the first couple weeks in the Sierra involved Lanacane, the ointment we smeared on insect bites to ease the itching. He thought he had packed a full tube, but in fact it was only half full. I, on the other hand, had made the same mistake with the bottle of sunscreen. In the end, we had plenty of both with just a small effort at rationing. And by the time we reached northern California, we had quit using either one. I have always reacted strongly to mosquito bites, thus my anxiety at having inadequate Lanacane along. When I first met Gary in 1988 and went backpacking with him in Shenandoah National Park, I would go home after a two-day trip with dozens of bites, some of them swollen to the size of a quarter, and the itching would drive me crazy for a couple weeks. Somehow, my body adjusted to the plethora of mosquitoes in the Sierra, and itching was minimal. I had the same experience with poison oak. I'm normally extremely sensitive to it, but on the PCT, I just didn't react to it. (Unfortunately, that immunity didn't last, as I discovered the hard way three months after we returned home.) As for sunscreen, we plastered it on religiously in the southern desert, but I still got sunburned, and Mary did, too. By the time we reached the Lake Tahoe area, we found that a little on our noses and ears was enough. And despite months of sunshine, we neither tanned nor burned. (The thick layer of dirt we wore on our skins may have had something to do with that.)

The animal everyone talks about on the trail isn't the marmot, or even the mosquito. It's the bear. This creature forms a sort of leitmotif to every long trail. There are Bear Creeks and Bear Valleys up and down the PCT, and Black Bear restaurants off the trail in nearby cities. And wherever trail people gather, there are bear stories.

I began our PCT trip partly hoping we'd have a bear encounter worth sharing later, but mostly hoping that the only part of a bear we'd see would be its tail, rapidly receding in the distance. We had all read Bill Bryson's *A Walk in the Woods*, with its opening tale of a 12-year-old boy being carried off and killed by a black bear in Quebec in 1983. Dayhikers who met us on the Tahoe Rim Trail in 2003 eagerly told us about recent bear attacks in western states. We had spent hours

Day 20

We're in Bear country, now. We had yet more uphill, into a saddle. In the saddle, there was a great campsite me and Mom found. Later this evening, we heard weird groaning noises.

They might be BEARS

discussing how to protect our food from ursine marauders, eventually settling on the new, improved Ursacks that a California company manufactures from extremely tough fabric similar to what is used in bulletproof vests. Compared to hard-shell bear canisters, Ursacks worked well in terms of bear protection, and were vastly more practical on a long trip. We also avoided much-used campsites along the trail, knowing from experience that the more heavily used sites were more likely to have furry visitors. The only bear problem we had ever experienced before was during our Section I hike in 1999, at Glen Aulin High Camp, about 6 miles north of Tuolumne Meadows in Yosemite National Park. There, in the cloak of darkness on our last night, *Ursus americanus* snagged our food bag. Mary never forgot about that bear, which ate up the Gummy Bears she'd been saving for our last day. A package of freeze-dried chili and another of freeze-dried blueberries—mistakenly left in my backpack in our tent—provided us with our only food for that last day. What made the bear's theft especially frustrating for Gary was the fact that he had carefully hung our food from a bear pole the night before. We concluded that the Glen Aulin bears had learned to shake the bear pole supports really, really hard whenever they saw food bags hanging from the crossbar, and our bag was the first one to fall.

Our closest 2004 encounter with bears occurred one day in late June, about halfway between Pinchot Pass and Mather Pass. The evening before, we had spent a long time looking for a suitable campsite—suitable meaning one that hadn't been used before, was out of sight of the trail, and showed no signs of bear activity, such as fur or claw marks on the trees. We were beginning to worry we didn't have enough food to get to Vermilion Valley, our next resupply and the only source of provisions on a very long stretch of trail. If we ran low, there was no place to get more, so we decided to go on short rations, beginning that evening. We knew we had to let nothing go to waste—or to bears. The weather was warm, so we went to sleep with the tent door pulled back, giving me a good view through the mosquito netting of the tree where Gary had attached our Ursacks about 5 feet off the ground with a chew-proof Kevlar line.

About 5 a.m., I awoke to a crunching sound. My first thought was of footsteps. A ranger on very early patrol? We had passed the Bench Lake seasonal ranger's tent cabin the previous afternoon. It was fully light as I peered through the tent's screen. But it wasn't a ranger. It was a bear, big and furry and cinnamon-colored, the classic black bear of the backcountry, gnawing away at an Ursack. I shook Gary hard (he's difficult to wake up and uses ear plugs as well) and shouted, "Gary, there's a bear trying to get our food!" That got him out of bed. He scrambled out of the tent, with me right behind him, grabbed an ice ax, and shouted at the bear to get away. Unimpressed, the bear kept gnawing. "Get some rocks!" Gary ordered. Wouldn't you know, that site was practically bereft of rocks. After all the time and effort we'd spent moving rocks out of other tent sites, all I could find here were soft, half-rotten pinecones. Also, I was barefoot and walking was painful. After some scouting around, I managed to find four or five rocks, which I handed to Gary, who heaved them near (not directly at) the bear while continuing to shout. The idea was to scare the bear without injuring it; Gary figured actually hurting the animal might inspire it to hurt him back. Luckily, the bear was scare-able, and after a few suspenseful moments, it dropped down on all fours and ran off. By that point, Mary was wide awake and watching the action from inside the tent. We gave her strict orders to stay put.

Breathing hard from the excitement and sudden exertion, Gary and I climbed back into the tent and wriggled into our sleeping bags to rest. And 20 minutes later, the bear was back—with a friend. Another couple rocks, and the original visitor lumbered off, but the newcomer was made of sterner stuff. This one, although smaller than the first, was also grumpier, growling at Gary as it continued gnawing fruitlessly on an Ursack. It took several more stones and a lot of shouting to send it on its way. Or perhaps it was the sight of Gary in his navy blue long johns that frightened it off. But finally, go it did, and we felt safe enough to exit the tent and eat breakfast. The bears had failed to open any of the Ursacks or gnaw through the Kevlar line. One bear left a set of fang impressions on the bag containing the garbage, which we proudly showed off to other hikers all the way north.

In July, in a wilderness area south of Yosemite, a ranger we met was the only person who ever asked to look at our permit. She also asked to see our bear canisters. Acknowledging to her that we knew about the canister requirements, Gary explained why we were carrying Ursacks instead. She let us off with a warning, which we considered very generous. But the fact is, we were willing to risk a fine just to avoid using canisters, which we had used in the past and discovered to be cumbersome and too small. Ursacks (especially the newer versions, which have been redesigned to thwart bears even more effectively than before) suit us much better. Rangers always have blood-chilling bear stories to tell backpackers, in an effort to encourage compliance with food-storage rules. This ranger told us bears have become so accustomed to finding food in tents that they'll walk right in, whether there's any food there or not. That seemed to suggest it was immaterial whether campers stored their food properly. But we didn't argue. We like rangers, we just don't like the bear-canister regulation, which they're required to enforce.

A week later, in the little California town of Bridgeport, we had our first encounter with the thru-hikers we came to call the Friendly Four: Nocona and Bald Eagle, a married couple from Texas, and Crow and Sherpa, two women who at that time lived in Colorado. They'd had more bear encounters than we had, and their encounters were more serious. Mary asked Sherpa about the two bear claw marks on her shoulder, of which she was very proud. A few days earlier, she and Crow had made camp in Yosemite Valley during a side trip to see the sights. Following regulations, they had stashed all of their food in a bear canister outside their tent. A bear visited their camp anyway—they could hear it. The animal walked through camp, wandered off, and then returned. On its fourth visit, it tried to take the canister with it.

Crow and Sherpa both started to get out of their sleeping bags to chase the marauder away, but at that instant, the bear slapped the tent on Sherpa's side, knocking her on top of Crow. The bear's claws went all the way through the tent fabric and left a deep puncture wound on Sherpa's shoulder. Then it ran off. Crow applied first aid, and in the morning the two continued with their trip. They hadn't let Crow's broken wrist earlier in the trip knock them off the trail—they sure weren't going to let some little puncture wounds get in the way.

The two women showed remarkable presence of mind on another occasion on this same PCT expedition when the Friendly Four were camping in Evolution Valley in Kings Canyon. This time, a pair of bears ran off with the packs, even though they contained no food. The two women were sleeping outside, so they didn't even have to unzip their tent before they leaped into action. Grabbing headlamps and trekking poles, they struck out in hot pursuit, yelling and shouting as they followed a trail of spilled gear. Not only did they catch up with the bears, but by throwing poles and rocks at the beasts, they scared the animals into dropping the packs. Crow spent the rest of the night sewing up her pack to repair the bear damage.

In late July, when camping with three other backpackers at Richardson Lake, near Lake Tahoe, we had barely settled into our tent when a bear climbed the tree where our three companions had hung their food. (Our own food and toiletries were in Ursacks tied to trees within sight of our tent; the bear ignored them.) The other backpackers were so frightened that they were ready to pack up everything and leave. Gary calmed them down and suggested they wait for the bear to come back down the tree and then throw a few rocks at it. Sure enough, the bear soon descended and disappeared into the darkness.

Our other bear encounters were even less exciting, but still memorable. About 170 miles north of Richardson Lake, Gary glimpsed a bear running away from us on the trail north from Belden on a terribly hot day. He urged us to grab the camera and join in the chase. I expressed the opinion that it would make more sense for us to run in the opposite direction.

Another 400 miles north, on August 20—the first day of bow-hunting season for bears in this part of California—we were walking along a dusty trail on a 25-mile trek from a point near Etna Road to Grider Creek. That morning, we had met a bow hunter from southern California who claimed to have killed a 600-pound black bear a few years earlier. (I have no interest in hunting, but it struck me that going after a black bear with a bow and arrows is a much more sporting proposition than, say, going after a mule deer with a rifle. Bow hunters have to get close to their prey to get a good shot—and bears can fight back.) That afternoon, I was trudging along in the lead, thinking to myself, "Gee, there are an awful lot of bear prints on this trail. Some are adults, and a lot are cubs ... maybe I'd better start paying attention." So instead of staring at my feet, I started looking around a bit. Just in time. About 40 feet in front of me, I saw a cloud of dust above the trail. A split second later I realized what had made it—a dark brown cub had run up the hill on my left, pivoted on a dime, and rushed down the trail away from me. I gathered my family and described what I had seen with great excitement. They were excited, too; they wanted to see the bear. What is it, I wondered, with this hikers' death wish? Camera at the ready, we strode on. Mary spotted the sow, a big brown one, downhill from us, between the trail and the stream. The dark cub I had seen was hard to spot in the shadows of the trees. Mary then saw the second cub, the color of its mother, also well down the hill from us. We quietly took our photos and then scooted on down the trail. Mary wrote about the experience in her journal that evening:

> **Day 110:** *Today we saw three bears! There was a sow and two cubs! (No Goldilocks.) They were eating berries, probably. The sow was a very nice, cinnamonny color. She had a little black cub and a bigger brown one. Ma saw the first one, and I saw the other two.*

The animal I saw a few days later was a dog, at first. And then it was a human. But in hindsight, I think it was a bear. Here's what happened: Mary and I had left camp ahead of Gary and we were just walking along, fairly quietly for once. At a curve in the trail, I saw a flash of motion, which I thought at the time was a large, black, shaggy dog with a shuffling sort of gait. We were 10 or 12 miles from the nearest paved road, and I thought it likely the dog was with a human. In that case, we could expect to meet the human fairly soon. Whoever it was could have walked in from the trailhead early that morning, and by now would be looking for a break spot. We saw no humans. But a mile or two later, I found a good-quality, lightweight, black jacket draped over a bush. Where was the owner? Could it have been a human that I saw, running around on all fours, which caught my eye earlier? Somewhere deep in my subconscious arose centuries-old stories, from my ancestral home of forested Germany, stories about men who could turn into animals ... or, more likely, I was remembering the Harry Potter tale in which Harry's godfather, Sirius Black, turns himself into a large, black, shaggy dog. I think now it was a bear, and the black jacket was just a coincidence.

The only other animal mystery occurred the morning after our hundredth day on the PCT. Mary and I had hiked up a half-mile side trail from our campsite between a logging road and Tate Creek. Gary was behind us, struggling with an aching knee on a day that promised to be a scorcher. As we reached a trail intersection, Mary and I caught a split-second glimpse of a small, furry creature bounding across a clear patch between shrubs. I remember it as catlike in shape and running style, and very dark. Mary remembers it as more silvery-gray, and resembling a giant squirrel. We agreed it had a roundish head, a long back, and short legs, and that it was too big for a weasel but too small for a bobcat. It was probably a fisher or a marten, large, seldom-seen relatives of the otter and the mink.

Our favorite animal story is about Henry the mule. Mary loves telling this story. She starts out:

Day 16: *Today, we walked 2 or 3 miles through ice and snow.*

The ice and snow were on Fuller Ridge in southern California, where we had camped the night before on the only remotely adequate tent site for some distance. It was bitterly cold. While looking for a place to set up camp after dark, we reached a spot where we could see the lights of a city way down on the valley floor. Mary remembers thinking, "Here we are, freezing our tails off, and down there people are sitting around and cranking up the air-conditioning!" Backpackers often swap stories of that moment in their outdoor experiences when they realize they could be dying of cold, thirst, or heatstroke, while only a few miles away, unsuspecting couch potatoes are complaining that they've run out of ice for their soft drinks.

Then we walked 16 miles down a hill. It was 16 miles because we'd go WAAAAYYY this way and BAAAACCKK that way and so on.

Imagine a huge slope of sandstone and dirt, carpeted with prickly desert plants, with a drop in altitude of well over 6,000 feet. It's exposed to the broiling hot sun for the entire day, and there's no shade. It's also liberally supplied with rattlesnakes. At the bottom, at the mouth of Snow Canyon, is a water fountain. Now imagine some sadist has decided to draw out, for as long as possible, the trail that winds down this hellish landscape to that longed-for fountain. The path zigs one way for about a mile, then zags back the other, losing hardly any altitude in the process. Short-cutting is out of the question—if the yucca, cacti, and other vicious vegetation weren't enough to discourage it, the rattlers curled up in the dry grass would do the job. We concluded the trail could have been made about half as long if the designer hadn't wanted to re-create the inner ring of the seventh circle of Dante's Inferno—the one with the burning sands.

The only thing that broke the extreme monotony was Henry the mule. He was a large, chestnut mule, and we were taking a break. We had got far off the trail, but the mule wouldn't pass.

Horses are notoriously afraid of backpackers, but I had expected more common sense from a mule. We couldn't get off the trail on the downhill side—the ground dropped precipitously, and the trail was edged with small but nasty yucca—so I directed Gary and Mary to climb above the trail and perch on some boulders. The mule stopped, and his rider introduced his steed as "Henry, a genuine Missouri mule." We never did learn the rider's name. We chatted for a few minutes and learned that Henry was even more afraid of rattlesnakes than of backpackers. Henry refused to pass a rattlesnake, even at a safe distance. His rider was in the habit of dismounting whenever he spotted a rattler. He would throw rocks at the offending serpent until it slithered away. Finally, the venerable rider tried to get his mount to head on up the trail. No luck. We squatted on the boulders, trying to look as small as possible. Still, no forward movement on Henry's part. The situation was rapidly deteriorating into a frustrating impasse. We couldn't move down toward the water fountain with the mule in the way. And I wasn't sure the beast could even turn around on the narrow trail.

Finally, his rider dismounted—right into a yucca bush.

Ouch!

He cajoled this big, strong mule to walk with phrases like, 'You can do it, sweet wittle mule!' Finally the mule walked RIGHT TO THE EDGE! The rider backed him up. Then they went the right direction, but Henry just casually shoved him off the side with his nose.

Ouch again!

When they finally left, we all burst out laughing.

Thanks to Henry, I stopped envying equestrians. It's hard enough to get myself moving down the trail. Having to persuade a 1,200-pound animal to "git along" would be too much.

The mule encounter had its humorous aspects, but the scene we saw another day involving horses and mules very nearly became a tragedy. We had camped at Woods Creek, a popular site in Kings Canyon with bear boxes and the scariest suspension bridge I've ever seen. High above the deep, rushing stream, it was made of skinny cables holding together skinny slats. It looked like it could fall apart at any moment. The signs admonishing hikers to cross one at a time didn't do much to inspire confidence. Each slat was an inch or so apart from the next, providing an excellent view of the water far, far below. The bridge scared even Gary, who (unlike me) has little fear of heights.

Soon after we got across, we saw a Park Service wrangler riding toward the stock crossing at the head of a long line of pack animals. We figured the supplies were intended for the backcountry ranger's tent cabin we'd seen the day before. Gary asked him if we could watch the crossing. The wrangler, a lean young man in blue jeans, a cowboy hat, and cowboy boots, directed us to a spot about 50 yards upstream. We scrambled through brambles to get there, and then quietly settled down to watch. The Park Service worker looked over at us a few minutes later from water's edge and asked, "Could somebody help me, here?" Gary volunteered. The wrangler handed Gary the reins of the lead horse. Behind that horse was another, standing in the water. Behind the second horse, half a dozen or so mules stood along the trail. Gary obligingly held the reins while the wrangler went back along the line, tightening packs and shoving mules into position.

After several minutes, the second horse started pawing with a front hoof at the rocks in the stream. I've had just enough experience with horses to know that means trouble. The restless animal graduated from pawing to plunging to panicking. Gary hung on to the lead horse, but soon all the rest of the animals were in the stream, with its rocky, slippery bottom and cold water above their knees. Within moments, two mules fell over. One got stuck against the rocks, unable to gain its feet. The second ended up in an even worse position, almost on its back, barely able to keep its head above water. Shouting and swearing, the young man waded in. His hat was the first casualty. It floated downstream at a rate that revealed the current's strength. Pulling out a knife, he began sawing through harnesses, trying to cut the animals apart from each other. Then he started cutting the trapped animals' loads from their backs. In a few minutes, the first mule got to its feet and ran onto the opposite bank, where the troublemaking horse and the loose mules had already fled. The man turned his attention to the second mule, which was in danger of drowning. He alternated between holding up the animal's head so it could get a moment's respite to breathe, and shoving at the poor thing's body to get it unstuck. Mary was in dread of the beast's imminent demise. But finally, the wrangler got the mule free. It staggered to its feet and splashed onto the bank. Coming back to our side to fetch his lead horse, drenched from head to boot, he made just one remark to us: "That's not the way you cross a river." Assuring us with a nod that he now had the situation under control, he mounted his horse, and rode across to capture the rest of the stock, which we could hear squealing at each other in a nearby grove.

I finally discarded my previous idealized impression of trail mounts a couple months after our PCT adventure, when I read Joseph LeConte's *A Journal of Ramblings Through the High Sierras of California*, in which the University of California professor describes a monthlong adventure in Yosemite, Lake Tahoe, and points in between. I had assumed that back in 1870, at a time when personal transportation was mostly four-footed, men tackling the mountains would have steeds worthy of the challenge. But LeConte described his companions' mounts as far less than ideal. One large, mud-colored monster had what LeConte called "vicious" eyes and a sprung knee. "He stumbles fearfully, and bucks whenever he can," LeConte reported. Another, a dark gray pinto with "imbecile-looking eyes," was "serviceable," except for the fact that he had a distinct cow shape, so every time he went downhill, his ill-fitting saddle would slip down around his neck. Of a companion who traded his horse for a mule, he wrote: "He no sooner mounted than the mule started off in the contrary direction, kicking and plunging, and jumping stiff-legged, until he threw off—not the Captain, indeed, but the pack behind the saddle." And finally, he offered this description of a typical trail diversion: "Phelps and his mare entertained us while getting off this morning with an amusing bucking scene. The interesting performance ended with the grand climacteric feat of flying head foremost over the head of the horse, turning a somersault in the air, and alighting safely on the back."

Sounds like LeConte's party would have been better off trying to hitch rides on wild mustangs. Speaking of which, thanks to a note about them in the guidebook, I was on the alert for the wild horses of Oak Creek Canyon near the town of Mojave. These dark brown descendants of animals lost by Spanish explorers in the Antelope Valley area left Mary in awe:

> **Day 40:** *Today we got out of the canyon. We windily hiked out of the wilderness to a very windy windmill farm. The windmills were huge. I was afraid a blade would fall off on me! When we came out, I saw two wonderfully beautifully gracefully running horses. They curiously looked at me and Ma and Dad, then galloped off. Instead of galloping, they flowed, because they were so fast and graceful! They could be wild! Then we had a fairly normal but windy walk to where we were picked up and taken to White's Motel.*

Of course, some horses we met on our journey were so docile, Mary treated them as household pets. Here's what Mary had to say about Rick and Emmy, a pair of horses trail angel Donna Saufley calls her "gentle giants:"

> **Day 33:** *Today we were up at 5 (me at 6), very early. We walked through very impressive Vasquez Rocks and then, perhaps equally impressive, we saw crows soaring. Then I found a snake skin, and we had a break where we were short of food. By 3 p.m. we were in no way short of food. We gorged ourselves on exceptional egg rolls, awesome apricots, and succulent sandwiches. For dessert we had nice ice cream! Then we went to the Saufleys where we took SHOWERS and I met two horses, Rick and Emmy.*
>
> ***Rick:*** *Rick is a gelding. He's very handsome—almost black, with very shiny fur. He's a bit face shy, but quite nice.*
>
> ***Emmy:*** *She's a mare, so she's registered. Her registered name is Shalynka Emerald Moon. She's very nice, too. She's a dapple gray. I met [dogs] Buddy, Lucky, Bitsy, Nally, Fozzie, Sammy, and Shady. I helped Donna feed the horses, and we had a painfully filling meal at Maria Bonita's.*
>
> *P.S. They are both purebred Percherons, so they are huge. Emmy weighs 2,100 pounds. Rick weighs 2,300 pounds.*
>
> **Day 34:** *This morning we had breakfast at the Saufleys. Then we got first-aid stuff and two books for me:* Anne of Avonlea *and* Racso and the Rats of NIMH. *Then we had pizza at Vincenzo's with Leprechaun. When*

we drove "home," Donna was riding Rick. And she ASKED ME to
RIDE WITH HER! I did, of course. It was one of the best things ever!
(No saddle or pad, so riding this Giant was my introduction to riding
bareback.) I'm glad I rode bareback. He was warm and velvety. We
rode around the yard three times and then I got off. Instead of just
watching, this time I actually helped feed them. I love horses! (And
Donna.)

Of the seven dogs, only one was simply acquired as a pet. The rest had histories of one sort or another, with the happy ending of being rescued by Jeff and Donna. My favorite story is about Nally, whom Donna describes as a "tall, slender, short-haired, jet black dog." She told me Nally's story in an email after we got off the trail: "Nally is the one rescued by the hikers after she followed different groups of them across the Mojave Desert, reportedly from just north of here. Where the trail crosses Highway 58, Stretch, Yucca, Kimber, and a few other hikers, managed to catch her and bring her to the White's Motel with them. She was too emaciated and exhausted to continue on with them, so they called us. One of the hikers that was here recharging his physical batteries drove to Mojave to get her and bring her home. They called me about her the same day we learned of the death of another hiker at the White's. His name was Neil Ball, and 'Nally' is based on his name." The Saufleys' nickname among animal lovers should be the "Soft-hearted-leys." They nursed the creature back to health, and when we met her, she was the sweetest and happiest of a crowd of seven sweet, happy dogs.

Animals continued to entertain and amaze us as we headed north. Coveys of quail, trotting across the trail with their little plumes wagging, always made me smile, as did the bleating goats some hikers used for pack animals. Non-poisonous king snakes and rubber boas stopped us in our tracks while we admired their slithery beauty. The deer inside national parks were comfortable enough around humans that we could watch them from fairly close up, unlike their much-hunted relatives under Forest Service jurisdiction. In the desert, legions of lizards startled us with their instantaneous transition from immobility to streaks of lightning. We were especially fond of the glossy black ones doing push-ups on boulders. Captain Critter, a small dog, steered the ferry at Vermilion Valley Resort, or appeared to. As a child, I loved to catch horny toads (the common name for horned toads, which are actually lizards) in the dry mountains of east-central Nevada. They don't live near our house in Sunol, although we've seen plenty in the dusty hills of nearby Henry Coe State Park, our favorite training ground. We delighted in noting their varied colors and sizes along the PCT. But none of us had ever seen horny toads mating, as we did in the southern desert. Naturally, we made a point after that of telling everyone we met about the very "horny" toads we had seen.

One of our biggest surprises came near Cienega Creek Ranch. We had camped a short distance away from a dirt road one April evening. Here's what Mary wrote before she went to bed that night:

Day 20: *We're in bear country now. We had yet more uphill into a saddle. In the saddle there was a great campsite me and Mom found. Later this evening, we heard weird groaning noises. They might be BEARS.*

Mary was sincerely frightened, and it didn't help any when Gary and I debated in front of her whether they were bears or cougars. Mary was feeling a lot more cheerful when she wrote in her journal the next night:

Day 21: *We walked DOWN this morning to a private zoo with bears and tigers!*

Sure enough, there behind bars were the kinds of big predators normally seen and heard—in zoos.

Animals that live around popular campgrounds and trailheads become dependent on human food. And they become downright demanding. We became adept at chasing away the rodents and birds that came to beg, borrow, or steal. But nothing prepared me for the birds at one road crossing in northern California. It was a hot day (as was almost every day in northern California) and when Gary called a rest break, I immediately got out the food bag and my water bottle and plunked myself down on my pack. I had barely unwrapped my candy bar when a bird tried to grab it—right out of my mouth! All I saw was a flash of feathers, but Mary saw the entire scene. She said the bird flew in on a banked turn, like a stunt pilot at an air show, as though intending to grab my Baby Ruth bar with its feet. I was scared half out of my wits when this thing flew in my face. Gary and Mary were merely amused, and Mary quipped that only a birdbrain would try to steal food from a hungry thru-hiker.

The grandest animal thieves of all are at Drakesbad, a century-plus-old resort within Lassen Volcanic National Park in northern California. Mary calls them chipmunks. I think they're golden-mantled ground squirrels. Whatever they're rightfully called, these animals were on top of their game. At Drakesbad, where the food is excellent and plentiful, these critters don't even bother begging. Once the other customers had been through the buffet line, we were invited to chow down at half price. It had been days since our last shower or change of clothes, and we smelled pretty bad, so in consideration of the other patrons, we sat on the patio. In a flash, the rodents were on us. The cutest little robbers in the world, they were incredibly impudent. At first, I brushed them away from my plate with the wine list (which contained some pretty fancy choices for a resort smack in the middle of one of the lesser-known national parks). Here's what happened next, as Mary described in her journal:

Day 94: *One even got to licking up Dad's mayonnaise off his plate—until Dad threw it! Then one (I don't know if it was the same one) waited till he left and stole an entire cookie of his!*

Gary told me later that when he realized a rodent had the effrontery to steal a thru-hiker's food right in front of him, he instinctively grabbed the little pest. But then in the next second, it flashed through his mind, "I'm holding onto a rodent! What do I do now?" As the words "bubonic plague" flitted through his head, he gave the creature a robust toss. It landed several feet away, apparently unhurt, and promptly returned to the fray. The stolen cookie must have weighed as much as the thief did. The resort's other guests could only stare as Mary and Gary pursued the animal all the way to his hidey hole, which was too small for his booty.

A flock of educable birds lived in the chaparral near Highway 18, not far from Big Bear City. We were walking away from our campsite one morning in late April and listening to the birds sing a simple three-note call. They'd been doing it all morning. Gary imitated the bird call until he got it just right; he would whistle, and a bird would whistle back. Then he added another note—and the bird imitated him. For quite a distance, Gary kept up his avian school. I was a little regretful when we reached the highway and had to leave Gary's musical disciples behind. I sometimes wonder: Did any of the birds keep up the new call?

Always, in the backs of our minds, was the chance of running afoul of small but dangerous animals: rattlesnakes, scorpions, black widow spiders, centipedes, and wasps. Our first close encounter with a rattler came early. Mary's journal entry reads:

Day 2: *Today we saw a RATTLESNAKE! It was rattling like crazy and it was coiled and reared up! I was really scared, but my Dad took a picture of it!*

Before long, rattler-sightings were frequent enough that we didn't bother recording each one in our journals. We had seen plenty of the creatures before we started the PCT, and we knew that bites commonly occur when young, (usually) inebriated (usually) men stupidly pick up snakes and then get bitten on the hand or arm. But we also knew that there is no good backcountry treatment for snakebites, especially for someone as small as Mary. Trying to get a straight answer from the "experts" on what to do if Mary suffered a venomous snakebite was the most frustrating part of our first-aid preparations. Every source said the exact same thing: Get the patient to a hospital as quickly as possible, preferably within an hour. Yeah, right. What if we're halfway through Section I and three days from the nearest road? We took a snakebite kit, figuring that trying to remove the venom from the wound with a small suction device would be better than nothing. (Gary and I knew that the old treatment methods we had learned growing up—cutting the wound and sucking out the venom, or applying a tourniquet—have since, fortunately, fallen out of favor.) Snakes, along with smaller creepy-crawlies, are the main reason we always used a tent in California. Sleeping outside "under

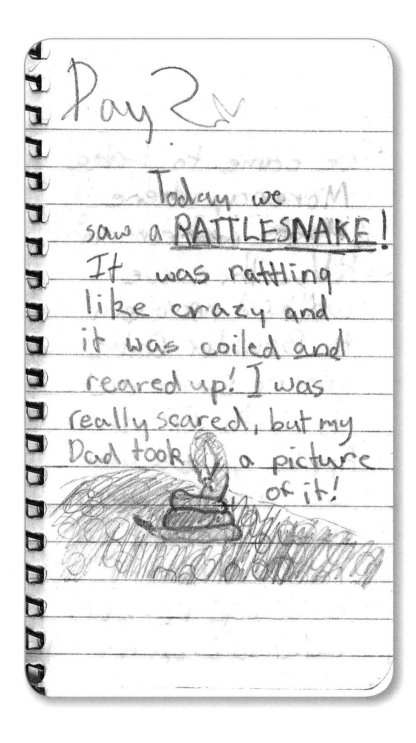

Day 2.

Today we saw a <u>RATTLESNAKE</u>! It was rattling like crazy and it was coiled and reared up! I was really scared, but my Dad took a picture of it!

the stars," as people say, sounds wonderfully romantic, and on really hot nights, it's probably more comfortable than being inside a tent. But I wouldn't be able to sleep, wondering what might decide to creep into my bag or, worse, Mary's. Besides, I'm a living mosquito magnet. The nasty critters invite their second and third cousins to the party when I'm around. Let the ultra-light types go with a tarp, or less. For me, a tent is just common sense.

One of my biggest concerns was anaphylactic shock—the potentially fatal reaction some people have to the odd insect sting, foodstuff, drug, brush with latex, and even bout of exercise. If one of us suffered severe breathing difficulties as a result of an allergy, death could occur before help could be found. Luckily, the only bite or sting that caused a bad reaction occurred close to Belden Town Resort.

It was Day 90, and some mysterious bug stung Mary on her wrist, which proceeded to swell suddenly and painfully. We had just held a circle cheer for having exceeded 25 miles the previous day, and had sat down on some handy boulders for a snack break before descending the steep hill to our next resupply. (Circle cheers are how we celebrate a major accomplishment. We hold hands, jump up and down, and shout, "Hurrah!" I sometimes wonder what the neighbors think.) Mary put her hand down on a rock and immediately started screaming. We could see a red dot where something had bitten or stung her. Gary spotted a wicked-looking black insect, perhaps some kind of wasp, but he couldn't be sure it was the culprit. The pain was bad, but much more alarming was how quickly Mary's wrist became puffy and red, so swollen that she had trouble moving her hand. I half expected her to develop trouble breathing. However, she seemed all right otherwise, the pain gradually subsided, and by the time we reached Belden, her wrist hurt just a little. The stiffness, however, lingered for days.

Nature provides the PCT with an amazing variety of plant life. We were fortunate enough to hit the wildflower season at its peak in the southern California desert and again in much of the Sierra Nevada. We saw scores of different flowers, only a few of which I could positively identify. Most we just admired as we walked by, but some stood out for their beauty or unusual setting. Some were notable for their rarity, others for their abundance.

In the far south, the Mojave yucca was in bloom, with its yard-long clusters of white flowers guarded by stiff, spiny leaves. Like many desert plants, the yucca comes equipped with spikes, thorns, or needles to fend off browsers. I refer to such blood-drawing vegetation as carnivorous because I've donated my share of blood and flesh to them. Also fully adapted to hot and dry conditions is the ocotillo, a shrub that looks like a giant twig broom sitting in the desert upside down. After a rain, the leaves suddenly spring to life, and the red flowers on their tips bloom briefly. Closer to Palm Springs, we began seeing the brilliant red of the vermilion phase of the desert mariposa tulip. Shaped somewhat like California poppies or sego lilies, these silky red flowers on their short stems stand out like drops of blood on snow. It was near a cluster of these flowers that we paused to watch a colony of ground-dwelling bees. Another desert flower bears the delightful name of pussypaws. This strange little plant stretches out on the ground, with the pink cat's-paw flower clusters forming a circle.

Sky pilot is named for its lofty home among the boulders on the highest peaks. To come upon a patch of these little blue flowers on the approaches to Mt. Whitney was a delightful surprise, and an inspiration. If such delicate blossoms could thrive in the thin air, certainly I could, too. The crimson columbine, whose red and yellow flowers I was used to seeing among the aspens in eastern Nevada, also graces streams in the Sierra Nevada. But for a change, I was treated to a hillside of Coville's columbine, a larger, pale blue flower much like the Colorado state flower. I saw them only on the interminable hill leading down to Edison Lake; they made the endless series of switchbacks a little easier to bear. Another familiar flower alongside alpine lakes and streams was the shooting star. Once seen, it's never forgotten, but it sure is hard to describe. Some say the lavender, white, and black blossom resembles a rocket; others say it looks like a mosquito's beak. Lupine grows along many portions of the PCT, sometimes in bushy masses of blue and lavender, other times in white or yellow. There's even a harlequin lupine, which sports rose-pink, yellow, and white on its sweet-pea-shaped blossoms. Lupine, which frequently provides a backdrop for orange monkeyflower or golden California poppies, is so common that I thought at first the Professor Lupin in the Harry Potter books was named after the flower. Then I remembered that the word actually derives from *lupus*, Latin for wolf. Just as J.K. Rowling's Professor Lupin is unfairly feared and stigmatized, so too were lupine plants, according to my Audubon field guide to wildflowers. Lupine were thought to be "wolf-like," devouring nutrients. But they actually prefer poor soils, and don't deplete them further. Now you know.

One of the pleasures of taking friends on first-time backpacking trips in the Sierra Nevada is witnessing their reaction to their initial sight of two flowers that flourish in the deep shade of the ponderosas: snow plants and pine drops. These two members of the wintergreen family don't look anything like traditional flowers. Pine drops, with their leafless brown stems and tiny brown flowers, look dead even when they're alive. And because the dried stalks remain standing for years, hikers are likely to see many more dead pine drops than living ones. Snow plants, so named because they appear as the snow drifts melt, are a brilliant red all over. They look more like vegetables than flowers, perhaps distantly related to brussels sprouts. Imagine the tip of an asparagus spear, dipped in bright red candle wax. Now imagine that spear about 6 inches high and 2 or 3 inches in diameter, loosely wrapped with red curling ribbon, and you've got a picture of *Sarcodes sanguinea*.

With a few exceptions, the flowers petered out around the Lake Tahoe area, as the northern Sierra's hot, dry summer settled in. One exception was the skyrocket, whose bright red, trumpet-shaped flowers defied the intense heat. Near Mt. Shasta, we were delighted by the large, fragrant white flowers of the Shasta lily, looking like Easter lilies growing on large shrubs. And in boggy patches north of Castle Crags, we came upon the West Coast's truly carnivorous plant, the California pitcher plant. Tubular leaves grow together to create attractive traps for insects, which creep inside to get at the nectar. The intruders drown and rot, and are absorbed by the plant.

Color returned to the forest in Oregon, and again in Washington—only it wasn't flowers, it was an amazing variety of mushrooms. I've never seen or even dreamed of such fungal variety. Mushrooms popped up from the ground, sprouted from fallen logs, crept up tree trunks, and dangled from branches overhead in an incredible and almost nightmarish array of shapes and colors. We don't know a thing about choosing edible mushrooms, and as a result tried to avoid touching them, much less eating them. In the San Francisco Bay Area, where we live, someone dies every few years from eating "death caps," an intensely poisonous mushroom that bears a striking resemblance to an edible mushroom in parts of southeast Asia. Immigrants go mushroom hunting, as they did in the old country, and end up destroying their livers by eating *Amanita phalloides*. We did our collecting with a camera and left the mushroom picking to the professionals. In Washington state, mushroom pickers (many of them immigrants from southeast Asia) had been making money hand over bucket a few years earlier when restaurants paid top dollar for morels, matsutakes, and other delicacies. In our year, the bottom had dropped out of the mushroom market, and suddenly pickers who had paid $50 for a Forest Service permit were regretting the expenditure. One exceptionally unpleasant day in central Washington, I saw a Russian family venturing out to pick mushrooms from the PCT trail crossing at Stampede Pass. The older woman of the group wore a calf-length housedress, heavy boots, and a scarf over her head. It was raining hard, and the high for the day was 42°F. Perfect weather for hypothermia. I felt so sorry for the old woman. At least Gary and Mary carried proper rain gear, even if they did have 18 miles to walk.

We weren't quite so paranoid about berries, but there were only two that we ate: blackberries, which seem to grow wild practically everywhere, and huckleberries, which we found in Oregon. Northwestern huckleberries look rather like purplish blueberries, and they're delicious. We ate only a few, figuring that the birds and the bears needed them more than we did. Huckleberries can't be raised commercially, but stores and restaurants in the Pacific Northwest typically offer wild huckleberry jam or ice cream.

Trees were almost constant companions along the PCT, except in parts of the southern desert and the passes above timberline in the southern Sierra. I've always loved trees. Most in my childhood experience were small: pinyon pines and stunted junipers that characterize the landscape around my Nevada birthplace. Big trees were a rarity: tall but spindly aspens, with their golden leaves in autumn, and more substantial cottonwoods in the creek bottoms. Above 10,000 feet, bristlecone pines grew to 3,000 years old and older, enduring fierce winter winds and bitter cold. My youthful idea of a forest was one that was easy to walk through, with widely spaced trees and limited undergrowth. The year I spent in Maryland introduced me to the thicker, hardwood forest of the Appalachians. This forest limits the view and shuts out much of the sun, making me a little claustrophobic. But that was nothing compared to the dense forests of Oregon and Washington. Heavy rain and abundant snow create thick forests of fir, tamarack, hemlock, spruce, and pine, towering over the trail and creating a twilight effect even at noon.

One day in Oregon, we crossed a small meadow in bright sunlight. The trail appeared to plunge into a cave, the inky darkness under the trees was so complete. Even just a couple feet away from the forest's edge, the scene gave us a *Twilight Zone* feel of walking directly from noon into midnight. And on days when the sun hid and a steady rain fell, the Northwestern forests brought to mind words such as primeval, monolithic, impenetrable—even hostile. But even when the forest was at its darkest and deepest, there would be some moment of startling beauty to remind us why we were out there. The day we came to a break in the Oregon forest and I caught my first view of Mt. Hood—freshly frosted with snow, with blue sky above and swirling mist in the valley below us—I knew again why I treasure backpacking as a fundamental part of my life. Having Gary and Mary along to share it with me made for a perfect moment.

One of the beauties of nature that I didn't contemplate as much as I'd hoped was the night sky. On earlier desert trips, we would sit up late to see the stars and try to identify the constellations. On the PCT, by the time we had the tent up and dinner eaten, all we wanted to do was climb into our sleeping bags. But in the desert, I would frequently take a minute just before following Mary into the tent to gaze up at the sky and locate the Big Dipper and the North Star, pointing toward Canada. Today, anytime I see the Big Dipper, I again experience that intense longing to reach my goal.

Weather was a constant concern of ours, but it also provided some of the trail's most beautiful moments. We had experienced a rough night in southern California thanks to a sudden ice storm, and in the morning I was thinking gloomy thoughts about scraping the ice off the inside of the tent and drying out our wet ponchos.

Mary had a different reaction, which she described in her journal:

> **Day 11:** *When I put my head out the door of the tent, I saw ice tipping burned manzanita—like white flames! It was so BEAUTIFUL, and there was frost on the trees, too.*

Snow is a rarity in the San Francisco Bay Area, where we live, and early sights of snow were special for Mary. On Day 45, she wrote,

We got our first glimpse of the snow-covered Sierra. It was very magnificent!

Later, as we were getting close to Mt. Whitney, we watched a storm move through the mountains several miles east of us, creating a dramatic landscape that reminded Mary of scenes in *The Lord of the Rings*. She wrote

Day 53: *We had beautiful views. The most spectacular was something I named the Dragon Mountains. The Dragon Mountains were so misty and mysterious. It looked like orcs could pour out any minute! But in front of them were sunny, sandy mountains, the opposite of the ominous, softly lighted mountains.*

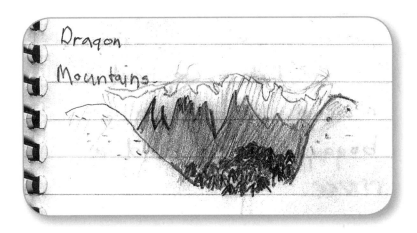

Months later, I called a halt to a day's hike a few miles short of our goal because dusk was falling, and in my state of heat-induced exhaustion, I didn't think I could safely navigate the upcoming rocky tread. We were all plenty tired as we set up camp at a wide spot next to the trail, but Mary was never too tired to appreciate everything she saw. In her journal, she wrote:

Day 108: *We saw a sunset, bats, and a crescent moon. The sunset was red, orange, and purple. The moon was beautiful and bright. There were many bats.*

Toward the end of our time on the trail came one of those days when I especially appreciated having a child along. Despite the depth of her experience as a backpacker, Mary still had a child's knack for seeing something ordinary in a new and wonderful way. We were struggling through the snow of Washington's North Cascades on what I was beginning to regard as a losing effort to get to Canada before we all froze to death. Gary was breaking trail, then came Mary, and I was bringing up the rear, thinking doleful thoughts. Mary pointed out how the little clumps of snow that we dislodged with our boots would roll down the steep slope to our right, pick up speed, and become miniature snowballs, carving erratic channels on their way down. Some would stop fairly quickly, while others would pick up speed and travel surprising distances. Once in a while, Mary would knock off a clump about the same time as I did, and the tiny snowballs would race downslope like competing skiers. Occasionally, one would change course and knock the other off track. This quickly became a little game for us, predicting which snowballs would roll the farthest. I cheered up in spite of myself. Mary's talent for introducing an element of play into almost any situation made all those miles I used to carry her on my back worthwhile.

CHAPTER 7

PaiN aND SuFFeRiNG

Day 125: *Today Dad's knee hurt him very badly. He fell. We had a heckish time getting water.*

—from Scrambler's journal

THE FIRST INDICATION OF SERIOUS PROBLEMS on the trail came at Olallie Lake in northern Oregon. The best scenery along Oregon's section of the Pacific Crest Trail is supposed to be in the northern half of the state, where the trail meanders through the Olallie Lake Scenic Area and Mt. Hood National Forest. Guidebooks tout the visual wonders of Mt. Washington, Mt. Jefferson, and Three-Fingered Jack. We had seen nothing of them. Rain had fallen for several days, and clouds and mist obscured our view of everything but the nearest trees. Creek fords had become deeper and colder. Our boots were constantly wet. Concerns about dangerous stream crossings had persuaded us to take a long detour around Russell and Milk creeks, requiring a short but risky road walk. Breaking camp meant packing up under a tarp, a difficult and back-breaking process. Setting up camp meant more of the same.

Hand-numbing cold had replaced northern California's mind-bending heat. And I mean *numb*. A few days earlier, I had felt an urgent call of nature as we plodded along through a drizzle. As usual, I told Gary and Mary to go on without me; I would take a quick pee and then catch up. But when I tried to get my pants down, I couldn't unfasten my belt buckle. It was the kind of buckle where all you have to do is push in from either side to release it. It's meant to be easy to operate even with mittens on. But I couldn't do it. My chilled hands refused to cooperate, and Gary and Mary were too far ahead to hear me shout for help. Luckily, I discovered that I had lost so much weight, I no longer needed to open the buckle and unzip—I could just pull my pants down right over my hips, do my business, yank them back up, and catch up with the rest of my family.

On this particular September day—our 138th on the trail—we had experienced not only rain, but snow and sleet as well. The PCT wasn't so much a trail as a navigable waterway. I half expected to see a flotilla of canoeists paddling by. We tried at first to walk around the worst of the puddles, but eventually we gave up. Our boots and socks weren't just wet; they were soaked. Saturated. Waterlogged. And that was just within the first mile. We eventually reached a dirt parking lot where we took shelter under the tiny roof of a forlorn outhouse.

Desperate for something to eat, the three of us jammed into an area the size of an old-fashioned phone booth. With our packs and my trekking poles, there wasn't much room to maneuver. I wriggled out of my pack and attempted to hold it above the wet ground with one hand, while opening the buckles on the pack lid, loosening the drawstring, and rooting around in the food bag with the other. I eventually managed to fish out three energy bars while Gary and Mary tried to grab their water bottles without taking off their ponchos or their packs. Houdini would have found this a challenge. The outhouse hadn't been cleaned in quite some time, judging from the smell, and after about 10 minutes, Mary announced that she was feeling faint. With some cajoling, Gary convinced her she was OK, only to have me complain a few minutes later that I was about to pass out. I abruptly opened the outhouse door, plunked myself down on the rusty metal lid, and tucked my head between my knees. We had reached a new low.

• • • • •

THIS WASN'T THE FIRST TIME we had experienced physical agony and mental suffering along the PCT. A certain amount of discomfort is inevitable during an effort of this magnitude. We had dealt with blisters and joint pain, heat, cold, rain, and snow. Looking ahead in the trail guides, we had worried about how to deal with dangerous stream crossings and difficult navigation. But so far, we had suffered these discomforts one at a time; it had been the pain *or* the uncertainty *or* the weather that had been hard to bear. On this day in central Oregon, they all hit at once. Nonetheless, like every other day on the trail, we had no choice but to continue. The dirt road that led away from our temporary refuge might not see a vehicle for weeks. And that night's proposed shelter was just a few water-logged miles away.

As we left the outhouse, dusk was falling right along with the rain, and we passed a series of ponds—now overflowing onto the trail—that indicated we were getting close to Olallie Lake Resort, our resupply destination, where we also hoped to get a cabin for the night. Beyond the constant downpour, it was cold and we were very tired. We found the store where rooms could be reserved just before the clerk locked up, and just in time to grab the last available housing. I

138

Today ~~in other~~
it rained all day.
We finnally
got to Ollallie lake.
After we got
our cabin and
A fire going in
the stove, Chris
(Hiker 816)
came in.
816
Stayed
with us. We had
hot Dinner!

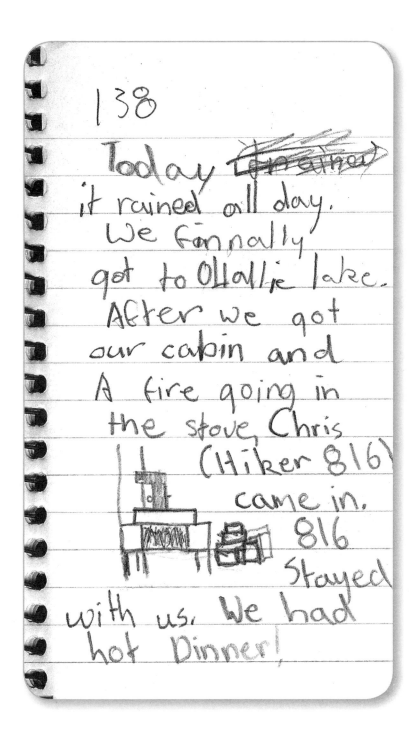

imagined we could soon relax in a "charming lakeside cabin," as advertised in the resort's website, with light and warmth and comfort. Don't get me wrong, I was glad to have any kind of roof over my head at that point. But the accommodations fell somewhat short of the picture in my mind. Our cottage reminded me of the cabin in which author Jack London spent the winter in the Alaskan backcountry: small, dark, and cold. The lighting consisted of a pair of dim gas lamps that together produced about as much illumination as one votive candle. There was no bathroom—the outhouse was about 50 yards away—and for water, there was an outdoor tap. Fortunately, there was firewood. I'm a past master at starting a fire in a wood stove, having relied on one for six years in northern Nevada's Washoe Valley, and I soon had a blaze going. We pushed the two benches close to the stove and gathered around it, arranging boots, socks, ponchos, jackets, and most of the rest of our belongings around the fire to dry them out.

We were just starting to get warm enough to relax when there came a knock on the door, and out of the cold, rain, and wind, a section hiker appeared. With no cabins left, Hiker 816 had come to us to seek refuge from the storm. We took him in, of course, and he turned out to be a very considerate house guest. He settled down in the corner nearest the door, offered intelligent conversation, and insisted on sharing the cost of the crowded, smoky lodging. But even his cheerful endurance couldn't mask the fact that we were huddled around a wood stove in a tiny, mouse-infested cabin, while outside, the terrain through which we would soon have to travel became colder and more sodden with each passing minute. And the rain just kept falling.

It's hard to explain to non-backpackers why we hate rain the way we do. As we learned in Oregon, of all possible weather conditions, rain creates the most sheer wretchedness, especially in cold weather, and also the most petty annoyances.

A rainy day begins with the unpleasant task of breaking camp without getting everything wet. Imagine us in our little home away from home, our 6-by-8-foot Eureka Zeus tent. There's enough room for the three of us to lie comfortably abreast, and there's a little extra room at the head end—plenty of space normally, but cramped if we have to pile our packs inside, instead of keeping them under the vestibule at the tent's entrance. Besides the empty packs and gear at the head end, we must stack our bear-proof Ursacks at the foot end, where they provide a waterproof barrier between our sleeping bags and the tent wall. The remaining space comprises our living, dining, and bedrooms. At breakfast, we sit up, keeping as much of our bodies inside our sleeping bags as possible, while we eat Pop-Tarts, using Ziploc bags for placemats to catch the crumbs. We then take our two pack towels and wipe the frost and condensation off the inside of the tent, so we don't rub against it and get our clothes and gear soaked.

Getting dressed is awkward, especially for me, for two reasons: First, I sleep in the middle, and anytime I stick out a foot or an elbow, it's likely to connect with a member of the family; and second, my knees are stiff and don't want to bend. Eventually, we're suitably attired for the weather and it's time to stuff our sleeping bags and roll up our sleeping pads. There's just enough head room for sitting up, but none for standing, and no room to maneuver. So in order to pack, we must dodge around each other to grab the clothing and gear that have become scattered all around the tent. Done with the easy parts, we put on our rain ponchos (still damp from the previous day), go outside, and take down the tent while bending over, underneath the rain fly, in an effort to keep the tent and our packs dry. Finally, we put on our packs, drape our rain ponchos over them and us, and start walking. Sometime during this process, we each in turn answer nature's call and try to keep our skin and clothing from getting soaked in the process.

That gets us out of camp. Walking in a light rain on a wide, well-drained trail isn't so bad. Soon, however, the rain comes down harder, the trail becomes muddy, the rocky portions get slick, and our boots and socks become soaked. Invariably on rainy days, the trail narrows and we have to push through the wet leaves of overgrown brush, which deposits water on our pants. Rain ponchos don't do much to keep our pants dry—if we wear them so that they hang down enough to protect our pants, they catch on twigs and trip us; instead, we remove the zip-off legs and just put up with the wet, slimy, and occasionally thorny branches slapping our legs. Of course, then our socks and boots get even wetter. Pretty soon, we're hungry, but there's no shelter, so we wait until the rain lessens before stopping to grab some candy bars out of the food bag. But as soon as we sit down and unwrap our bars, the rain picks up and we have to move again, trying to shove a few bites into our mouths as we walk.

When we find a place to camp, we have to set up the tent and get everything inside it while keeping our gear dry—almost impossible in a heavy rain. Gary has to filter water, regardless of the weather. At least I don't have to cook in the rain; when the weather is bad enough, we eat energy bars or Pop-Tarts in the tent and skip the hot meal. But that still means stooping under the rain fly, getting out of our wet ponchos and boots and damp clothes, and trying to get warm without getting water on or in our sleeping bags.

For Mary, rain was the worst part of the PCT, and the "Olallie day," as it became known in our family, epitomized our misery. "The trail was a river, ankle deep," Mary recalls. "There were waterfalls on the trail, and then we went over the pass (it was snowing), and after that, we went through territory with lots of pretty little ponds—supposedly—but they formed one continuous lake about 2 feet deep, and it extended over the trail. Mom and Dad waded, but I tried to hop across. It was really awful."

To say Mary hates wet boots is an understatement along the lines of saying that she finds mosquitoes slightly annoying. By the time she crossed Oregon and Washington, she developed such an aversion to cold, wet boots, that even now she'll do anything to avoid hiking in the rain.

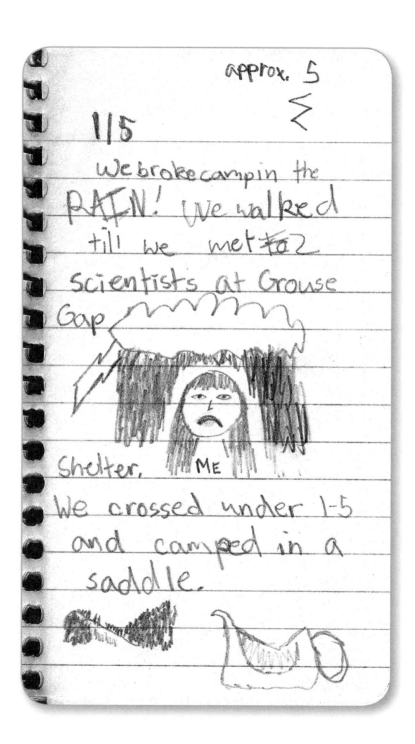

approx. 5

1/5

We broke camp in the RAIN! We walked till we met Foz scientists at Grouse Gap

Shelter. ME

We crossed under I-5 and camped in a saddle.

For Gary and me, rain wasn't the biggest challenge. Our primary trail nemeses came from our own bodies. While I temporarily lost my tendency for lower back pain and my sensitivity to poison oak while hiking the PCT, I developed new, unexpected maladies. During July, I was able to work through fairly severe pain in my right leg in the southern Sierra, thanks to Gary and Mary taking some of my pack weight, and thanks to my mule-headed determination to avoid seeking medical advice. But the blisters were another story.

My problems began at the border. Some thru-hikers boast about how long it takes before they develop their first blisters—or even that they never endure any

at all. They chide those of us (mostly older) hikers who develop blisters or other foot problems early on. But I began the trail already afflicted with blisters. I had acquired them during a weekend training hike a few weeks before beginning the PCT, and they hadn't had time to heal. While planning our hike, I had expected that most foot problems would occur early on, and then they would clear up, leaving me with tougher feet for the duration of the hike. Foolish me. I started out with this big, painful blister under the ball of my right foot—and not only did it fail to clear up, but I developed others as well. After a few weeks, I noticed that I seemed to have a lump underneath the spot between my big toe and the one next to it, on my right foot. I kept shaking out my boot to get rid of whatever was causing the lump. A rock? A twig? Eventually, I looked at the foot itself and discovered the source of the discomfort: an ugly, pink sore between the two toes. Just looking at it made me queasy.

Basically, my feet hurt all the time. Remember that scene in the movie version of *The Da Vinci Code*, where Silas removes his "cilice," that barbed thing he wraps around his thigh for some occasional mortification of the flesh? While everyone else in the theater was going, "Eeeuugghhh!!!" I sat there unmoved. He could take the thing off any time he wanted. I couldn't very well take my feet off.

When Gary began the PCT, he also had blisters on both feet, which he had to attend to every day. Unlike me, Gary really is a stoic. So when the pain was severe enough that he was complaining about it after only a week, I knew these were no ordinary blisters.

Gary had been experimenting with different footwear right up until we started our PCT hike. The boots were no problem, but he was still trying to find just the right inserts. During a training trip just a couple weeks before we started, Gary tried out a different pair of inserts. They fit badly and pinched his heels, so he started out at the Mexican border with a blood blister on one foot and a cluster of ordinary blisters on the other. Hot weather and 20-mile days didn't help. One day, Gary had run through a burned-over area to catch up with Mary and me after taking some photos. We took a break, and after 45 minutes on the trail, his foot pain failed to dissipate as usual. After an hour and a half, his feet still hurt. When we finally stopped, Gary took off the bandages and discovered that blisters had bubbled up under his calluses, painfully pushing up the dead skin and causing more irritation. The blisters were too deep to pop, so Gary took a knife and trimmed off the calluses before lancing the blisters. We called it the "Christmas Turkey Blister" because the way he sliced off the skin in layers reminded Mary of carving slices off the turkey at Christmas.

Mary's feet hurt occasionally in the first few months, but in northern California she developed cracks in the skin where the toes meet the foot. Ordinary first aid didn't cure them, so Gary began applying a product called New Skin. Mary remembers very well the burning sensation from New Skin being applied to the "horrible open sores" on her toes. They did clear up, eventually.

Strangely, it wasn't steady walking that hurt the worst; it was the stopping and starting. During the first couple weeks, Gary would call a break every 60 to 90 minutes. That was as long as Mary and I could tote full packs in the desert heat. We'd sit down, eat and drink for 15 or 20 minutes, and then pack up and get moving. There would be this excruciating period during which our feet screamed for relief. Then they'd get a little bit numb and walking was merely unpleasant.

As we became stronger, we were able to walk longer between breaks, which meant we could not only cover more ground, but suffer a little bit less as well. While our legs and lungs got stronger and healthier every day, our feet stubbornly refused to do the same. After a few weeks, Gary and I had so much moleskin and bandages on our feet, we could hardly see any skin. At first, Gary took care of my feet every morning in the tent, and then his own. Eventually, I learned to be my own podiatrist. Gary insisted on a high level of cleanliness for foot treatments: alcohol wipes, a clean needle for lancing blisters, and large quantities of triple antibiotic ointment. Thanks to that, we avoided infections, despite the fact that our feet were filthy much of the time.

We had problems above the ankles as well. An anti-inflammatory medicine I was taking for my knees at the beginning of the trip made me extra sensitive to sunlight, and after a few days, I developed a severe rash on both legs. It looked and felt like a second-degree burn—red, bumpy, and painful. I had to quit taking the medicine and wear long pants until the rash cleared up. I've had chronic bursitis in my hips for years—ever since I took up backpacking, in fact—and my hips ached many nights while I tried to sleep. Worse were my knees. Before we started hiking, I went through six months of physical therapy for those wretched joints, but within days they were aching again. They also kept me awake many nights. Trekking poles helped, but not enough.

Because Mary slept so soundly once she got into her sleeping bag, and because I lost so many nights of sleep thanks to aching joints, I assumed Mary didn't have any problems of that nature. What I didn't know was that she endured aching muscles and stiff knees just as I did, she just did so in silence. A 10-year-old doesn't spend much time agonizing over what might happen if her joint problems get worse, or if a scratch becomes infected; she deals with the here-and-now. As with so many of the conditions that arise on a major outdoor expedition, the anticipation that things will get worse can be as bad as the immediate problem. Mary trusted her parents to deal with any issue that might arise, from bears to blisters, rather than wasting mental energy worrying about the future.

Aside from his feet, Gary didn't suffer any major problems until we reached Highway 49 in northern California. My older sister, Carol, met us there and took us back to her home in Carson City, Nevada. We stayed the night, and the next day borrowed her pickup truck to run errands in Reno. I exchanged my trekking poles for a new pair at the REI store, where we bought socks and a few other items. That evening, Carol hosted a barbecue, and the rest of the family gathered around for a big dinner. We went to bed with full tummies, eager to hit the trail the next morning. But Gary woke up nauseated, dizzy, and thoroughly sick with what I suspect was some kind of inner-ear problem. He curled up on the floor of the guest room—even climbing back into bed was too much—and lay there for hours. I was alarmed, but Gary refused to see a doctor, rationalizing that he wasn't capable of moving very much anyway. So we delayed our departure, and I spent the afternoon brushing out Mary's hair with the help of an entire bottle of detangler. And suddenly, about 5 p.m., Gary got better. Not entirely better, but well enough to finish packing. The next morning, we were back on the trail.

As Gary recovered from whatever hit him in Carson City, he started having serious trouble with his knees. They both hurt badly at times, and the right one was especially troublesome. A stubbed toe meant agony; the pain traveled all the way up. And sometimes his knee would give way and he'd fall. He came close to dropping out at Burney Falls State Park at Mile 1,423. The previous day, we had hiked 25 miles through part of northern California's notorious Hat Creek Rim—known for heat, lack of shade, lack of water, and overgrown brush. At one point, the thermometer on Gary's altimeter watch read 107°F. My heat-addled

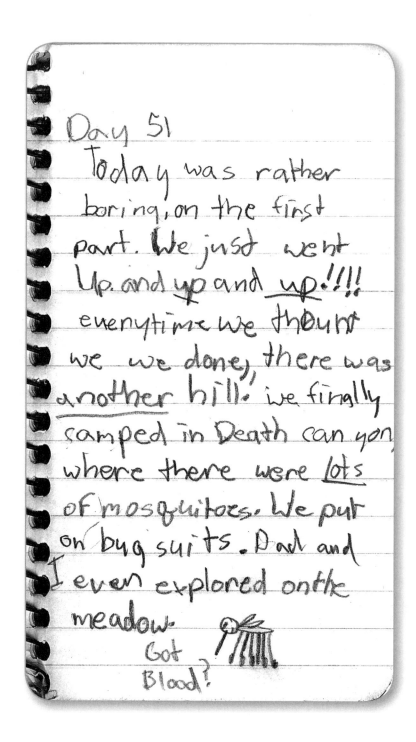

Day 51
  Today was rather
boring, on the first
part. We just went
Up. and up and up.!!!!
everytime we thount
we we done, there was
another hill. we finally
camped in Death can yon,
where there were lots
of mosquitoes. We put
on bug suits. Dad and
I even explored on the
meadow.
        Got
        Blood?

brain seemed to have forgotten simple arithmetic, and I miscalculated the distance to our first source of water. We didn't run out, but the frustration added to the general agony of the day. After 13 miles, we reached Rock Spring Creek, where, if anything, the heat felt worse because we walked past a large water pipe with a leak in the top, causing water to spray out in a fountain. Mary and I fantasized about abandoning our packs and running through the spray, like children with a lawn sprinkler, but with another 12 miles between us and our evening's campsite, we couldn't linger. All three of us were having foot trouble. Gary had a splitting headache. After filtering and drinking water at Rock Spring Creek, we traipsed over rocky tread before finally reaching the backpacker camp at Burney Falls. I've rarely seen Mary so tired. She fell asleep literally the moment her head touched the bundled up pile of clothes she was using for a pillow.

The next morning, Gary could hardly stagger out of the tent. He barely made it the few yards to the picnic table. "I don't think I can go on," he told me. He turned to our daughter. "Mary, I might have to drop out." We had often discussed what to do if one of us became disabled. We all agreed Gary was the keystone. I could keep going with him if Mary dropped out. Mary could keep going with Gary if I left. But any idea that Mary and I could keep going without Gary had disappeared in the first few weeks of our trek. Whenever I found terrain too confusing to choose the correct route, or fell while crossing a rushing stream, or began shivering uncontrollably in bad weather, I realized that I wasn't equipped to lead the expedition. Thus, Gary's announcement was really alarming.

I fixed Gary's breakfast (translation: I handed him a package of chocolate frosted Pop-Tarts and refilled his water bottle from the tap). We packed up and headed for the hot dog stand a few hundred yards away, sparing a glance along the way for thundering Burney Falls. "What a waste of water," I thought as we surveyed the beautiful cascade. Why wasn't it around when we really needed it the last few weeks? Gary, shuffling along behind me, was more vocal. "I can barely walk," he moaned. "My knee's killing me. We might have to get a ride out of here. What's the nearest town?" At one of the tables in front of the drive-up eatery, our trail buddies, Vice, Spreadsheet, and Dumptruck, were relaxing in the sun, filling their stomachs and waiting for FedEx to arrive with a new set of trekking poles. We joined them for a second breakfast, and somehow, Gary's knee began to knit. When we finally got going in late morning, we moved slowly, but we moved.

Gary's knees continued to give him considerable grief as we traipsed through the infamous Section O, an 83-mile stretch of trail that is overgrown with tough, chest-high manzanita and poison oak and that is exposed to the broiling sun for much of the day. However, we were all feeling pretty good when we got to the well and its big pump at South Brown Mountain Shelter early one afternoon in late August. This stretch of trail in southern Oregon is severely lacking in natural water sources, so we were pleased to find that the well was functioning. Mary didn't like the look or taste of the water, but Gary told her to drink it anyway. Water from a developed well, we figured, should be safe. To set a good example, Gary drank a lot of it, I drank less, and Mary just drank a little. (This was one of those times when we should have paid more attention to her opinion.) The next day, we all had some indigestion, especially Gary, who went to bed that evening with an upset stomach. He awoke at 5 a.m. feeling terrible: nauseous, weak, with a headache and severe joint and muscle pains. By a tremendous act of will, he managed to pack up and stagger several miles down to Mazama Village in Crater Lake National Park. I rented a room there and Gary hobbled inside. He turned up the heater as high as it would go, and spent the next few hours huddling in front of it with severe chills.

In spite of our bout with stomach sickness, we three had the good fortune to avoid giardia, a debilitating illness caused by microscopic protozoa that results in diarrhea, abdominal cramps, and general wretchedness that occasionally felled other backpackers on the trail. It was so widespread in 2004, and so concentrated in southern Oregon, that yo-yo hiker Scott Williamson came up with a name for it: the Crater Lake Curse. On a cold, drizzly day in southern Oregon, a few days after Gary had become really ill, we ran into Scott, who was heading south. We recognized each other right off. (To be honest, we were pretty recognizable, being the only threesome on the trail that included a 10-year-old.) As he headed south from Canada, Scott had met about 100 backpackers—and about a third of them had reported getting sick. Of those who had bothered to get a diagnosis, all confirmed that it was giardia. And they shared one or two things in common: They had all drunk the well water at South Brown Mountain Shelter, or the water at Mazama Campground in Oregon, or both. (Scott himself managed to avoid the giardia epidemic on this trip, but in 2006, during his second PCT yo-yo, he spent five days severely ill with giardia, losing 25 pounds from his already lean frame.)

Although Mary did the best of us all physically, she didn't get a free ride. What worried me the most was when she tripped and fell. She took some nasty falls, usually while walking on perfectly safe tread. Not paying attention, she'd catch a toe on a rock or a root and land face first on the trail. We finally realized that her habit of hooking her thumbs through the shoulder straps on her backpack kept her from catching her balance, so we banned the practice. It was a hard habit to break, but she fell less that way, and if she did trip over something, she usually caught herself.

More than the falls, Mary remembers a morning near Horseshoe Meadow in the southern Sierra, when she got sick. "I'm the only one who ever threw up on the trail," she told me later, with some pride. We had camped at a trail intersection where Gary could run down a couple miles to a parking area where we had cached nine days' worth of food in a bear box. The next morning, Mary felt nauseous and threw up a little bit. Then she had dry heaves for a couple minutes.

Finally, she felt a lot better and ate something. In fact, she felt so much better that 10 minutes later, she was balancing on a log while playing her recorder, the flute-like musical instrument she had brought along for entertainment

The toughest part of the trail for Mary was the weather. She suffered from the temperature extremes more than I realized at the time. When I asked her later about the hot days in California, she replied, "Heat is miserable." She remembered how thirsty she became in the heat, as well as how hungry she felt in the cold. There were plenty of times when the only thing that made up for her misery was the occasional lovely view. And even that wasn't always enough in Washington's snow-choked North Cascades. "The worst thing," Mary recalls, "was that we'd be walking through snow and big chunks of snow would get in our boots, but they wouldn't even melt because our feet were so cold." On another day in Washington, during which we walked 26 miles through deep snow and finally camped shortly before midnight, Mary recalls that her dad's boot laces were so frozen and matted with snow that he couldn't untie the knots. He had to cut the laces to get his boots off.

Sometimes the weather was so miserable, we pined for an abandoned cabin to hole up in. Unlike the Appalachian Trail, with its spacious lean-tos every 10 miles or so, the PCT doesn't have any official shelters along the trail. But a few times we were lucky enough to find shelter. In northern California, near where Interstate 80 crosses Donner Pass, we arrived at the Sierra Club's Peter Grubb Hut right at dusk, and we enjoyed sleeping in the loft and not having to set up the tent. In Oregon, we stumbled across a building maintained by the Mt. Hood Snowmobile Club on a rainy day after leaving Olallie, and gratefully accepted its shelter.

In Washington, where I had to leave the trail for a time to deal with some health problems, Gary and Mary had high hopes as they walked through cold, wet weather on their way to a primitive campsite, because the map for that section included the word "shelter" in tiny type. But what they found near Suiattle Pass was a sorry excuse for a structure, open to the weather, with rat and mouse droppings everywhere. Gary broke the news to Mary that there would be no roof over their heads that night. It was quite a blow. "Mary was crying, and I had to leave her there in the dark, with the drizzle turning to snow, for an hour, while I went off to filter water," Gary recalls. "She's such a trouper, she got the tent up and the rain fly on, and all the bedding ready, while I was gone." But even the lack of a shelter wasn't the last disappointment of the day.

Gary pulled out the little fuel canister he had purchased months earlier at Vermilion Valley Resort in California, but it wouldn't burn properly. What should have been a strong, hot blaze instead resembled the flicker of a candle. After a long time, the water in the pot reached what might be described as room temperature, if there had been any rooms around—a far cry from the full, rolling boil needed to turn a bag of freeze-dried food into a good meal. Gary poured the

Day Ten
   This Morning,
a thick Marine
Layer moved in.
By 2:00 PM, we
had to find a
campsite. It was
actually snowing!
It was not that
great, though. The
20mph (aproxi-
mately) wind blew
the snow
horizontally right
into our faces.

We actually got
a fairly good
campsite, but
Mom was shiver-
ing, so she had to
get warm inside
her bag (which
was really mine)
We will sleep in
two zipped to-
gether bags. We'll
pry stay up real
late tonight.
I was very

cold, as well, and
was scared of
the weather.
The wind may
still break the
poles. But I
am happy it
showed, because
it's dryer and
prettier than
rain. We pry
hiked only 8
miles, though.

tepid water into the waterproof food bag, stirred it up, waited a few minutes, and they choked it down. They didn't have any choice—they needed those calories, unappetizing as they were, to generate enough energy to walk 20 miles the next day. Mary laughs now about the "crunchy rice dinner" they ate that evening, but it sure didn't seem funny at the time.

Most long-distance hikers can recall an experience in which they were struck by the enormous contrast between their struggle to survive and someone else's blissful ignorance. Our moment came on southern California's Fuller Ridge, when we were hunting through the dark, the snow, and the bitter cold for a usable campsite, while far below, we could see the lights of Palm Springs, where we knew most people were cranking up the air-conditioning.

For Scott Williamson, one of those moments arrived as he was crossing the Mojave Desert near the completion of his first successful yo-yo. Scott was wrapping up a 40-mile day during an October storm that featured rain driven by winds gusting, he estimates, up to 50 miles per hour. Far to the north, this same storm killed two Japanese climbers stranded on a ledge on El Capitan in Yosemite National Park. Near a ranger station north of Agua Dulce, Scott set up his tarp alongside a road, using a few shrubs for a windbreak, and quickly ate dinner. "I was just curling up in my sleeping quilt, and the wind screaming through the power pylons was so loud it sounded like a freight train," he remembers. "As I was falling asleep, a gust pulled off my tarp, pulled out all the stakes, and broke both the guy lines." The tarp flew off about 100 yards. Just then a family in a huge SUV slowly drove past. "It was a couple with two kids and a DVD player," Scott says. "They had the dome light on, so I could see inside. They were all watching a movie, and I could tell the heater was blasting." As Scott huddled against the wind and the father in the car fiddled with the DVD controls, the contrast struck Scott as ironic, to say the least.

Time heals all wounds, says the proverb. As the months passed after our return home, I found it harder and harder to remember just how badly my feet hurt, even though I had plenty of reminders. Ten of them, in fact—my toenails. Most of the nails were black and purple, and I continued losing toenails for months after we returned. (Even worse, the toenails grew back deformed. I'll never wear open-toed sandals again.) At first, I suspected that if I had known ahead of time how much pain I'd have to endure, I wouldn't have started. Now, I think I would have gone anyway. But I would have done a few things differently.

First, I would have worn men's boots from the beginning, instead of waiting until I had suffered the entire length of California before realizing that I needed wider footwear. Would I have switched from boots to running shoes? No. My ankles and knees needed the extra support boots provide. Also, I would have been too sore-footed in the rockier sections with only running shoes.

Second, for stream crossings, I would have carried a pair of slip-on water shoes, the kind available at sporting goods stores for use on boats. We had debated this at length and Gary persuaded me that the extra weight wasn't worth it. But I came close to catastrophe many times, trying to cross streams without getting my feet wet. Often, they did get wet, and I had to hike in blister-promoting wet socks and boots. I would have been better off wading streams in the water shoes, and changing back into boots afterward.

And finally, I would have insisted that Gary filter that tainted well water and not drink so much of it. We don't know for sure that's what made him ill, but it's our best guess.

The fact is, Gary and I could have avoided a lot of problems entirely, and most of our foot trouble, if we had chosen to hike the PCT 10 years earlier. I never got blisters at all until I was 45. But then we wouldn't have had Mary along, and it wouldn't have been nearly as much fun.

CHAPTER 8

TOWN STOPS

Day 8: *We got to wonderful Eagle Rock. We took a lot of pictures. Then we came to Warner Springs where we ate at a restaurant and slept on beds! There were also two enormous pools, one from the hot springs and one cooler, that I swam in.*

—from Scrambler's journal

BY THE TIME WE ARRIVED at the Warner Springs Ranch resort, our first town stop, we thought we were hot stuff. We'd been on the trail a whopping eight days, and in the space of 110 miles had already braved a long list of backpacking challenges: heat, rattlesnakes, crazy drivers, alarming appearances by strangers, sunburn, and dehydration. We felt like real veterans of the trail. We were among the first of that year's thru-hikers to stay at Warner Springs, and the only ones with a child, of course, and as such we received plenty of attention. Everyone was so curious, helpful, and admiring—we felt like royalty.

We were gratified that our first stop went so smoothly. We reached Warner Springs on a Thursday, when plenty of rooms were available. (Other thru-hikers who arrived on Fridays and Saturdays weren't always so fortunate.) The thru-hiker's discount gave us a comfortable cottage for less than we'd normally pay at a Motel 6. We got to the post office early in the afternoon, and our first resupply box was right there waiting for us. An older couple we met on the trail and again in the restaurant, the French Gourmet, took an interest in us, asking about Mary's schooling in particular. The staff was attentive and friendly. Our waitress, Phyllis, mentioned that the resort had two big swimming pools; when Mary mourned the lack of a swimsuit among our backpacking supplies, Phyllis promptly phoned the pool staff and announced that a loaner swimsuit was available. Mary was thrilled.

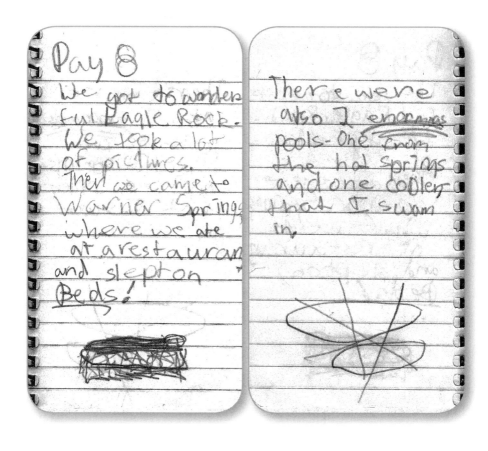

Day 8
We got to wonder
ful Eagle Rock.
We took a lot
of pictures.
Then we came to
Warner Springs
where we ate
at a restaurant
and slept on
Beds!

There were
also 7 enormous
pools-One from
the hot springs
and one cooler
that I swam
in.

After supper, she and I walked over to the pools, one at normal temperature, the other about 104°F, thanks to the hot springs for which the resort is named. The pools are big (or, as Mary described them, "gargantuan") and made a beautiful picture under the night sky.

Warner Springs set a pattern for laundry that we followed the entire trip. I showered first, then put on my "town clothes"—spare shirt, spare underwear, and fleece pants. Then I gathered up everyone's dirty clothes, leaving Mary and Gary wrapped in towels. Mary showered next and got into her town clothes. Gary, who takes longer showers than Mary and me put together, went last. At Warner Springs, the laundry room was in a building that housed, among other things, a small library. In between checking the progress of the washer and dryer, I sat in the library and read the first chapter of Randy Shilts' *And the Band Played On*. Every 10 or 15 minutes, I would check on the clothes and take the dry ones back to our room. Eventually, everything was clean and dry, and so were we.

Our lodging was delightful. Warner Springs dates back to 1844 as a ranch, and to 1900 as a resort. Families own shares in the cottages, which can be rented out when not in use by shareholders. Our little cottage had a double bed, a single roll-out bed for Mary, a small bathroom, and plenty of closet space, plus a little porch and a lawn. Mary loved the bay window, big enough for her to sprawl in comfortably with a book.

There was no telephone in the room, and no television, which suited me just fine. Many Warner Springs shareholders must agree that getting away from televisions is a good thing; there was only one TV set in the entire place—it was even marked on the map given to visitors—and it was tucked out of the way in a games room behind the library. I saw no one using it while we were there. Although the cottages lacked phones, for essential communications, there was a pay phone between our cottage and the laundry/library/games building. That's another pattern we set at Warner Springs: I would dig out a phone card and our list of phone numbers, and make calls to friends, relatives, the travel editor at the *Los Angeles Times* (which ran a four-part series based on my trail journals), and possibly a motel at our next town stop. Gary hates making phone calls, so that became my job at each stop. (Mary loves using the phone, but we didn't want her using up all our phone card time, so we limited her calls.) We slept well at Warner Springs, and the next morning ate across the street at the Golf Grille, where I obtained something I'd been craving for a week: a daily newspaper. Then we opened our resupply box, repacked everything, mailed excess food and medications to the neighbor who was taking care of our house, and donated a roll of toilet paper to the hiker box at the post office.

· · · · ·

WE DIDN'T KNOW WHAT TO EXPECT from town stops—it's one of those experiences that can't be fully understood from reading other people's descriptions. Gary had spent many hours planning each stop, poring over trail guides and the internet. He paid particular attention to the days and hours during which backpackers could pick up their boxes, whether at post offices, motels, stores, or even gas stations.

A wonderful town stop, Warner Springs gave us confidence that our resupply boxes would be waiting for us at each stop (they were) and that we could take care of all of our town chores and still get in some relaxation time (not always the case). But even when our town stops were rushed, they provided us with a chance to fulfill our three major desires: get clean, eat more food, and sleep in beds.

Not all backpackers find town stops so rewarding. For some, they are almost more stressful than they're worth. Some thru-hikers get to the post office and discover their resupply boxes failed to arrive. That launches them into a frenzied search through hiker boxes and stores, trying to find enough food, first-aid supplies, and additional gear to reach the next town. If something essential is in the missing box—the next section's maps and guidebook chapters, for example, or an ice ax—the thru-hiker must consider staying in town an extra day or two, wasting time and running up motel and restaurant bills, while making frantic phone calls to track down the wayward resupply box. Some thru-hikers buy their supplies along the trail, rather than sending boxes, and they too must find enough food and supplies for the next leg of the trip from the often slender amenities in little resort town stores. For those who do send boxes, post office hours become a limiting factor. Sometimes a post office located within a store or gas station is open only a couple hours a day. Even regular post offices close on Sundays and usually have short hours on Saturdays. For three days in a row in northern California, we got up at 4:30 a.m. in order to make the mileage necessary to wind up at Seiad Valley before the post office closed on a Saturday. We knew we would have stuff to mail back—books and some extra first-aid supplies—so we had to get there in time to retrieve the box, open it, sort everything, repack the box, and mail it. Only after those chores did we buy quarts of Gatorade at the store next to the post office and sit down in the shade to read the personal letters and color comics my sister had thoughtfully added to the box before sealing it. For hikers who have become accustomed to the freedom of determining their own schedules on the trail, having to comply with post office and store hours all of a sudden is a major downer.

These stresses are small compared to the pressure some thru-hikers feel at town stops to drop out. The pressure comes from two directions: from themselves and from the relatives, sweethearts, and friends they call on the phone. If a backpacker is having a lot of foot trouble or is falling behind schedule, worrying about the weather, running out of money, or just losing interest in the trail, a town stop is where the temptation arises to call it a trip. Especially in southern

California, town stops are located on or near major east-west highways from which one can easily zip into Los Angeles—with its airports and bus stations and car rental agencies—in just a few hours. Phone calls home can ratchet up the pressure tremendously. We had a huge advantage in this regard—my relatives were incredibly supportive of our trip, as was Nancy, the neighbor taking care of the house and pets. And the travel editor at the *Los Angeles Times*, of course, was always eager for more material. But often, a thru-hiker makes those obligatory phone calls and discovers that a sweetheart is lonely, a spouse is wrestling with unexpected problems at home, an elderly relative is ailing, or a job possibility has suddenly opened up. A town stop is sort of like a holiday, one that recurs every week or so—you get to open a box of goodies and talk to friends and eat a lot, but you also have to deal with all the scheduling and relationship stresses that make some people dread the holiday season. Town stops are where homesickness, doubts, and guilt can really take hold.

While Warner Springs was a well-run, smoothly oiled resort catering to the well-off, our next stop, on Day 14, was the funky but friendly Tahquitz Inn, up in the San Jacinto Mountains, in the resort town of Idyllwild. We got off the PCT at Mile 179, followed the steep Devil's Slide Trail down to the edge of town, and hitched a ride to the motel. Mary didn't care if the lights didn't all work or if the flooring was worn. She considered the place cozy and was happy to be under a roof, with a new activity as well: cataloging the kitchen gadgets. Here's what she wrote in her journal:

> **Day 14:** *We hiked to Idyllwild. I got my own bedroom! Our room even has a fully equipped kitchen: stove, silverware, dishes, cups and glasses, baking sheets, crock pot, colander, freezer, refrigerator.*

A couple days later, we got off the trail and caught a ride south so we could attend the Annual Day Zero Pacific Crest Trail Kick Off. This event at the end of April is held at a big county campground just 20 trail miles from the Mexican border. We took our first zero day, loaded up on the free food that trail fans provide for thru-hikers, and picked up the all-important water report. Gary and I enjoyed talking with other thru-hikers and becoming part of the PCT community. Mary enjoyed playing with a little girl about her age and pigging out at a nearby store. Then we got a lift back north and resumed walking.

Our next true town stop was Big Bear City, on Day 22 and Mile 274. The high point there, at least from an entertainment point of view, was our post office visit. At every other post office, before and after Big Bear, we were treated well and often received valuable help from postal employees who enjoyed helping thru-hikers. Occasionally, we photographed our visits to show us signing the trail register and receiving our box. At Big Bear, Gary headed in to retrieve the supply box, while Laurence, the trail angel who had given us a ride to town, carried the camera. Mary and I waited in the back of the pickup truck. Much sooner than we

Day AOZPCTKO

This morning we had pancake breakfast. It was good. Then we puttered around for a while, and Lawrence introduced me to Anna. Anna is a 9 yearold section hiker. She is nice, and has short brown hair.

I played and looked for cater pillars with Anna, and then walked to the store with her, I had a chocolate shake!

Then me, Mom, Dad, and Law- had lunch, then

got in a picture.

class of

expected, Laurence came hurrying back to the truck, a rueful expression on his face. It seems the postmistress had taken the Patriot Act and Homeland Security a little too seriously. She had chased Laurence out with threats and declarations that it was "against the law" to take photographs in a U.S. post office. (I found out later that there isn't any law forbidding picture taking; it's at the discretion of the postmaster or postmistress.) Laurence beat a hasty retreat and Gary left a sarcastic reference to the postmistress in the trail register.

By the time we reached Cajon Pass on Day 26, with 342 miles accounted for, we had the essentials down pat: get the supply box; rent the room, take showers and wash clothes; eat and drink (although not necessarily in that order); then eat and drink some more. Cajon Pass isn't a town, exactly. It's more of a wide spot on the road between Los Angeles and Las Vegas. Interstate 15 is a very busy freeway, and the wide spot is home to a gas station, McDonald's, and a motel. McDonald's presence is even noted on the trail, where a sign notifies hikers that the Guffy Campground is 22.1 miles straight ahead, but McDonald's is only four tenths of a mile to the right. What backpacker can resist the lure of cheeseburgers and cold drinks less than half a mile off the trail? Usually, we cleaned up before entering an eating establishment, so as not to offend the other customers. The weather had been very hot and we were a week away from our last showers. But McDonald's clearly wanted our business, and it was right along the way to our motel. We marched in, propped our packs against a table, and got in line. This was the first time we had eaten out while still in full backpacker regalia, so it was the first time we witnessed other diners' reaction to our scruffy presence. People looked at us askance, but quickly returned to the business of eating. We, on the other hand, could barely keep from staring. Accustomed to each other's emaciated appearances, everyone else looked so fat!

Next on the itinerary was Agua Dulce, 454 trail miles from the border, on Day 33. We stayed at Jeff and Donna Saufley's Hiker Heaven, of course, which lived up to every possible expectation for trail magic. But the town of Agua Dulce itself deserves mention. In this hiker-friendly community, we felt at ease the minute we saw the big sign welcoming PCT backpackers on the porch of the Sweetwater Farms grocery store. (*Agua dulce* is Spanish for "sweet water," a phrase picked up by the grocery store and by another hiker-friendly establishment, the Sweetwater Café.) The staff was kind, the sandwiches delicious, and the store well-stocked. First we ate our sandwiches and fruit smoothies, on the large porch with its inviting tables and chairs, and then we moved on to dessert. Gary handed Mary a bag of Toll House cookie bars—which are a lot closer to candy than cookies and are very good—and offered Mary a dollar if she could eat the entire bag. A woman at a nearby table looked horror-stricken at the image of a father bribing his daughter to overindulge in calorie-laden snacks. If she had known that Mary had lost several pounds from her already slender frame, she might not have been so shocked. That night, we dined at Maria Bonita's Mexican restaurant, where, to our surprise, we actually had trouble eating all the food on our plates, the servings were so large. The next day Mary made friends with a cat with the accurate but not particularly creative name of Beige Kitty, the friendliest of the pets in the hardware store. Meanwhile, Gary and I bought duct tape and got directions to the nearest town where we could purchase items the store didn't stock. And in nearby Santa Clarita, which we visited with a loaner car from the Saufleys, we found a large used-book store and replenished Mary's dwindling supply of reading material.

Then it was back into the desert for six days of heat on the way to the town of Mojave, at Mile 558. Many thru-hikers take their town stops in Tehachapi, which is bigger and more pleasant than Mojave. But many thru-hikers count on doing a lot of hitchhiking. We had decided ahead of time to hitchhike as seldom as possible, so on Day 40 we were left with Mojave, where White's Motel offered free transportation from trailhead to motel and back.

We avoided hitchhiking for three main reasons: First, it's easy for a single person to catch a ride, and not much harder for two. But how many drivers in the mood to pick up extra passengers have enough room for three people with bulging backpacks plus a pair of trekking poles? Not many, we figured. Second, hitchhiking is too unreliable. Backpackers who move really fast can afford to waste an hour or two (and sometimes much more) waiting to catch a lift into town, and then getting back to the trail. But we were plodders, by comparison, and tortoises can't afford to waste half a day sticking out their thumbs. And third, although Gary has extensive experience traveling by thumb, he agreed with me that it might not be safe. The stories we heard from other backpackers certainly bore that out. A high percentage of the drivers willing to give rides are either drunk or loony, we concluded. A married couple told us about the man who gave them a lift in the back of his pickup truck. As they perched on his load of fruit from eastern Washington, they wondered which would kill them first: the biting cold or the man's reckless driving.

Our thru-hiker buddy Chacoman told us about a couple of his experiences that reinforced our decision to avoid hitch-hiking. In one case, a young man of about 19 gave him a lift at Sonora Pass in the central Sierra, a particularly remote spot notorious for poor ride prospects. The young man, who was driving, seemed normal enough, but his passenger, who was also his father, was anything but. The old man appeared to have already imbibed a couple drinks and repeatedly ordered his son to make senseless stops or detours. What started out as a long hitchhike ride began to seem interminable. Finally, as they drew near to Chacoman's point of departure, the old man began talking about wanting to murder someone. All this time, the son had been calm and patient, and the father had been drinking and ranting. But when Chacoman asked why he wanted to kill this particular individual, it was the son who turned around and said, "Because he tried to kill my brother." Suddenly, Chacoman felt a chilling certainty that this was no joke on the father's part, taking advantage of a captive audience to pull the leg of some gullible stranger, but was serious business. By the time they stopped at a parking lot in Sonora, the old man had passed out, and Chacoman quickly went his way.

His second cautionary hitchhiking tale involved a driver who believed he was being followed by a police officer. The driver had an open container of beer in his truck, and was grateful to pick up a passenger who could pretend that he, not the driver, was the drinker. At one time, many states allowed open containers of liquor in vehicles, as long as the driver wasn't indulging. (Go back far enough, and people could legally drink while they were driving.) By the time of Chacoman's experience, all West Coast states had passed laws prohibiting open containers, period, but this driver may very well have been unaware of the change and viewed a hitchhiker as divine intervention. That he himself was no angel was proved by a brief conversation at the end of the drive. "Later, when he dropped me off and I couldn't open the door because there was no door handle, he told me that his wife had broken it off earlier in the day when they had been fighting," Chacoman recalls.

So we were relieved in Mojave to have the promise of transportation. We were hot, dry, and thirsty as we approached Tehachapi-Willow Springs Road and I used our cell phone to call the motel owner, who promised he'd be right out. Sure enough, we barely had time to take off our packs when he drove up in a van with plenty of room for our gear. Our motel room was modest but comfortable. I had to walk a couple blocks to the laundromat. But McDonald's was right next door!

Besides offering rides, White's Motel provided us with the additional benefit of meeting other thru-hikers. Leprechaun and Leatherfeet, whom we first met at Agua Dulce, showed up there. We also met Pineneedle, whom we subsequently ran into off and on all the way to Kennedy Meadows. Our Mojave stop exemplifies the changes that can occur from year to year. We had a good experience at White's, but during a later year, some thru-hikers reported a much less pleasant time. Soon after that, it changed hands and now probably provides an entirely different experience. These little motels tend to change ownership frequently. The big chains maintain certain standards, but the character of the small-town, individually owned motels can vary dramatically depending on who's in charge.

Mojave—at least the part of it we saw—had the look and feel of a dying town. I'm a small-town native, and I know what a community looks like when it's on the skids. Storefronts were either empty or rented by businesses catering to people with little disposable income. The laundromat was untidy and not all the machines were functioning. The sidewalk and street seemed too big for the amount of traffic they had to bear. Thrift stores were the sole growth industry. Now, I have nothing against thrift stores. We visited two in Mojave looking for a used paperback for Mary, and found what we needed on the second try. When Mary was little, most of her clothes came from thrift stores; we didn't have much money to spare, and buying her clothes there meant it didn't matter if her outfits became stained or torn. Even today, if Mary needs a costume for a school play, Goodwill is my first choice, followed by Salvation Army outlets, and I have found some real deals for myself, too. But it's a bad sign when the thrift stores appear to be providing the bulk of a town's sales tax revenues.

And then we reached Kennedy Meadows, the Holy Grail for serious backpackers. It's the end of the beginning, and for some, the beginning of the end. By the time we got there, after 703 miles and seven weeks on the trail, I had abandoned most of my standards concerning schedules, nutrition, personal cleanliness, and comfort. They didn't matter anymore. The important thing—really, the only thing—was that we got there, in high spirits and good health. Mary expressed our common feeling in her journal:

Day 48: *Southern California done!*

Kennedy Meadows is a major landmark along the PCT. It's where the desert ends and the Sierra begins. It's where thru-hikers pick up their ice axes and crampons, and mentally prepare for ice, snow, and mountain thunderstorms, not to mention bloodthirsty mosquitoes and hazardous stream crossings. It's where some backpackers begin their treks, choosing to skip the southern desert section entirely. And it's where some backpackers drop out, deciding that they've been through more than enough on the first portion of the PCT, and aren't ready for anything more challenging.

Kennedy Meadows had particular significance for us: We had arranged to get off the trail there for a few weeks. The main reason was to visit the East Coast. Gary refused to miss "Mensa Walks Across Maryland," an annual event in early June, in which he had participated for every one of its 18 years. I had joined his friends on their three-day hike on the Maryland section of the Appalachian Trail several times since we married, and Mary had completed it every year of her life, whether carried by her parents or walking on her own. How could we possibly miss that?

A second reason to get off the trail temporarily was to complete our resupply boxes. Despite all our planning, we had managed to pack only enough boxes for those first seven weeks. On our break, we would pack about 20 more, after shopping trips to Costco, Trader Joe's, and Albertsons.

Just knowing my brother, George, would meet us in Kennedy Meadows turned the little town and its general store into our Big Rock Candy Mountain. When we got there, we discovered that the showers were outdoors—not an ideal situation with an electrical storm approaching—and the towels were thin, and getting a restaurant meal that night was very iffy. But hey, we didn't care. We got to Kennedy Meadows!

We received a generous portion of trail magic at the general store. As we were more or less trapped on the big porch by an afternoon rainstorm, we were fortunate to share it with people we very much enjoyed being with, such as Steve and Sara, the Canadian father-daughter team, and Pineneedle. We gorged ourselves on junk food and got to know the local cats and dogs.

Eventually, the rain stopped and everyone else started walking toward a restaurant about a mile and a half away called Irelan's (not Ireland's, there's no "d"), in hopes that it might be open. The store manager had phoned down there for us, but repeated calls had failed to elicit any certainty about the arrangements. Gary, unwilling to commit to what might be a fool's errand, decided we should stick around the store a little while longer. Luckily, a woman who had been using the pay phone while Mary made friends with her dog offered us a ride, so we drove down there in style. Even better, she came back an hour later, figuring we would have finished, and gave us a ride to our campsite.

The restaurant would have fit right into a television sitcom, maybe *Fawlty Towers* meets *The Outer Limits*. The owners were out of town, and the cook and waitresses apparently had to be called in at the last minute from the surrounding neighborhood. Although they worked within a couple miles of the PCT, the waitresses didn't seem to know anything about it. Most of the menu items weren't available. If you didn't want beef, you were out of luck. And the collection of kitchen gadgets adorning the walls looked like they hadn't been dusted since the Reagan administration—governor, not president. Halfway through the meal, Leatherfeet arrived, and we told him about the menu situation. He didn't mind. He just ordered two of everything they did have. So there we sat, eating fresh food, with congenial companions and the knowledge that the next morning George would drive up in a real automobile and take us to Carson City. Life was good.

Most thru-hikers plan to stay on the trail, with occasional zero days, until they finish or drop out, but longer breaks aren't unheard of. Some are planned, such as weddings that must be attended. Others are unplanned—funerals, say, of relatives close enough to require attendance but not so close that the loss means the end of the thru-hike attempt. Our hiatus was somewhat of a glorified town stop. We first flew to the East Coast for the Walk Across Maryland, where we added crab cakes, fried chicken, and other Maryland specialties to our menu. (The South Beach Diet was popular that year, so Mary gleefully referred to our eating plan as the South Beached Whale Diet.)

Back in California, we still had to pack all those resupply boxes and take them to my sister's house for her to ship. Mary saw her friends and visited the local swimming pool. I made lots of phone calls. And the entire time, we felt that familiar town stop pressure to attend to every detail, so we wouldn't get back on the trail and discover we were missing something important.

Our three-week sabbatical from the trail ended June 21, when Gary's rock climbing friend, Janice, drove us back to Kennedy Meadows. We were well-rested, with healthier feet and fuller waistlines, and eager to resume trail life. We had enjoyed our Maryland visit, and being home was pleasant, especially for Mary, who had missed her friends, the cats, and her usual summertime activities. But for Gary and me, the PCT, in some ways, felt more like home than home itself did. So we were glad to get back.

Before, we had been ahead of the pack. Now, at least 175 backpackers had steamed through in our absence. All the better, we thought. The snow has had time to melt, and what's left will have a well-marked trail running through it, pointing straight to our next stop: Vermilion Valley Resort. We had allowed 13 days for the 173 miles and six major passes between us and the resort that marketed itself as the place "where the pavement ends, and the wilderness begins." According to the resort's website, "Vermilion Valley Resort at Edison Lake is the type of rustic paradise that John Muir would have truly treasured!" That's only if Muir could have afforded a stay. Previous thru-hikers had written glowing praises of the hiker-friendly attributes of Vermilion Valley—and one *Fresno Bee* reporter referred to it as "a backpacker's best friend"—but our 42-hour experience matched the trail chatter warning that it's all too easy to "spend a million at Vermilion."

Just getting to Vermilion Valley was quite the accomplishment. We had made fairly good time the first few days after rejoining the trail at Kennedy Meadows, heading into the mountains with our bodies strengthened by those three weeks of home cooking, hot showers, and adequate sleep. On our third day out, we camped a couple miles from Horseshoe Meadow, at an intersection of trails for New Army Pass, Mt. Langley, and other Sierra destinations. Gary ran down to the parking lot where, a few days earlier, we had stashed a nine-day supply of food in a bear box. We thought we had plenty of supplies. But the heavy loads, the difficult treks over passes, and our side trip up 14,495-foot Mt. Whitney slowed us to the point that we had to ration our supplies. By the time we got to Vermilion Valley on Day 64 (counting days on the trail and zero days, but not our three-week vacation), we were getting pretty desperate.

Our entire Vermilion Valley experience could have been an episode from *The Three Stooges*. If a movie were made of just our VVR visit, the TV listing might read something like Mary's journal entry for the day we arrived:

Day 64: *We're finally at Vermilion Valley Resort! We had a hard time getting there because of an enormous hill and overshooting the ferry. Then the fuel line on the ferry malfunctioned and Dad had to hold it in place. Mom christened the ferry 'the Henry.' Good supper. Good night!*

The VVR ferry picks up backpackers, and anyone else who wants a ride to the resort, twice a day at the east end of Edison Lake, near PCT Mile 877. We were determined to make the afternoon's 4:45 ferry, so we pushed ourselves very hard, wading Bear Creek in our boots, suffering through battalions of mosquitoes, pushing up a steep ridge, and then hurrying down dozens of switchbacks on the other side. We reached the lake in plenty of time but somehow managed to walk right past the sign directing us to the ferry's landing. Our friends Paul and Alice, John Muir Trail thru-hikers, were already there, and we all got on the ferry together with a couple picnickers. We also greeted three thru-hikers, including Chacoman, who were disembarking from their VVR stay and hoping to get in a few trail miles before dark. The other two hikers were the intriguingly named Rot 'n' Skirt. Skirt was one of the few women whom we met who wore a skirt for serious backpacking (it's becoming more common every year), thus her trail name. (We met no men wearing skirts that year, although we have since.) Rot, we gathered, earned his name because Skirt told him he smelled like something dead that had been lying in the hot sun too long. Strong hikers, they stayed ahead of us all the way north, and we never met them again.

The ferry started to leave about five minutes early, without the customary horn-blowing, but just as the captain pushed off from shore, a hiker came bounding down the side trail, waving his arms and shouting, "Wait! Wait for me!" He barely made it. I'm guessing if he'd known what was coming, he might not have been so keen.

As it turned out, the captain may have been anxious to get going, but the ferry was in no hurry. The motor coughed. It sputtered. It stopped. As I settled back on the boat's bench, ready for a relaxing, no-stress trip across the lake, certain that I was about to be transported to a hikers' paradise of hot, delicious food and hot, running water, the ferry slowly drifted away from the shore. When we were about 40 feet out, it dawned on me that floating out onto the lake in a powerless boat was a whole lot less pleasant than staying on shore. I gazed longingly at the solid ground we had left behind so gleefully just minutes before.

Next, a man and a woman in a small aluminum motorboat with "VVR" stenciled on it rowed up to the hapless ferry. They explained that they had run out of gas and asked for a ride back to the resort, with the ferry towing the boat. "Sure!" the captain replied. So they clambered aboard, trusting the crew—the captain and one other VVR employee—to tie the boat to the ferry. Bad idea. As the ferry floated toward the middle of the lake, the line tying the boat came loose, and the boat promptly slid off in the opposite direction. "The boat!" the woman yelled frantically. "The boat! My purse is on it ... my wallet ... my driver's license!" The captain barely acknowledged her. "Who tied up that boat?" he asked rhetorically. (Paul, an experienced sailor, muttered, "No one, obviously.") Finally, the captain acknowledged the problem, assuring her that "someone will come back for it," and then he returned his attention to the recalcitrant engine. Sputter. Cough.

By that point, the ferry was heading straight toward the granite boulders lining the lake. Gary asked the captain if he could help. Motioning to a couple poles used for hauling fish on board, the captain told Gary, "Why don't you keep us away from those rocks?" Gary and another passenger grabbed the gaffs and started fending the wayward ferry off the boulders. Once the immediate danger passed, Gary walked aft to where the captain was becoming more desperate and more red-faced. "What's happening with the motor?" Gary asked. "It's the fuel line," the captain replied. "Here—hold this." He handed Gary the broken fuel line and instructed him to hold it together so the gas could pour through the line instead of into the lake. To do this effectively, Gary had to climb over the railing and crouch on the platform extending beyond it, with one arm linked through the rail for security. With Gary precariously positioned holding the fuel line together, the captain finally succeeded in starting the engine, and the ferry kicked like a mule before roaring off across the lake. As we zipped along, I whispered to Mary that this ferry should be called "the Henry," after the recalcitrant mule we met above Snow Canyon.

For 15 minutes, Gary clung to the rail and the fuel line, with the spray flying around him and the afternoon breeze getting chillier by the moment. When we reached the dock across Lake Edison, the owner of the resort acted as though this sort of thing happened on every trip. The crew member, on the other hand, was grateful for Gary's help, and scurried around digging up extra shampoo, soap, and towels for us to show her appreciation. I began to suspect such equipment failures and creative fixes were the rule rather than the exception at VVR. Finally arriving at Vermilion Valley, we were eager for a room with real beds and a shower, not just space in a crowded tent cabin and a turn at the community bathing facility. So we signed up for a room and headed straight for the restaurant's patio, where Paul and Alice had already established themselves at a picnic table. They didn't mind that we ate before showering, and neither did we. The food was good and so was the service. The chef and the waitress took great care of us, and we cheerfully tipped them more than adequately. Chef John's brown sugar-dill sauce for the salmon was so good I wrote down the ingredients in my journal.

Otherwise, we found ourselves nickel-and-dimed at every opportunity. I understand that isolated resorts have to charge top price for supplies. But it didn't occur to me that some of these top-dollar supplies would be defective. We purchased a fuel canister at VVR, only to discover a week later when we looked at it more closely that someone had scratched "not for resale" on the bottom with the tip of a knife blade. We guessed that a previous thru-hiker had left the canister in the hiker box out in front for a needy hiker's use, and that the management had retrieved it, put a price sticker on it, and charged money for something that was meant to be free. And on top of that, the canister was defective, which we discovered, too late, months later. Up until Vermilion Valley, our town stops had cost us maybe $100, roughly half for a room and half for food. Because we took a zero day at VVR, the bill was bound to be higher, but I was still surprised when I saw the total for a room for two nights, four meals, two ferry rides, and a few incidentals: a whopping $556. Spend a million, indeed! With friends like that, who needs collection agencies?

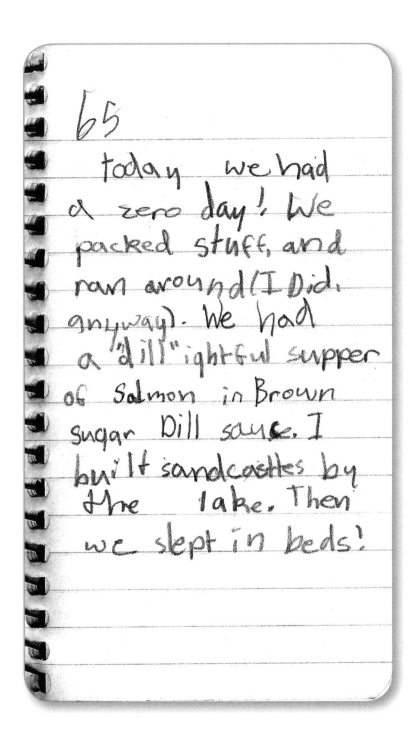

65

today we had
a zero day! We
packed stuff, and
ran around (I Did.
anyway). We had
a "dill"ightful supper
of Salmon in Brown
sugar Dill sauce. I
built sandcastles by
the lake. Then
we slept in beds!

Our next several town stops were relatively uneventful, but notable in part because during two of them we got the chance to visit with loved ones: Lipa, a friend and retired park ranger, and my sister Carol and her family, including her first grandchild, whom we were meeting for the first time. Those stops in Bridgeport, California, and Carson City, Nevada, were among our more relaxed town stops, with people like Lipa and Carol looking after us. And then came Belden, at Mile 1,289.

Belden Town Resort is a small community along California State Highway 70. It straddles a narrow piece of land, with the highway and the Feather River on one side, and the railroad on the other. The PCT drops down a steep hill, cuts across the railroad tracks, and finally meanders into the little resort . We had phoned ahead to reserve a cabin, but when we got there, we couldn't find anyone who knew anything about it. Here, my small-town background came in handy: I knew to hang out near the bar, and the person in charge would show up eventually. "In charge" may be an exaggeration. The two young people running the place seemed overwhelmed with it all. Restaurant hours were apparently decided at the whim of the cook. The small store's supplies were stacked on the floor in the same bags and boxes in which they had left the nearest discount food warehouse. Our resupply box? "Well, gee, I don't know, dude, it's gotta be around here somewhere ... Why don't you try the office?"

Back in the main room, we leaned against the bar to wait, admiring the bills of various monetary denominations tacked to the ceiling and dodging the locals who approached us. One such denizen was a potbellied fellow with a hairy chest, who swaggered up and shoved a shaky hand in Gary's direction. "Hello, there!" he bellowed, while ogling Mary. "I'm John." About the time he wandered out of sight, another guy walked up and launched into a long story about how he and his fellow band members had run an extension cord through the bedroom window of the cabin we were renting for the night so that he could operate an open-air tattoo parlor out of the back of the band's old school bus. Eventually, we did track down the acting manager and got the key to our cabin.

At our cabin, we weren't terribly surprised to discover the meager sanitation and maintenance standards of the resort. Whoever cleaned the cabin apparently never looked above eye level. Doing laundry later on, I found that one of the resort's washing machines was capable of delivering a nasty electrical shock. On the other hand, we did get some cooked food at the bar, augmented by canned goods that we could heat up in our kitchen. There were plenty of clean towels for our showers, and plenty of hot water. By the time we got to bed, we were feeling pretty good (and possibly a little high, as well, what with the sweet, skunky smell that intermingled with the already strong tobacco and barbecue smoke wafting through town).

By 10 p.m., Belden Town was delightfully quiet, and the three of us fell into a deep, profound sleep. At 2 a.m., I awoke, startled by the sensation that the entire cabin was trembling. I heard a rumbling. Having lived in California for 20 years, my first thought was that we were experiencing an earthquake. But this didn't feel like any earthquake I remembered. Rumble, rumble, shake, shake, RUMBLE, RUMBLE. My mind turned instead to the distinct possibility that this was The End of the World. The noise was deafening, and the vibrations in the pitch-black bedroom were downright disorienting. For a second, I was truly frightened. Gary with his earplugs and Mary with her 10-year-old's ability to sleep through practically anything left me alone to deal with this bizarre situation. Finally (maybe 20 seconds later), it dawned on me that a train was running through town, on the tracks above Belden. That was reassuring—until it occurred to me that if the train were to derail, not just we but the entire town of Belden would be history. Judgment Day is a one-time event, but trains derail every day. I eventually fell asleep again—until the next train rolled through. I know people can get used to this sort of thing, but our night in Belden wasn't the kind that would make me want to return. I had to wonder how the families with children I had seen earlier coped with the train noise at night. Maybe they were from large cities and a freight train booming and banging down the tracks during the wee hours wasn't any more disturbing than a Boeing 747 with its landing gear nearly touching the roof, or an ambulance with lights and sirens blaring, tearing down the street.

Our last experience in Belden was a very good one. We headed out in midmorning, leaving what felt like a ghost town. About a mile up the trail, Mary and I took a short detour down to the post office while Gary stayed behind to guard our packs from bears. Dorothy, the postmistress, was friendly and helpful, and when she heard our names, she exclaimed, "You must be the famous family." We felt so good.

Our next stop, at Old Station, was like celebrating Christmas in August. It was Day 95, and we were 1,378 miles along. We caught up with Vice and Spreadsheet, and met Dumptruck for the first time, as he had just returned from a break while recovering from injuries. A friendly postmistress helped us retrieve our unusually large and heavy resupply box. Opening the box was like opening Santa's pack: new boots for Gary, a new water purifier, and for Mary—not one, not two, but *three* sets of color comics from Sunday newspapers of weeks gone by. A helpful clerk let us store our packs at the store while we dined at the Coyote Cafe. That night we stayed with Georgi and Dennis Heitman, and the next morning had our second breakfast at the Coyote Cafe.

Our next stop was at Castella on Day 103, when the smoke from forest fires added a little anxiety to our lives. Forest fires often close sections of the PCT, forcing thru-hikers to skip sections and then return later to hike the burned-over trail after the fires are out. One morning, we had awakened to find a fine layer of white ash sprinkled over our tent from a distant conflagration. But the fires never came close enough to stop our forward progress.

Soon after we left the trail at Mile 1,506 for the side road into Castella, a gentleman named Ted gave us a lift to the post office in his pickup truck. (We weren't as lucky later in the day. No one offered us a lift back to the trail, so we had to walk the 2 miles or so.) That night, Mary wrote about the stop in her journal:

Day 103: *Castella has very good burritos and a multitude of cats on the store patio. Afterwards we walked a few more miles with food-laden packs.*

A master of understatement, that girl. The burritos at Ammirati's are justifiably famous in the backpacking community. One is a meal and two are enough to fill up even a thru-hiker. The well-equipped store provided us with several bottles of Gatorade and plenty of other goodies. "The Guys"—Vice, Spreadsheet, and Dumptruck—were there ahead of us, and we joined them on the store's shady patio. The shade was important—that day was a real scorcher. Even the half-feral cats stayed out of the sun, occasionally deigning to play with Mary. We picked up a nine-day supply of food in Castella, which made for very heavy packs.

Castella—at least the small part of it we saw—seemed like a pleasant little town, with a good location, right next to Castle Crags State Park and its magnificent scenery. But the town, like the surrounding area, was dominated by the noise of Interstate 5. It was amazing. Long before we got to town, we could hear the freeway, and long after we left, we could still hear the constant hum of traffic. It was downright strange to be hiking and camping in surroundings that at least appeared to be remote, and yet every time I stopped to think, I was aware that thousands of vehicles were rushing by not that far away, their drivers completely oblivious not only to my existence, but to the natural beauty that lay all around. The only thing comparable was our experience in the southern Sierra, where, for several days after leaving Kennedy Meadows, we were frequently bombarded with the noise of military jets zipping in and out of the peaks and canyons. We rarely saw the planes, but commercial aircraft don't behave like that. My guess is that they were pilots from Edwards Air Force Base honing their skills at the expense of our eardrums.

Fortunately, there were very few sonic booms. A low-flying plane breaking the sound barrier can knock rocks and ice loose, as had happened to us a few summers earlier on a perilous stretch of trail leading up to New Army Pass. We were climbing that pass in the southern Sierra because Mary and Gary wanted to give me a chance to bag my first "fourteener"—a peak of 14,000 or more feet above sea level. Mary had already conquered two fourteeners: 14,162-foot Mt. Shasta and 14,026-foot Mt. Langley. Langley was easy to reach from Highway 395 on our way home from attending a wedding in Long Beach, California, so we took a side trip up to Cottonwood Pass and hiked into a backpacking area at about 12,000 feet. We spent a day getting used to the altitude, and the next morning headed up the rocky switchbacks toward New Army Pass. We were about a quarter of the way up when a plane came over, low and fast, and we heard a sonic boom. Within a minute, we heard some rattling on the cliffs above the trail, and we looked up to see a block of ice coming down. One of the pieces that broke off was the size of a bowling ball and could have killed someone easily. Gary yelled at the guy in front of us to get behind a rock, and then he yanked Mary down behind a big rock. I also dived behind a boulder, but the other man remained motionless until it was all over.

My quick reaction to the threat probably stemmed from a scary mountaineering experience Gary and I shared before Mary was born, when we were on Mt. Shasta making an unsuccessful attempt at the summit. We were strapping on crampons at the bottom of a snow field a little way above Helen Lake when Gary heard a noise and pointed up the slope. A dark brown boulder about the size of an oil drum was bouncing down through the rocks and heading straight for us. We both scrambled for cover, handicapped by the fact that our crampons were only halfway on. The boulder stopped short, but it looms large in my mind whenever I'm on similar terrain.

After Castella, our next layover was in Seiad Valley, the last town stop in California, at Mile 1,662. In order to reach the post office in time on Day 111, we had 12 miles to walk, on a day when the heat felt like a hostile entity. The last 6 miles along a paved road seemed endless. But once we arrived, Cindy, the post office worker, was friendly and helpful. Better yet, she was babysitting a puppy and Mary got to play with it. We didn't pause for showers or even cold drinks until our return box was in the mail. And then we collapsed in a rare patch of shade, guzzled down more Gatorade, and relaxed with the newspaper. At last, I could sit and reflect on the new state we had entered. No, not Oregon, not yet. Today we had entered the State of Jefferson. I knew, because it said so on the side of the post office, on people's houses, and even on the blade of a bulldozer parked along the road going into town.

As recently as 1941, residents of this area were serious about forming a new state. Resentment in southern Oregon and northern California over neglect by the respective state governments had been festering for a long time, with a State of Shasta and a State of Klamath proposed even before the Civil War. Bernita Tickner and Gail Fiorini-Jenner describe those efforts in their pictorial history, *The State of Jefferson* (Arcadia Publishing 2005). Legislation setting up a separate state was introduced in California in 1852, when the state capital was still Vallejo. The idea of separation stayed alive, although the legislation did not, and another serious revolt materialized in 1935 in Curry County, in southern Oregon. Yreka, in California's Siskiyou County, was designated the capital of what then would have been the 49th state (although I think it's safe to say the movement wasn't taken very seriously in Salem or Sacramento). By November 1941, however, there was real progress made toward a State of Jefferson, with local government involvement, a gubernatorial election, and a declaration of secession. But in politics, as in life, timing is everything. The new state was to proclaim its existence to the world in early December, but on December 7, the Japanese government bombed Pearl Harbor. The necessity of exploiting the remote region's timber resources and strategic minerals for the war effort resulted in the construction of roads and bridges; and since better transportation was the main grievance behind the secession movement in the first place, the movement lost momentum.

In the end, the State of Jefferson got what it wanted, at least temporarily. But the problems of unemployment and governmental neglect haven't disappeared from northern California, or from most of the rural parts of the state. Unemployment is high; incomes are low. Ranchers and farmers share realistic worries over water allocations, and residents in general find their concerns ignored because there are so few of them compared with the millions living in the major population areas. Even today, when a bridge is washed out in a storm, there's no guarantee it will get fixed quickly, whereas when the Northridge earthquake unraveled Los Angeles' freeway system in 1994, the entire state's wealth paid the overtime for construction workers to rebuild the damaged roads.

The State of Jefferson movement is primarily a libertarian movement, toward less government and, in particular, fewer environmental regulations governing resource exploitation. This brand of politics is not uncommon along the stretches of California, Oregon, and Washington through which the Pacific Crest Trail wanders. But it's not the only political ideal. There's also the Cascadia movement, an idealistic frame of mind that envisions the area as the future home of a peaceful and sustainable community based on environmentalism and social justice. Ernest Callenbach wrote his book *Ecotopia* in 1975, and while the book is dated in many ways, his ideas are still popular in some coastal sections of California, Oregon, and Washington. As it turned out, timing wasn't the secessionists' best friend in this case, either. The Cascadian National Party, devoted to a separate nation-state encompassing what is now Washington and Oregon, was launched on September 10, 2001, just one day before the tragic events of September 11.

Outside of its politics, Seiad Valley is famous among backpackers for two reasons: It's supposed to be the hottest and driest point on the California section of the PCT, and it's supposed to offer food that excels in both quantity and quality. It failed on both counts.

Seiad Valley was certainly earning its hot-and-dry reputation when we arrived. It must have been well over 100°F, and humidity was probably hovering around 9 percent. But that evening, Rick, who owns an RV park where thru-hikers can camp for free, mentioned there was rain in the forecast. Rain seemed about as likely as 4 feet of snow, but I told Gary, and he rigged the rain fly in such a way that it let in plenty of air, but could be pulled over the tent in minutes if needed. The next morning at 6 o'clock, I awoke to the feeling of rain on my face. Felt good, actually. Gary pulled the rain cover into position, and we went back to sleep for an hour. The precipitation slacked long enough for us to pack up, but when we settled in at the cafe for lunch, it was raining hard. We were lucky: By the time we started walking, the rain had finished falling, but had cooled things off enough that our long, steep climb out of town was fairly pleasant.

Seiad Valley's pancake challenge is nationally known (as seen on TV!): Eat three of these monsters and they're free. We knew eating three was out of the question for any of us—we'd heard how big they were—we were just hoping for some good food, and lots of it. But the meal we were served the night we arrived was so disappointing that when our waitress saw Mary and me standing on the sidewalk the next morning, she insisted on paying us back out of her own pocket. I was using the pay phone, deep in a discussion with my sister Liz, when the woman drove up and hurriedly parked. She jumped out of her car, ran over, and said, "I felt so bad about your dinner last night—here, take this," shoved a $20 bill into my hand, and rushed off before I could react, much less give it back.

Sunny California. Rainy Oregon. I never dreamed these stereotypes would be so true for us. The rain really began for us the day before we reached the California-Oregon state line, a day I described in my journal as cold, wet, and miserable. The next days were worse. Much of the trail was overgrown, which meant pushing through waist-high vegetation all day, and getting our pants soaked. It was worse for Mary, being shorter. We got warm and dry again on Day 116 at Hyatt Lake Resort, near Mile 1,750, and from there pushed on to Mazama Village in Crater Lake National Park on Day 120, at Mile 1,830. There, we took an unplanned zero day for Gary to recover from his chills, nausea, aches, and general wretchedness. The staff—mostly retirees making enough money as seasonal workers to keep up their RV-oriented lifestyles the rest of the year—treated us very well. They may have been a little slow-moving, but they made up for that by treating Mary as though she were their collective grandchild. Our next stop was Bend, Oregon, named for its location on a double curve of the Deschutes River. When Californians talk about moving to Oregon (as lots of Californians do; it's sort of a state hobby), Bend is the city they name if they really don't like fog and rain. (The fog-and rain-tolerant ones talk about Ashland and Portland. People who simply adore fog and rain fantasize about moving farther north to Washington and living in Seattle.) Bend is about 30 miles away from the PCT, but our retired-ranger friend, Lipa, picked us up at Mile 1,958 and drove us there for a much-needed rest. Our Bend experience is nicely summed up in Mary's journal entry:

Day 128: *Today we hiked in and met Lipa. We drove down to a motel room next to the laundry. McDinner!*

Detroit, Oregon, also is nowhere near the PCT, but it turned out to be one of my favorite town stops. We got a cheap but comfortable motel room right across from a restaurant that offered both good food and good service. The town had a clean, cozy, welcoming feeling to it. Everything about Detroit combined to sooth our nerves, frazzled by too many days of cold, wet conditions, and uncertainty about how much worse they would get.

128

Today, we hiked
in and met Lepa.
we drove down
to a motel room
~~the~~ next to the
Laundry.

ⓂⓒＣ dinner!

We didn't visit Detroit on Day 136 because we had a sudden desire to sleep in motel beds and eat restaurant food. Well, OK, we always had a more or less constant desire to sleep in real beds and eat real food. But it wasn't an intensification of that desire that sent us off to Detroit. It was an intensification of the rainfall and the creek depths along a section of the PCT already notorious for difficult stream crossings. Specifically, Russell Creek and Milk Creek had reputations that made us think twice about fording them with Mary along. A man hiking near Pamelia Lake with his chocolate Labrador retriever showed us on his map how to hike out to Highway 22, follow the pavement 7 miles to Whitewater Creek Road, and follow that 4 miles back to the PCT. Quite a long detour, but we were really worried about those two creeks.

Once we got to the highway, we hitched a ride into Detroit with a ski patroller from Bend on his way to the coast to learn sea kayaking. Soon we were sitting comfortably in the Cedars Restaurant, warm, dry, and well-fed, watching a light rain fall and reading *The Oregonian*. And what I read in the newspaper made me wonder if we should ever go back into the woods. Oregon, I discovered, takes a liberal position toward people with physical handicaps who want to obtain hunting licenses. Based on the policies set forth in the Americans with Disabilities Act (ADA), the Oregon Fish and Wildlife Commission had some years earlier decided that residents confined to wheelchairs weren't the only disabled individuals who should be able to enjoy the pleasures of hunting. Oh, no. The enlightened commissioners decided that blind and sight-impaired people are just as entitled as anyone else to take a powerful weapon capable of shooting a bullet at 3,000 feet per second and head into the forest.

Oregon also decided that disabled hunters could sit in a parked vehicle anywhere but right smack on a public road, sense that a deer or an elk was somewhere nearby, and direct a companion to pick up the .30-06 in the back seat, and blast away. And he could blast away at just about any animal, regardless of gender, even when ordinary sportsmen slogging through the mud were restricted to the males of the species. I grew up in a hunting area and it was sort of understood that keen vision was a prerequisite for going into the woods and firing at elk or mule deer, so as to avoid shooting the cattle that roamed the range, not to mention the ranchers who owned those cattle. This has to be some kind of Oregon aberration, I thought, the liberal coastal element's eagerness to comply with the ADA combined with the inland passion for hunting. But months later, I discovered that other states have accommodations for handicapped hunters, and that hunters with physical limitations are constantly working to expand those provisions. Able-bodied hunters, naturally, worry that the rules are being abused, and that hunters perfectly capable of carrying a rifle or drawing a bow are obtaining special treatment under false pretenses.

This is a difficult issue for fish and game departments all over the country. I wouldn't want to be the commissioner deciding if a man with one arm and limited vision should be allowed to hunt deer with a crossbow and a mechanism that allows him to cock and fire it with his teeth, especially when that man has a national organization and a set of lawyers supporting his interpretation of the ADA. But neither would I want to be another hunter pursuing a white-tailed deer through the underbrush when the one-armed, one-eyed man with the powerful crossbow is out there as well. It's easy—especially for a non-hunter like me—to dismiss people who insist on being given hunting licenses in the face of common-sense safety issues, or who try to take advantage of the system by accentuating an old injury or claiming that using regulation gear during the official season brings with it the risk of a new injury. But I've come to realize that for many people, hunting is as essential to their pursuit of happiness as backpacking is to mine. I've asked myself sometimes what I would do if I could no longer hike. Buy a horse? Invent a trail-ready wheelchair? I have to hike, and these people have to hunt.

But even so, after Detroit, I never urged Mary to be quiet while walking in the woods. I let her talk as much and as loudly as she wanted—sing, shout even—anything to let the hunters know that humans, not ruminants, were approaching.

From Detroit, we hitched a ride back to the exact spot we'd left the day before, and walked across a bridge through a construction zone with no shoulder and high-speed traffic. In the end, it was probably a greater threat to our lives than the stream crossings would have been, but at least if we'd been hit on Highway 22 an ambulance would have arrived quickly. We were walking in the rain, and the weather steadily worsened, which made us more grateful than we might have been to get a cabin at Olallie Lake Resort, just off the trail at Mile 2,053, on our 138th day.

We were sick of walking in water. So before we left Olallie Lake, we mapped out an alternate route on a series of Forest Service roads that would take us to Clackamas Lake in a day and a half. At that point, we had taken an alternate trail a couple times, but we were determined nonetheless to maintain our thru-hike philosophy of linking up all our steps. The maps we had picked up in Detroit showed an abundance of back roads, all of which, we figured, had to be better drained than what we'd been walking on. We started out with ice and frost everywhere, and about the time the air warmed up a little, it started to rain, sometimes heavily. Late in the day, during a brief break in the downpour, we started looking for a stream from which to filter water, and a place to camp. Gary walked one way, and found water. Mary and I walked the other way—and found a cabin! We were so excited. It was like half a town stop—shelter minus the fast-food and laundromat. The sturdy, two-story structure had been built by the Mt. Hood Snowmobile Club for "winter recreation," and I decided the cold, rainy weather we were experiencing matched perfectly what we call "winter" in the San Francisco Bay Area. Inside, there was firewood and a fine stove built out of a 50-gallon drum. I started a fire without using a single match; someone had used the stove the night before, and there were still enough embers among the ashes to ignite the cardboard I shoved in for tinder. Mary and I brought in some more kindling to dry out overnight and be ready for the next person's use, but otherwise we stayed close to that wonderful wood stove. We slept upstairs in the loft, lulled to sleep by the sound of rain on the roof, while our ponchos and jackets dried downstairs.

A few days later, we stayed overnight at Timberline Lodge, and then it was time to head for Cascade Locks, the last stop in Oregon. We were enjoying fairly good weather, for a change, but as we descended the 3,500 feet toward the Columbia River and the Washington state line on Day 145, I began limping. My shin splints were finally catching up with me. I also had a severely aching jaw that I couldn't ignore, either. But we still had Washington to go.

CHAPTER 9

TOWARD THE NORTH STAR

Day 176: *We got over Buckskin Pass and down the other side. We managed a hot dinner. I wish I were Henrietta, warm at home!*

—from Scrambler's journal

DURING THE LAST FEW DAYS in Oregon, something changed for me. Gary noticed that I became downright wolfish when it came time to eat, as though my body were suddenly crying out for much more nutrition than I could give it. Chronic calorie deficits are the norm for thru-hikers, but we had recently had more chances than usual to replenish, during our stays at Olallie Lake and Timberline Lodge. So my change in mealtime behavior seemed odd. It worried us.

At our cabin at Olallie Lake, our trail buddies Nocona and Bald Eagle had dropped by for a chat and admitted that they, too, were becoming discouraged. "Everyone's dropped out except you guys, us, and Chacoman," Nocona told us. They especially missed Crow and Sherpa, with whom they had become close friends. Bald Eagle and Nocona had recently made a side trip to buy cold-weather gear at the Portland REI, and it looked as if another shopping trip would be in order if they wanted to continue. "At some point, I have to ask myself: Why are we doing this?" Bald Eagle said. "We're here to hike the PCT and have fun. But what if it's not fun anymore?" Gloom was in the air. Quitting was beginning to sound like an attractive option to me, too.

Gary and Mary would have none of it. We had hiked 2,053 miles and had only 597 to go. Gary made his position plain: "I've had enough fun to last me until Canada. What I want to do now is finish." He announced he would complete the trail even if he had to walk on snowshoes all the way across Washington state. Mary declared her equal determination. "I'm going to finish," she said, "no matter what." All I would commit to was reaching Cascade Locks, 102 miles away, the last stop before crossing the Columbia River into Washington. Considering how determined I had been at the beginning to complete the PCT, and even considering the really horrible conditions we had endured since entering Oregon, I was surprised at myself. Unbidden, the thought began occurring to me late at night: Should I get off the trail?

As we approached Cascade Locks, I developed crippling shin splints in my left leg, so painful I could barely hobble. It was much worse than what I had endured in July in the right leg, and it was accompanied by a severe pain in my upper jaw. When we reached our motel room and I looked in the mirror, I made the shocking discovery that I had a big, bleeding sore on my gums—about the size and shape of a cranberry. Same color, too. I'm convinced that those heretical thoughts about leaving the trail were my body's way of telling me my left shin was developing tiny cracks that my strong muscles wouldn't be able to compensate for much longer, and a serious infection was building up in that tender jaw.

I finally faced up to the fact that we had walked 2,155 trail miles—roughly equivalent to the entire Appalachian Trail—but I personally couldn't go any farther without at least a temporary break for medical treatment. Suddenly, our situation was totally changed, and all bets for a successful PCT thru-hike were off.

• • • • •

OUR IMMEDIATE PROBLEM was transportation. I had to get to Hood River to fill a prescription my dentist had sent by phone for an antibiotic, and short of hitchhiking on the freeway (legal in Oregon, but hardly safe), there didn't seem to be any way to get there. It's only 20 miles from Cascade Locks to Hood River, but it might as well have been 120 miles. Getting by without a car is nearly impossible in small Western towns. I don't know what small Eastern, Southern, and Midwestern towns are like—maybe they have buses, or each town is self-sufficient, with all services within walking distance, the way I imagine a New England village would be—but way out West, you need a car. In some communities, people are in the habit of driving 45 miles or so to buy milk or go to church or watch a high school basketball game. You want to talk to a friend in town who isn't home? You get in your car and drive around until you see his car parked in front of someone else's house, and you park alongside and go in, with a quick knock on the jamb as you walk through the door and shout your hellos. So there we were in Cascade Locks, which boasted bus service to Portland—twice a week—but no other public transit.

Trail magic kicked in at the grocery store, where I was buying juice, milk, and doughnuts for breakfast. As the clerk rang up the groceries, I asked about public transportation. "We're thru-hikers, and I need to get to Hood River to fill a prescription," I explained. The sympathetic clerk suggested I talk to people at local businesses, in hopes that someone might know someone who might be heading out of town and be willing to offer a ride. That didn't sound very likely to get me to Hood River any time soon, especially on a Saturday, but I thanked her for the tip. Outside the store, I paused to scan the headlines on the news rack, and a tall man walked up behind me. "I overheard you asking about how to get out of town," he said, before I could get anxious about a stranger approaching me. "My wife has an Avis agency in Portland and she could arrange to get a car to you." Sure enough, Troy called his wife from his custom fishing rod business in the next block and, within a few hours, Gary, Mary, and I were on our way, in a bright, shiny, air-conditioned vehicle, gobbling up the miles that had seemed so vast an impediment that morning. We picked up my penicillin in Hood River, and then went the opposite direction to reach Portland, where we bought a two-person tent, cold-weather gear, and food at the REI.

At this point, I subconsciously understood that I was going to be off the trail for more than a few days. Consciously, we all figured that I would be able to run down to California, get healed up, and rejoin the rest of the family in less than a week to continue walking. But looking back, I can see how my mind shifted gears from thru-hiker mode to helper mode sometime during that weekend in Oregon. I began seeing everything from the point of view of a manager, not a participant. For example: That afternoon, after making the appalling discovery that the Bridge of the Gods over the Columbia River had no sidewalk—in fact, no way to separate hikers from traffic—I used the rental car to hold up 13 other cars and let my family walk across in safety. (I confess I derived a perverse pleasure from holding up all that traffic.) Once across the bridge, I found a motel room in the little town of Stevenson, checked on Gary and Mary (who were taking an alternate route recommended in the guidebook that involved a long road walk), and at dusk picked them up and took them to the room, where I had food waiting.

The next day, we awoke to a sunny and mild morning. After a large meal, I dropped off the rest of the family at the point they had stopped walking the day before, and headed home to California. Gary and I had agreed there would be no tears at our parting, that it was very important for Mary that I be cheerful. So I put off the weeping and wailing until later. Instead, I stopped the car alongside the road, made sure we agreed on the date, time, and place I would see them again (the following Saturday, early afternoon, where the PCT crosses U.S. Highway 12 near White Pass), delivered quick hugs and kisses, and drove away, waving out the window until I disappeared around a curve. Scrambler and Captain Bligh dutifully displayed good spirits as I left.

I made up my mind not to spend the entire day worrying about Gary and Mary. I certainly had plenty of other things to worry about. My joints and muscles, accustomed to walking for hours every day, couldn't adjust to sitting for the 12-and-a-half hours it took to drive to Sunol. They just ached. I also worried whether I'd be able to see my dentist and doctor right away. I had promised to meet Mary and

155

M

Today we bade
a tearful farewell
to mom. Sigh.
We hiked 6 miles.
We camped at Buesfach lk.

Gary six days hence, and I would have no way of getting word to them if I were delayed. With my aches and pains, a loud radio, and substantial amounts of caffeine from convenience stores along the way, I got home that evening just before midnight, greeted our two surprised cats, and fell into bed.

The next morning, the first order of business was to become reacquainted with the cats, Hank and Henrietta. I feared they'd be aloof or even hostile, as some house pets are when the owner goes away for an extended trip. Not these two. Every time I sat down, they'd leap onto my lap, purring loudly and practically wearing their fur off as they rubbed their heads on me.

I was on the phone for hours on that brief visit, and conversations would go like this: "Hi, Liz, it's me. The endodontist—Ouch! Get off my lap, Hank—sorry about that. The visit to the endodontist went fine. I'm going to take the antibiotics for a few more days—Henrietta, stop chewing the phone cord. What? Oh, it's penicillin. Yeah, and I got some Vicodin, too—Stop that, Hank! What? Oh, I didn't mean you. It's the darn cats; I should have put them in the bathroom. I—OK, Henrietta, you can get on my lap, sheesh! I hardly have any pain. Just took one before bed last night—Hank, are you going to try to fit up here, too? Oh, all right. The Forest Service? Yes, I called the ranger in Stehekin. She says everything's pretty well shut down this late in the—Ouch, don't claw!—this late in the year, and ... What? Oh, yes, I'm running up to State Farm this afternoon. She'll have the Canadian insurance form for me. What I really need are copies of our birth certificates, but I can't—Off! Get off! Darn cats, they can't both fit in my lap at once, I hardly have any lap left! The weather? Yeah, it's good up there right now, but you'd be surprised how cold it's getting at night already—hold on a minute. Come here, you two. Dang it, now I've got you, you little pests! (Sound of me walking down to the bathroom with a cat under each arm, tossing them inside, closing the door, and running back up the stairs.) Where was I?"

My dentist was able to fit me in the very morning after my return, and he sent me off to the endodontist that afternoon. The next day, I returned the rental car and saw my doctor, who told me to get off the trail and stay off until the shin splints healed—and if I didn't, a stress fracture would follow. I didn't cry in the doctor's office, although I felt like it. I saved the tears until that evening, when I called my sister, Liz, with the news. "It wasn't supposed to end this way!" I blubbered.

I felt like a big wimp, leaving the trail just because of severe pain and a serious infection. I felt a little better after I met Liz, her husband, Marq, and their younger son, Michael, at a Mexican restaurant in San Jose. My dental visit had confirmed that, indeed, I had an abscessed tooth. The endodontist had opened up the tooth to let it drain, and I had a return appointment scheduled for just a couple hours after I met my relatives for lunch. Marq looked at me closely. "You don't seem very nervous for someone who's going in for a root canal," he remarked. After a pause, he added, "I guess after what you've been through ..."

That was the best laugh I'd had in weeks. And it was true. After five months of the Pacific Crest Trail, the dental procedure that summons up fear in the hardiest souls had struck me as nothing more than a minor annoyance.

During my four days at home, I resolved that upon my return to Washington, I would be the best trail angel I could be, while I took time to heal up. By meeting my family at road crossings, mapping a better route around the portion of the trail destroyed by floods, and otherwise supporting them, I would help Captain Bligh and Scrambler get through Washington in spite of the bad weather they were almost certain to face.

I prepared for my trail angeling before I returned to Washington. I borrowed some car-camping gear from Liz, continued the endless series of phone calls, visited the grocery store, and did a load of laundry. The night before I left, I gave the cats a final burst of affection, loaded the car, and went to bed early. The drive to Packwood, Washington, took 16 hours, and my legs and joints ached just as much as they had on the drive home. The Cowlitz River Lodge had left the key in the door as promised. I staggered into my comfortable room and fell into bed.

The next day, I embarked on one of the strangest periods of my life. I became Angel Mom, the super trail angel, shepherding my two precious backpackers through Washington state, running errands, picking up supplies, providing rides, arranging accommodations, and charting itineraries. First, I met them at White Pass, where I gave them the bad news that I wouldn't be continuing on with them—at least for now. The good news, of course, was that I'd be able to help them in many important ways.

While I emphasized the positive, the fact remains that losing me was a serious impediment to Scrambler and Captain Bligh as they headed farther north through Washington. Although I was the weakest link in the chain, I was a link, nonetheless. I was the one who got them up and moving in the mornings, who sorted and rationed and prepared the food, who set up the tent and arranged the bedding. Gary simplified the food arrangement in Washington so that boiling water was all it took to fix dinner, and Mary became an expert at erecting the tent and laying out the pads and sleeping bags. Three days after I left for California, she described her newfound task in her journal:

Day 151: *Today we walked quite close to Mt. Adams. We camped near a lovely waterfall. I only made one mistake getting the tent up all by myself: I got the rain fly backwards! Daddy showed me the moonlit mountain.*

But that still left them without a morning person to get them going. That is my job, no matter where we are. At home, I get up with the alarm clock, roust Mary, and make sure she eats breakfast and gets dressed in time for school. Gary keeps a clock radio on his dresser so that as soon as I wake him up, he can turn on National Public Radio and be goaded into action by the sound of his least favorite politicians being interviewed first thing in the morning. In Washington,

The mountain by Moon. scrambler.

they had to get up in the dark in order to take advantage of the dwindling amount of daylight, so they couldn't rely on the sun to awaken them, either. Gary had two wristwatches with him, an ordinary waterproof digital watch and his fancy altimeter watch—and both had alarms. At first, he tried setting one and relying on Mary to hear it and then to rouse him. But that didn't work out so well. As Mary reported in one journal entry:

> **Day 162:** *The tent was surprisingly dry this morning—partly because we slept two hours past the alarm!*

As Gary recalls, they often had to get up at 4 or 4:30 in the morning to keep their 20-mile days going. They would get up, eat frozen Pop-Tarts in the dark with ice on the inner walls of the tent, and often it was still dark when they started walking. After the first time they slept through the alarm, they began exploring other ways to get themselves up. First, they tried using both the wristwatch and the altimeter watch, with one near each of their heads. But they slept through even those alarms most of the time. Since Gary slept with earplugs, the noise wouldn't wake him, so it was up to Mary. They figured they had to get the source of the sound as close to her ears as possible, so they hung a spare piece of line from the inside top of the tent and tied a watch to the other end so it dangled just inches from Mary's head, like a spider descending from a web. They placed the other watch on the floor between their heads. At first, they set both watches for the same time and hoped for the best, but even then they occasionally slept right through the noise. Finally, they learned to set the second watch a minute or two later, so Mary couldn't go right back to sleep after the first one woke her up. It

162

The tent was suprisisi-
ngly dry this morning—
pry partly because
we slept 2 hours
past the alarm!

We did manage,
~~however~~
however, to do
22 miles.
we ended up at a
mouse infested site.

was her job to shake Gary until he could start talking, and then he was in charge of keeping them both awake.

Our original plan at White Pass, the first resupply point in Washington, was to get to a little resort called the Kracker Barrel in time to get our box there, camp somewhere nearby, and then proceed on to Snoqualmie Pass. We wouldn't be able to mail anything back, and we would have to carry five days' worth of food. With a set of wheels, however, I was able to pick up the box early in the day, take it back to the motel and sort it, then meet the rest of the family at White Pass in mid-afternoon. I took them to the motel in Packwood, fed them, did their laundry, and returned them to the trailhead the next morning. I camped in Mt. Rainier National Park that night, but when I met them the next afternoon at Chinook Pass, the weather was threatening, so we spent one more night at the pleasant Cowlitz River Lodge.

I spent the next night back at the Ohanapecosh campground in Mt. Rainier National Park and then moved my base of operations to the Summit Inn at Snoqualmie, a ski resort with a motel, restaurant, and gas station right on Interstate 90. The day before, on a pleasantly warm afternoon with just a few clouds, I had driven up the well-maintained, dirt Forest Service Road 54 to Stampede Pass to scout out the PCT crossing near Frog Lake. When I picked up Gary and Mary the following day, the weather had turned cold and rainy. They were glad to be indoors for the night. The next day was infinitely worse. I took them back up to the pass for 18 miles of slack-packing, with just enough food, water, and clothing for the day, while the tent, sleeping bags, and backpacker stove stayed in our room. From the motel, I could see a big sign over the highway that gave the temperature—I presume so that drivers could decide if they were likely to hit icy conditions farther on. It never rose above 42°F, and the rain never stopped falling: ideal conditions for hypothermia. But they made it, and spent another warm, dry night with full bellies. The next day, I saw them off again, and prepared to move my base of operations farther north.

Through all this, I scoured Washington for supplies, worked out a route around the flood-damaged area north of Stevens Pass, and made sure Scrambler and the Captain had a place to stay out of the rain every night I could manage it. I was busy! Dang, I said to myself once or twice (or maybe more) every day, this trail angeling is hard work! And, of course, I worried myself sick about them every minute we were apart. But thanks to me, Gary and Mary made good time with relatively light packs. They were able to sleep in towns rather than the tent on many rainy nights, catching up on their rest and their calories. They slack-packed some days, and avoided having to carry more than a few days' worth of food, in a state that's notoriously difficult for resupply. Their three days of slack-packing while we were based at the Dinsmores' River Haven in Skykomish provided them with a much-needed respite.

The morning after our last night at the Dinsmores, it was drizzling lightly. We drove back to Trinity, where Gary and Mary would tackle some of their worst weather, terrain, and route-founding conditions on the trail so far. In three days, they would meet me again at Rainy Pass on Highway 20. Gary was at the wheel. As we passed several deer hunters' camps, he remarked on the difficulty he had getting the car to stay on the road going up the muddy slopes. "When you leave," he advised me, "get a running start on these hills so you don't have to accelerate once you start. Otherwise you could spin out, slide off sideways, and end up in a creek bed, miles from help." I followed Gary's advice and got down the dirt road fine, but later, as I drove along paved Chiwawa River Road, the light sprinkle turned into a heavy rain. With every hour, the weather worsened, and I reached Mazama in a downpour. How were Gary and Mary doing? I felt plenty anxious— and a little guilty for spending my day inside a warm, dry vehicle.

In her journal, Mary described the day they left Trinity Trailhead, heading for Rainy Pass:

Day 168: *We left this easy life to do some true backpacking. At first, it rained very lightly, and then became heavier. It then commenced to snow thickly, about 2 inches. We finally found a wide spot in the trail. We set up camp there and ate a cold, substantial dinner. Lots of hills, including a 3,000-footer right off the bat!*

As I drove away, Scrambler and the Captain's worries about me gradually faded. Gary remembers those three days and two nights from Trinity Trailhead to Rainy Pass as the worst stretch in all of Washington. While they worried about whether I had spun off the dirt road into a ravine, the light drizzle that was falling when we parted turned to rain, and then to snow. Soon, Gary thought to himself, "If Barb's in the creek bed with the car, she might be better off than we are." Snow was falling hard as they reached Buck Creek Pass, and the footing was just horrible: a thin coating of ice over about 6 inches of water. Every now and then, they'd break through and get their feet even colder and wetter.

Finding the right trail was nearly impossible in the blowing snow. They found a signpost, but the words were covered with ice that refused to break off. A snack break under a tree, where they hoped to find shelter from the wind, was cut short because the wind kept knocking the snow off the branches and onto them. They managed to add another layer of clothing, and chose a trail that went downhill. The snow turned back to drizzle, the path went from snow-covered to just wet and muddy—and they still didn't know if they had chosen the correct route. By the time they reached an intersection with the original PCT and knew they were in the right place, it was dark and time to set up camp. The next day was equally bad, only longer. The day after that, I met them at Rainy Pass.

We were all happy to reunite in the tiny northern Washington town of Maza-ma, an oasis of liberal blue in a sea of conservative backwoods red, where Dick and Sue Roberts, who have since retired, ran the North Cascades Basecamp.

Mary has read J.R.R. Tolkien's Lord of the Rings trilogy two or three times (three or four times for me), and we sometimes drew comparisons between Fro-do's adventures and our own along the trail. Reaching Mazama would correspond with the scene in *The Fellowship of the Ring* in which Frodo and his companions, after much hardship and many perils, reach Rivendell and finally feel warm and dry and safe. They only leave because they have to, if they are to complete their quest. We only left because we had to, if we were going to complete our quest. The Roberts took such good care of us, on the one hand, and the weather and terrain were so forbidding on the other, that we felt we were leaving Rivendell directly for a frozen version of Mordor.

Mary described the North Cascades Basecamp as "a spectacular bed and breakfast." If she could build a dream house, it would probably bear a close re-semblance. The Basecamp has a delightful living room with a woodstove and car-peted steps around it, perfect for lounging. Comfy couches and chairs are ideal for reading or watching videos, in both of which Mary indulged. One night while we were there, two women who were staying overnight made friends with Mary and played board games with her after she finished helping her Dad waterproof our boots. One flight up, there were four bedrooms, and on the top story, there was a children's bedroom and also a playroom, with books and toys and a soft day bed with a view out the window. Our bedroom had a queen bed plus two bunk beds. (We wouldn't let Mary sleep on the top one at first, for fear she'd fall out, but later she got her wish.)

The Roberts loaned us gear, gave us rides, and tracked down backcountry rangers to help us plan a route through the wind and snow. And beyond that, the food was top-notch. But the best thing about our stay in Mazama was knowing that I was healthy enough to hike again. The abscessed tooth had healed up com-pletely, and my shin splints bothered me hardly at all. For this last stretch of 70 miles from Rainy Pass to the border, we would again be a threesome.

Our stay at the Basecamp gave us a chance to visit the nearby town of Win-throp, which dates back to the 1880s, when gold prospecting brought settlers to the area. Until the 1970s, the tiny town's only claim to fame was that author Owen Wister was inspired to write the 1902 Western novel *The Virginian* after spending his honeymoon there. But then Highway 20 was completed through the North Cascades, and the town reinvented itself as a Western-themed tourist destina-tion, a sort of Cascadia version of the Comstock Lode's Virginia City. Architect Robert Jorgenson of Leavenworth, a town in central Washington that resembles a Bavarian village, designed the false storefronts and wooden sidewalks.

Most of Winthrop might be only pseudo-historical, but there's real history be-hind the Duck Brand, a small restaurant with a big reputation and an odd name.

The original Duck Brand Saloon opened in 1891, identified by a cattle brand shaped like a duck. A fellow named Guy Waring started the saloon because he hated drinking. It seems he knew a saloon was inevitable, so he opened the first one, but he told the bartenders to eject any customers who appeared drunk. Waring also hosted author Owen Wister. The original saloon is now the Winthrop town hall, but the name lives on at the restaurant just down the street. Today, Winthrop is primarily a tourist town, but only for seven or eight months of the year, and less during heavy winters. Highway 20 is closed every winter, and the annual reopening of the highway is the occasion for great celebration among the community's business owners.

Winthrop's Wild West credentials may be only a Hollywood set, but its small-town friendliness is genuine. While Gary got maps at the Forest Service's visitor center, Mary and I played in the adjacent park. A woman walking her dog welcomed Mary's request to pet her pooch, and soon we were discovering mutual acquaintances and learning the history of the beautiful Methow Valley (which I quickly learned to pronounce "Met-how").

It's a very good thing Mazama was such a great place to stay. In spite of our best efforts to get to Canada, we couldn't seem to get any farther north. After a night at the Basecamp, we ate the extra-big breakfast Sue prepared, and then hit the trail from the Rainy Pass trailhead at noon on October 20.

At the trailhead, it looked like autumn, with fall colors and no snow on the ground. But as we gained altitude up a series of switchbacks, we began to see snow. Soon we were taking turns breaking trail as the snow became deeper and deeper. Just moving forward was exhausting. At some points, the snow was thigh-high on Gary, and almost waist-high on Mary. Little Scrambler would have to pick up a leg with both hands and set her foot down in the print left by her dad, who ended up leading most of the time. Worse, snow began to fall—flurries at first, and then dense flakes. Snow on the ground obscured the trail, and the wind and snow made it hard even to read a map. And still we climbed higher, contouring around hills and always searching for the vestige of a trail. Gary's route-finding abilities were stretched to the max as he guided us down into a valley in the gathering dusk, sometimes plowing through snow-choked ravines. It was completely dark and snowing hard when we set up camp at a flat spot below the trail. We tried to memorize our location in relation to what we thought was the trail, because in the morning, with more snow, everything might look completely different. It was very cold.

We set up the tent, arranged the bedding, had something to eat, and crawled into our sleeping bags as snow continued to fall. Gary was very worried. The pass ahead of us was higher than the one we'd crossed that day. He didn't know if we'd be able to find it, much less get over it. In fact, he was concerned about whether we'd even be able to backtrack to Rainy Pass, with the snow covering up our footprints.

Between the cold and the worrying, we didn't sleep much, but by the next morning, it had stopped snowing. Gary got us up early, and we headed north for a very long day. Our destination was the Pasayten Wilderness, more than 25 miles to the north through snowy forests where the path was often invisible. Gary kept up his route-finding miracles, relying on his compass, map-reading skills, and decades of experience finding trails by figuring out where they were most likely to go. Late in the day, we reached Harts Pass, where a dirt road from Mazama twists its way up to an intersection with the PCT before climbing gradually to Slate Peak's fire lookout tower about 3 miles away.

We arrived at Slate Peak in the dark. It was cold and getting colder. Gary began searching by headlamp for a trail slightly to the east of the crest, which would run roughly parallel to the PCT but at a lower elevation, thus avoiding the deepest snow. Unable to be certain where the trail was, Gary decided to turn back, camp for the night, and try again by daylight. We backtracked about a mile and a half to a parking area, complete with an outhouse, near Harts Pass. We got to bed past midnight, after our longest day—about 26 miles—and again it was too cold to sleep well. (Mary slept soundly both nights, just not long enough.)

It had been snowing when we set up our tent, and 2 or 3 inches had accumulated by the time we got up the next morning. It was still snowing lightly. Things weren't that bad at first, as we once again marched along the dirt road toward Slate Peak. But as soon as we topped the ridge, blizzard conditions set in. Leaning into the gusting wind, we headed across a steep slope, with Gary breaking trail through snow that was in places thigh-deep on him. The howling wind meant we could barely hear each other, even when we shouted, and the strong gusts made it hard to keep our balance. Mary and I followed Gary as closely as we could, as the snow lashed our faces and the wind pushed us all over the place. One gust knocked Mary flat on her back. "Stop!" I screamed to Gary. "We've got to go back! This is *crazy!*" Gary turned around at the sound of me shouting and Mary screaming (being knocked over by the wind had really frightened her). He gestured to us to indicate that he understood. Conditions really were too terrible to continue. With the roaring wind now at our backs, we slogged back up and over the ridge, and down the icy, slippery road. Dejected, we trekked back to Harts Pass and then began walking down the dirt road toward Mazama, 20 miles away.

That's when Eli showed up.

Trail angels come in all forms, but not many come armed to the teeth. Eli had not just one deer rifle, but two, lying on the front seat. He also came equipped with a long-bed pickup truck that had an extra seat. He was making one of his frequent trips into the Mazama area, where he and his brother had spent years sharpening their hunting techniques. He told us about his wristwatch GPS system and his methods of keeping in touch with his brother while they roamed the foothills in search of elusive mule deer. He showed us where deer fleeing the winter snows for the warmth and cultivated crops of the Methow Valley crossed the road, leaving obvious trails for anyone in the know. Mary was fascinated by the highly polished stock of one of the rifles. I was more interested in the probability that the rifles were loaded and the possibility that one of them would discharge accidentally as we bumped and bounced down the narrow, rocky road. When we arrived at the Mazama Store, Gary interrupted his profuse thanks for the ride with a caution to Eli about trying to lift his pack. No problem, Eli told us; the last time he'd carried a big pack, it contained an entire case of beer. Sure enough, he had no trouble lifting Gary's huge pack out of the back of the truck. If only Gary's spirits could have been lifted as easily.

Back in Mazama, the weather was lovely for October: warm, calm, and partly sunny. Yet only 20 miles away, the frigid wind was blowing the snow horizontally. Gary began to think we weren't going to make it to the border after all. That's when Scrambler delivered a pep talk. "Daddy, we can make it," she told her father. "We've never given up before, no matter how bad it got. And we're so close." Months later, Mary told me, "I knew that we were going to succeed. I thought what Daddy was saying about not being able to finish was absolutely ridiculous. I knew we were going to succeed."

I didn't. I thought we'd reached the end, 40 miles short of success.

We kept a stiff upper lip in public—meaning in the Mazama Store, where we consumed an excellent black bean and tomato soup—but after Dick Roberts gave us a ride back to the Basecamp, we let our true emotions show. Gary was really depressed at the thought we couldn't finish. But that morning's experience with the weather over Slate Peak had made a deep impression on both of us. I wanted to finish, too, I told Sue later as she drove me up to Rainy Pass to retrieve my car. But I wasn't going to let us head off into conditions like that. With even worse weather expected in just a few days, missing the trail and getting lost didn't seem merely a possibility; it seemed highly likely. And in the wind and snow, a bad fall for at least one of us loomed large in my imagination. By the time I returned to Mazama in my little red Ford, I had made up my mind: We're not going on.

Gary, however, had a different plan. After looking over the maps, he discovered a number of ways to reach Canada. If we started again at Harts Pass, but then took an alternate trail well to the east of the PCT at Buckskin Pass instead of Slate Peak, we'd miss the worst of the wind and we could drop into the Pasayten River drainage. Dick Roberts called a backcountry ranger and verified that even with the recent snow, this lower route should be possible. I still argued that we should give up. The weather forecast wasn't encouraging, and we'd already seen how cold and snowy it was up in the Cascades. But Mary wanted to go on with Gary, who was sure we could finish. My resolve to quit began to fade. "Think it over," Gary told me. I studied the map and concluded that it might just work.

Taking a zero day in Winthrop allowed us to rest up as well as to get a little more gear and some maps, plus lots of advice from the Forest Service. The hardest part was calling my sister, Liz, with the news that we weren't done yet. I had told her just a few days earlier that the next time we called, it would be from Canada, and here we were, still stuck in the States. It was also difficult to look at the weather forecast, which showed a narrow window of decent weather, followed shortly by yet another storm. Throughout the evening, Sue kept getting updated forecasts from the internet for us. They worsened by the hour.

The next day, Scott from the Mountain Transporter charter van service took us up to Harts Pass. He seemed honestly worried about us and spent much of the drive seeking assurance that we possessed adequate experience and equipment to have a chance. He asked us to call him when we finished so he would know we were safe. Due to his obvious concern about us, I was beginning to get a bit nervous myself. But as soon as we started walking, everything became much easier. Heading over Buckskin Pass, a few hundred feet lower than Slate Peak, we avoided the gusting wind that had turned us back two days earlier. The trail rapidly disappeared under the snow, but Gary was able to pick out a route through the snow banks and, sure enough, several miles later, as we dropped down to where there was less snow, he found the trail leading down to the Middle Fork of the Pasayten River.

We made good time and set up camp at 6:45 p.m., which seemed very early by the clock, but very late by the sky—it was already completely dark. It was very cold, but calm—that is, until a mouse ran into our toothbrush bag. I had just set it down for a second, but that's all it took. Don't those little pests ever hibernate? I made quite a racket, chasing away the tiny creature. Worried about contamination, Gary, Mary, and I shared the one toothbrush we were sure was clean: the one clutched in my hand.

At that point, I began to think we might actually make it to Canada, although the last weather forecast we'd heard still had me worried. Gary and Mary would be genuine thru-hikers. I would still have to come back in a year or two and hike most of Washington, but I could do that during good weather. And with the border tantalizingly close, I began to let my mind drift to the prospect of making the transition back to ordinary life.

Mary would be returning to school, after having missed more than two months of sixth grade. How would her friends and her teacher react to her long absence, and her unique accomplishment? How would Mary adjust to the regimented routine of dress codes, class projects, and homework, after the freedom of the trail? Gary would finally shed the heavy responsibility of keeping us alive and on track. But he would also be giving up his leadership role, and moving from a wilderness where he felt so at home, to a home where he sometimes felt surrounded by an impenetrable societal wilderness of rules, deadlines, and annoying phone calls. I would be returning to my newspaper job just days before a presidential election, and exchanging the simplicity and beauty of trail life for immersion in an electoral jungle. As success on the PCT started to look possible,

I began to realize we would be exchanging one set of uncertainties for another. But at that moment, exchanging the uncertainty about whether we would survive our attempt to reach Canada for the uncertainty about whether John Kerry could give George W. Bush a run for his money seemed like a pretty good deal.

The next morning, I was relieved to discover that the snowstorm that was supposed to blow in overnight had not arrived. It was crisp and dark when we left camp, walking by headlight. With luck, we would reach the border this very day. We set out with determination, rather than jubilation. Mary in particular remembers being cold and tired more than anything else. We eventually left the Middle Fork of the Pasayten River, turned left, and before long, the snow was again deep enough that the trail was covered and the route difficult to find. We crossed Frosty Pass, where the most recent storm had left thick, wet snow plastered against the trees like stiff white flags. The wind that created those frozen banners must have been ferocious. In mid-afternoon, we rejoined the Pacific Crest Trail at Castle Pass, only a few miles short of our goal.

Late in the afternoon, as the path curved gently downhill, we caught our first glimpse of the monument marking the north end of the trail. We crept up on it as though we were afraid it might run away if it saw us first. And then we were there. We touched the monument. We had reached the end of the Pacific Crest Trail, all together.

It was 4:30 p.m. on October 25, 176 trail days since we had left the matching monument at the Mexican border, 2,650 miles away, and we didn't even try to contain our excitement. We were dancing, cheering, shouting, high-fiving each other, jumping up and down—deliriously happy. We were so thrilled, not even the bitter cold could cool us off. We stood in front of the monument in the snow and sang the trail song we had composed over the last many months. Any animals not already hibernating knew something big had just happened at the border.

Our finishing was a surprise to a lot of people. In fact, the trail register for that year had already been removed from its home in the base of a small, hollow obelisk on the border, and a new one had been placed there instead. So we, along with the other late finishers who came through a few days ahead of us—Old Dirty, K-Too, Bald Eagle, Nocona, and Chacoman—signed the new register, carefully writing the complete date so that there could be no doubt about when we crossed the border, and no doubt that Scrambler and Captain Bligh had truly completed the trail in one calendar year.

We set up camp a few hundred yards north of the border. It was very cold, and we weren't very comfortable, but Mary nonetheless penned this jubilant entry in her journal:

> **Day 176:** *We finished! We are finally done! I am so glad! We just have to walk out, and it'll be all over at last, and I'll be warm and dry! I kissed the monument, and we are set up just inside Canada. I will be home soon!*

176

We finished!
We are finally done!
I am so glad! we just
have to walk out and
it'll be all over, at last
and I'll be warm and
dry! I kissed the
Monument, and we
are set up just inside
Canada. I will be home
soon!

I felt sorry for all those thru-hikers who finish up in glorious weather, after only five months on the trail, with hardly a blister, in the pink of health, and who feel sad and disoriented and rootless—disappointed that their trip is over and their trail friends are scattering and now they have to go back to ordinary life.

There was no such feeling of disappointment for us. There was relief that we'd somehow slipped through a window of opportunity in the weather. And there was joy and anticipation at the thought of telling all our friends and relatives that we had succeeded and were heading home. But our overwhelming emotion was triumph.

We spent our first post-PCT night back at the North Cascades Basecamp, after a large meal at the Duck Brand in Winthrop, during which Mary kept drifting off to sleep. Once in our room, Mary was comatose within seconds in her prized upper bunk bed, and Gary was soon in dreamland, too. It took a little longer for me to fall asleep. Because of the freezing weather during our last few days on the trail, I had worn my stretchy black balaclava over my head and neck the entire time, including in the sleeping bag. My jaw had to work extra hard every time I talked or ate. Now that the thing was finally off my head, my jaw muscles went into spasm, and my twitching chin kept me awake. But that was OK. We'd finished!

Epilogue

Months before finishing the Pacific Crest Trail, Mary, Gary, and I had talked about the best way to make the transition from trail life back to the routine of home, school, and work. We had planned to take three or four days to drive down the coast, staying in seaside campgrounds and getting used to being around people again. We knew from the trail journals we'd read, and the long-trail veterans we'd met, that the change could be difficult.

Mary and I had even created an imaginary resort at the Canadian end of the PCT in which thru-hikers would be able to spend a few days re-learning how to sleep in a bed, eat at a table, use a bathroom, and make small talk. We imagined a multistory restaurant, with trail food served on the top floor, for backpackers whose digestions had become accustomed to nothing but granola bars, freeze-dried meals, filtered stream water, and large quantities of chocolate. Diners would sit on their packs, logs, or boulders. The next floor down would feature the kind of fast-food on which thru-hikers typically gorge themselves during town stops. Diners would have to sit on benches and eat off tables, but they wouldn't have to wash up, and they could eat with their fingers.

The next floor down would feature "real" food, and customers would be expected to bathe first, use knives and forks, and discuss topics other than blisters, giardia, bear canisters, stream crossings, and the progress of other backpackers as discerned from trail registers. This floor would feature plate-glass windows through which non-backpackers dining in the next room would be able to peer in, and the thru-hikers themselves could look out to see how ordinary people dress and behave. In the bottom-floor restaurant, the two groups would be allowed to mingle. Outsiders would be permitted to ask the questions that everyone from the wider world seems to ask about the PCT, and thru-hikers would be obliged to answer them—without (ideally) laughing, snorting, or rolling their eyes. In turn, the outsiders would be encouraged to re-introduce subjects such as who's running for president and which teams are playing in the World Series. Upon successful completion of this course of adjustment, each thru-hiker would be handed her boots, backpack, and a bus ticket home.

Thru-hikers all have stories to tell about making the transition back to their ordinary lives after they get off the trail. For many, the transition is way too long—they may have to find a new place to live, apply for graduate school, begin job-hunting, or rebuild suspended relationships. We had the opposite problem. Our transition was way too short.

Because we finished so late in the season, and because I had promised my bosses at the newspaper that I would be back before election day, we packed up after our last night in Mazama and drove to Cascade Locks so that I could walk across the Bridge of the Gods and be able to say that I had completed all of Oregon. (Gary escorted me across with the car, the same way I had escorted the Captain and Scrambler a month earlier, although this time it was after dark.) We spent the night in a motel near Salem, Oregon, and the next day we drove the 500 miles home.

The day after that, I went back to work. That abrupt transition to the real world is not something I would recommend to other thru-hikers. I couldn't remember how to log on to the computer or even turn on the desk lamp, and I had to get up and walk around every 30 minutes, or my cramped muscles would lock my joints into place. I warned my boss that I might be a little slow adjusting to office life and advised him that if he saw me trying to dig a hole in the carpet, he should remind me that the *San Jose Mercury News* has flush toilets.

Mary had a more gradual reintroduction to her old life. She stayed home for a week, sleeping, eating, and getting caught up on material in her textbooks, before starting sixth grade two months late. And even then, it took some time for her to get used to her old friends and their lives. While Mary's classmates admired what she'd accomplished, they couldn't really comprehend it. But that period of feeling like an outsider didn't last long, and she quickly began enjoying the company of her friends and classmates again.

Gary would have had plenty to do even if no extra chores arose once we returned home. All of our gear had to be cleaned, sorted, and packed away, and all of our digital photos had to be loaded into the computer and organized. The furnace had to be put in order for the cold weather that had already arrived in Sunol. Our financial affairs required immediate attention, and the cats demanded constant petting to make up for the months of separation.

But that was only the beginning. The dishwasher broke the first time we used it, probably because the 10-year-old machine hadn't been operated for several months, and during that time, some normally flexible component had become brittle. Gary made a quick study of *Consumer Reports'* recommendations, bought a new dishwasher, and installed it in just a couple days. Then our computer began acting up, and he had to do more research, decide on a replacement, and get that up to speed. The Ford Escort and our household water filter broke down in rapid succession. Our 80-year-old house needed as much attention as our cats, being overdue for all the maintenance that had been put off for the past couple years while Gary made sure everything was in place for a successful thru-hike. And then there was the day Gary came home early from an errand and announced, "The van almost caught on fire!" We ended up replacing that, too.

Amid the stresses of our return to work, school, and the hassles of daily life, we welcomed the occasional reminders from other people that we had accomplished something extraordinary. Mary spoke to school groups and at the annual conference of the American Long-Distance Hiking Association-West. Months after our return, the *San Jose Mercury News* ran an article I wrote about our journey, accompanied by Gary's photographs. A sister paper picked up the story, so our words and pictures eventually ran in newspapers across the Bay Area. Shortly after the story appeared, we boarded an airplane in Oakland for our annual trip to the East Coast. Mary was looking around the cabin when she spotted a woman looking at a recent travel section from the *Contra Costa Times*. "Look, Mom," Mary said excitedly. "She's reading our story." The woman turned around, stared at Mary, and exclaimed, "You must be Scrambler!" She had saved the story to read on the plane, and promised that now that she'd met its subject, she'd make sure the young nieces she was flying to visit would read the article, too.

I was pleased that she planned to share the story with her family and hoped her nieces would be inspired by the accomplishments of a girl their age. About two years after we began our PCT trek, I was enjoying a little web wandering on my office computer, when I came across a father asking for advice about how to entertain his son on backpacking trips. He explained that he had resisted letting his son accompany him until the boy was "old enough." The child had finally reached this milestone at age 12. Poor man. He had it exactly backwards. He should have been taking the kid along since infancy. By the time the kid was 12, it would have been Dad struggling to keep up. And entertainment? For a child who has been brought up in the wilderness, the trail itself provides plenty of opportunities for fun.

This father's remarks got me thinking again about how much our lives had been enriched by sharing all of our adventures as a family. It would have been easier if Gary and I had tackled the PCT as a pair, leaving Mary with relatives. But 10 years of backpacking as a family not only prepared us for our long-trail adventure, it made it unthinkable that we would do it any other way. Then and now, we do things together. Even though they had finished the entire trail in 2004, Gary and Mary returned to Washington two years later to accompany me on a 320-mile journey toward my completion of the trail. I now have just one section of about 120 miles around Glacier Peak for my final PCT expedition, and I'm confident I'll finish with my family by my side.

Now, three years after our journey, while helping prepare Mary for her first year of high school, I find myself flummoxed when asked what we learned about ourselves and our family by hiking the Pacific Crest Trail. At first blush, we didn't learn anything. We already knew how to survive in the wilderness, how to function under stress, how to entertain each other, and how to watch out for each other's weaknesses. If we hadn't, we wouldn't have taken that first step on the trail. On the other hand, our knowledge in each of those areas became much deeper based on our experiences.

The lessons we learned about each other's personalities were more subtle. Gary and I learned that Mary could bounce unexpectedly from being a 10-year-old to an adult, and back, with dizzying speed. In a pinch, we knew we could rely on her to rise maturely to the occasion. Also, she developed an instinct for the trail much faster than we expected. By the time we reached Oregon, she was offering advice about practical decisions such as where to camp and whether to drink from certain water sources—advice that deserved to be taken seriously, even if Gary and I didn't always realize it.

This wasn't an easy trip for Gary. But Mary and I came to realize that no matter how frustrated he was with his ailments, or impatient with my map-reading shortcomings, or angry with some misbehavior on Mary's part, he would always take care of us. He never forgot his responsibility as the captain of our little crew. About myself, I learned that I can put up with just about anything if the goal is important enough. Pain, uncertainty, frustration, hunger, filth, exhaustion—the things I find hardest to cope with in daily life are things I can overcome. And that's a very good feeling!

The one big lesson we all learned was how to persevere in the face of uncertainty. As enjoyable as backpacking can be, often it's anything but. Much of the time, one of us was in acute pain or even feeling seriously ill, and the hardest part was not knowing whether it would get worse or better. But we supported each other and kept going, anyway.

Togetherness can be wonderful, but there were those times when being stuck with each other, day after day, was an ordeal. Hiking with a child was a great deal of fun, but it did add a big load of responsibility for Mary's safety to our heavy packs. No doubt, there were times when Mary felt that having her hyper-vigilant parents along was a huge burden on her, too. She could never decide to just do nothing for an afternoon, or even get away from us for a few hours of solitary rambling or reading. Those rare occasions in which she had a room to herself for one whole night were a major treat. Still, she persevered—and she succeeded.

Uncertainty can be exhilarating. It has to be for a thru-hiker, who would otherwise quit at the first close escape from disaster. Uncertainty leads to learning important lessons the hard way, and it's those lessons that keep you alive later. As Dusty tells his cowboy partner on "Lives of the Cowboys," my favorite *Prairie Home Companion* sketch: "Good judgment comes from experience, Lefty, and all the really useful experiences come from bad judgment." I would add that bad luck also leads to some important learning experiences. I had a severe fright in the southern California desert when an ice storm blew in and I came close to suffering hypothermia. Gary crawled out of the tent in his underwear during the worst of the storm in order to tie down the tent more tightly, and Mary crawled into my sleeping bag to share her body warmth. By the time we reached northern Washington, we were dealing with the possibility of hypothermia every day, but I don't remember being nearly so frightened about it. We just kept on moving through the snow, the cold, and the rain. That scary experience months earlier taught me how to prepare and to persevere against the uncertainty of late October's weather in the North Cascades.

While hiking the PCT meant persevering through bad days (not to mention the scary, frustrating, angry, and painful days), what I remember most is a good day. It was one of those velvety-warm summer nights when I paused outside the tent to find the Big Dipper and follow its pointer stars to the North Star. As I whispered to myself, "That way to Canada," I knew that the two people who mattered the most to me were right there, sharing my dream.

A couple months after we returned from Canada, we went for a walk in our Sunol neighborhood. It was pouring rain, and cold and windy. We quickly became soaked. Returning home, we changed into dry clothes and settled down at the window with cups of hot cocoa. We sat there watching the rain fall, and chuckled delightedly over our dry feet, warm hands, abundant cocoa, and, most of all, the knowledge that we didn't have to go back out in the rain unless we wanted to. We were deliriously happy with our good fortune. Because we remembered what it was like to be miserably cold and wet when more days of misery awaited us, we could enjoy the warmth and hot food and a roof over our heads more than ever before. But we also knew that when we wanted to, we could go back into the rain and hike for miles. Because we've done it. Because we know how to do it. And when the time comes, we'll do it again.

Appendix

The Future of the PCT

When we hiked the Pacific Crest Trail in 2004, 11 years after the trail was officially completed, 250 or so people were on the trail with us as thru-hikers, and thousands more were walking parts of it as section hikers, backpackers, and dayhikers. One old-timer told us that when he first hiked the trail in 1977, there were no trail angels or water caches, and the trail itself was not even completely constructed. Today, the trail is complete, fairly well-signed, blessed with enthusiastic trail angels, and still uncrowded.

I like to think we hiked the trail during what will come to be regarded as the Golden Age of the PCT, the early years of the 21st century. On the other hand, thru-hikers decades from now may very well look back on our time as the Dark Ages. "Those poor hikers!" they'll say. "How did they ever survive?" Gary and I will go to trail events, and the young folks will look at our white hair and wrinkled faces and ask incredulously, "What was it like without GPS? Constant radio communication? On-trail entertainment systems?" Gary and I will drone on about how it was back in the day, and Mary will pretend she doesn't know us.

It's hard to imagine what the trail, its thru-hikers, its angels, and its adjacent town stops will look like 25 years from now, but speculation about the future is a game we thru-hikers like to indulge in. Will the growing accessibility of backpacking, thanks to advances in gear and route-finding technology, encourage hundreds more to head north from Campo every year? Would this strain the trail and its caretakers beyond their capacity? Or will an increasingly out-of-shape and game- and internet-addicted public turn its back on the long-trail experience? And would that mean less official support and funding for a trail that's under constant threat from development and logging?

Trail angel Donna Saufley, who runs Hiker Heaven and likely sees more hiker traffic at her place in Agua Dulce than any other trail angel, isn't concerned just with the effects of crowding on the PCT in 25 years. She's worried about the effects of crowding right now. Every spring, she watches the majority of the 200 or 300 people who begin the trail at the Mexican border head through Agua Dulce in what is known alternatively as "the pack," "the herd," "the wave," and sometimes even "the clump." This concentration can strain the facilities, and the hospitality, of small towns along the way.

Donna believes that the trail gathering, the Annual Day Zero Pacific Crest Trail Kick Off (generally, but unpronounceably, known as ADZPCTKO), held at the end of April, contributes to the situation. At the time we hiked the PCT, the American Long-Distance Hiking Association-West had begun a tradition of hosting this party for thru-hikers at a county park 20.6 trail miles north of the border. It attracts former hikers, prospective hikers, trail angels, a few people selling gear, and a whole lot of people who turn out to show their support for the PCT and to enjoy the company of like-minded individuals.

Because of the kickoff's timing—the last weekend in April—and its location so close to the beginning of the trail, not to mention the free food and campsites provided for thru-hikers, many people make ADZPCTKO their beginning date. They get their copies of the all-important water report, listen to presentations from experts, buy extra sunscreen from the little store next to the park, consume as much food as possible, and then, on Sunday morning, catch a ride with volunteer drivers to the monument at the south end of the trail. Some of the thru-hikers start walking a day or two before the kickoff, stop at the campground for the weekend, and then continue on. Donna believes the overall result is that dozens of people begin right around the end of April and move north in a pack, stretched out over about three days.

Other people involved in PCT issues believe the kickoff has a minimal effect, and that clumping occurs because, as backpackers meet each other along the trail, at town stops, and during zero days, a group dynamic takes over in which the more sociable hikers begin traveling in a loose group. This isn't bad in itself; strong hikers can help the weaker ones until they develop harder muscles, and those with better route-finding skills can guide and teach the directionally challenged (among whom I include myself). One PCT backpacker, John Donovan, who died during his thru-hike attempt, would almost certainly be alive today if he had paid attention to what other hikers told him about getting through a snowy section of the San Jacinto Mountains in southern California. Donovan, a 60-year-old retiree from Virginia, had camped with a group heading toward Idyllwild in May, 2005. As they headed down the Devil's Slide Trail, he apparently wandered off in a different direction and became thoroughly confused. Instead of backtracking, he kept going in the wrong direction and then tried to work his way down an impassable, steep canyon choked with brush. He vanished so completely that months of intensive searching failed to turn up a single clue. Donovan's name became nationally known a year later, when two people wandered away from a group hiking down from a tramway near Palm Springs and got lost. The young couple from Dallas floundered through the boulders and thickets for three days and then stumbled upon Donovan's camp—one year to the day from his last journal entry. They used his matches (almost miraculously waterproof after a year) to start a brushfire, which quickly brought a helicopter rescue crew to their aid. Only then did searchers find Donovan's body.

Some clumping of thru-hikers is inevitable on the PCT because people schedule their start dates so that they arrive at Kennedy Meadows after most of the snow has melted in the southern Sierra, but early enough that they still have a chance to reach Canada before the autumn storms begin. That's a fairly narrow window, requiring people to leave Kennedy Meadows between June 1 and June 15 most years.

So whether the kickoff should be moved farther north and be held later in the year, as Donna and others have suggested, or remain at Lake Morena County Park in late April, as many others prefer, the end result may remain the same: a fairly compact group of thru-hikers in southern California, with smaller numbers in front and behind.

Donna and her husband, Jeff, plan to keep Hiker Heaven going as long as they can, and they say they'll never get tired of thru-hikers, even when 50 or more are camped in their yard, necessitating the addition of camp toilets and canopies to the trailer and RV. But Donna has seen some indications that other people are getting tired of the sudden influxes of backpackers. "The first indication was a busy Memorial Day weekend when we were having breakfast at a local place," she says. "I overheard one waitress telling another waitress about us: 'Those are the people who are hosting the hikers.' And she came unglued. Everyone has always been so positive, saying what a wonderful thing to do, but this woman was angry, because of the impact." This experience forced Donna to view the wave through the eyes of a busy waitress. "You have 50 hungry hikers in one place wanting breakfast, and you have locals to serve, and the place only seats 25, and they're running out of everything, running out of coffee mugs, running out of toast ... and you've got disgruntled people," she explains.

Donna will always be an advocate for thru-hikers, but she also knows how small-town residents feel about seeing disruptions to the very things that make small towns attractive. "If something interferes with getting their mail or their breakfast, they're really grouchy," she says. Portions of the trail have to be rerouted from time to time, and a bad reputation can cause trouble. The PCT was originally planned to run through the nearby town of Acton, Donna points out, but because of local opposition, it was rerouted.

Beyond the effect on trail towns, some PCT advocates worry that the growing size of the herd will lead to restrictions on the numbers allowed to use the southern desert's campgrounds, and a reluctance by post offices to hold hiker boxes longer than two weeks. Some people have begun complaining about the appearance of water caches—which, to the untrained eye, do look as though someone dumped several dozen plastic jugs alongside the trail and just left them there. The larger concern, of course, is the effect of all this on the trail experience itself. Some of the most popular destinations in the West—such as Mt. Whitney in the Sierra and the Obsidian Trail in Oregon—have quotas. If thru-hikers in the southern desert have too much of an impact on that fragile ecosystem, PCT advocates worry that limits may be imposed on the number of hikers who can start on any particular date.

ADZPCTKO coordinator Greg Hummel opposes any rationing of start dates. "I don't think the PCTA can do this, nor should they," he wrote to me in an email. "I think they should be a steward for the trail and encourage good etiquette. Even though they do issue hiking permits, I think that they can only encourage people to start over a range of dates. Each individual usually picks a start date based upon conditioning, expected hiking pace, and the weather conditions in the southern California ranges and the Sierra."

Scott Williamson, who, having taken nine trips border to border, has spent more time on the PCT than anyone else, shares the concerns about crowding. In 2006, his second successful yo-yo, he started in mid-May, well behind the herd, and immediately noticed the difference from previous years. "The number of thru-hikers is beginning to exceed the carrying capacity of the water sources in the first 700 miles," he says. "I saw a lot of garbage, feces, and toilet paper, but as soon as I got ahead of the pack, I didn't see it." Part of the problem is that use of the trail is getting ahead of the abilities of both professionals and volunteers to patrol and maintain the trail—and that's compounded by the remoteness of many trail sections. The U.S. Forest Service in recent years has received between $1 million and $1.7 million a year for the PCT, according to Liz Bergeron, executive director of the Pacific Crest Trail Association (PCTA). That amount is augmented by PCTA and other private funding. But it's not a huge amount of money for a trail that's 2,650 miles long.

Maintenance chores are shouldered primarily by volunteers who are limited in the amount of time they can spend hauling equipment miles into the wilderness in order to repair erosion or chop trees felled by winter storms. "It's an old problem, which the Appalachian Trail has already faced," Scott says. "They worked it out because of the large number of volunteers. The Appalachian Trail Conservancy can keep up with it. Here, volunteer efforts to protect the trail and get federal dollars are still in their infancy."

Other trail advocates cite concerns about the resilience of the trail angels as a major issue for the future of the PCT. Donna Saufley's waitress in Agua Dulce isn't the only person whose opinion of thru-hikers has dimmed with greater numbers. People who live near the trail, whether they help backpackers as part of business or as a hobby, are bound to see some bad apples occasionally. As the number of hikers increases, so will the number of bad apples. And some people who in the past were eager to provide rides to trailheads, post offices, and supply shops, will stop doing it. The trail angels who make helping hikers a hobby express great enthusiasm for continuing their generous ways. But sit and talk with them for a few hours, and they do have stories of occasional guests who became pests, whether by being drunk and disorderly or by inviting non-hiking friends to move in and take advantage of the trail angels' hospitality. These situations so far have been extremely rare. But even if most of the hikers stay on their very best behavior, there will be incidents, and word will get around.

Many trail angels are retired. Eventually, they might run out of the energy it takes to welcome all the backpackers who arrive at their doors, tired, hungry, and dirty—not to mention the energy it takes to pick up all the socks, sunglasses, hats, trekking poles, cameras, and gaiters that backpackers leave behind, wash them, sort them, and try to reunite them with their owners. When these wonderful people decide it's time to buy an RV and see the country, I worry that there will not be enough younger people ready to take their places.

Greg Hummel, who hiked the PCT in 1977, believes the trail will become much more popular, but he doubts it will reach Appalachian Trail status, simply because it's so much more difficult. I asked him what would happen if the PCT began to attract 1,000 northbound thru-hikers each year, as opposed to the current average of 250 to 300. What will be the effect on camping areas, water supplies, trail angels, and town stops?

"We are already seeing the impact of greater numbers on the trail and the supply points," he replied in an email. "An inn in Idyllwild has begun to refuse service to hikers due to a bad encounter, and there have been increasing complaints about rude hikers 'expecting' trail angel services. Thus, greater numbers are likely to cause fewer angels continuing their services. However, I think that there is a flip side: We, the ADZPCTKO organizers, began sending out letters to the Chambers of Commerce of most of the southern California supply points, telling them exactly what services and items hikers want [in order] to encourage their members to take advantage of this by stocking up on the items and offering the specific services."

As executive director of the PCTA, Liz Bergeron deals with the future of the PCT every day. For her, it's not so much an issue of whether this spring or that campground can handle a crowd of thru-hikers, as whether this stretch of trail is about to be surrounded by a housing development, or that mile of trail depends on an informal agreement that needs the legal protection of an easement, which a future property owner wouldn't be able to rescind. She has hiked several hundred miles of the trail (and her husband has hiked the entire distance), so she respects backpackers' concerns about individual points along the trail. But her job is to focus on the bigger picture. If you were to write down every single issue that could affect the PCT, you could paper a wall with issues—in fact, that's exactly what Liz did a few years ago, at a gathering of all the various groups interested in the PCT, from hiking and equestrian groups to land-use professionals and volunteers. Those issues ranged from damage to specific parts of the trail by off-road vehicles to damage to the Sierra Nevada by air pollution to broader issues, such as establishing a PCTA presence in more towns along the route.

When Liz looks at the trail, the first things she sees are the 30 or so small sections where private property issues of one sort or another have to be dealt with right away. "Our biggest problem is the 200 or 300 miles of trail that are not fully protected," Liz explains. "As you hike the trail, there are areas that cross private property. We may or may not have permission to pass. Typically, permission to pass looks like an 8-foot easement. When the property changes hands, the next owners may not honor the easement even though they're required to do so. We've seen fences go up across the trail."

When addressing very specific trail issues, Liz has to remind herself and others that her job is to protect the trail—or else there won't be one. "So our number-one priority is to protect, and number two is to keep the trail open," she says. "There is a possibility you would not be able to hike on a continuous trail from Mexico to Canada if we don't address these issues. You'd have to get off the trail and go around a new housing development and then get back on."

For sure, there's nothing like hiking down a heavily traveled highway or through a trashy trailer park to degrade the trail experience.

Liz and her staff have to know land-use issues as well as any big-city planning department. When I talked to her, she was negotiating a conservation easement to protect about a mile of trail in a crucial link in Oregon; keeping an eye on several parcels up for sale in Washington; and dealing with a southern California housing development that seemed likely to put some people's backyards right smack on the PCT. "If people are unaware they're going to have a national scenic trail in their backyard, that could be a problem," she notes wryly.

Scott Williamson agrees that the biggest threat in the next 25 years is encroaching housing developments, especially in the first 700 miles of trail in southern California. He is also concerned that residential development could threaten sections in northern California, near his home in Truckee. Formerly focused on logging, Truckee is turning into a popular location for retirees and owners of second homes, especially among skiers. He's worried that these new landowners will ignore easements allowing backpackers to cross their private property.

Scott's secondary concern, after residential development, is the effect of logging and the road building that goes along with it. "The road building is almost as bad as the logging itself, because, as you know, once you build a road through an area, you've permanently altered it," he says.

Logging is one of those issues that sharply divides thru-hikers from the residents of many of the small towns they travel through. Many residents see logging as a good thing, providing jobs not just for loggers, but for truckers, mill workers, real estate agents, and restaurateurs. However, like many highly mechanized extraction industries, logging companies tend to move into an area, take what they want, and then move out, providing a few temporary jobs while permanently damaging the forests and streams upon which many tourist-oriented businesses rely. Many city dwellers also defend logging, not just because they recognize the need for wood for home construction, but also because they perceive logging as equivalent to fire protection, thinning out the overgrown forests so that a lightning strike is less likely to result in a catastrophe.

What small-town and city residents alike don't see is what backpackers see when they walk through an area that's been cut over. Logging rarely makes an area more fire-resistant. Loggers take out the biggest trees, which are least likely to burn, and leave behind the smaller, less marketable but more flammable trees. Worse, they leave behind piles of slash—the limbs and tops that are cut off the trees before the trunks are hauled away. These piles of dead limbs and forest debris are a bigger fire hazard than anything the loggers remove. Perhaps worst of all for backpackers is the maze of dirt logging roads snaking through forests, encouraging erosion, wiping out trails, and making route-finding a lot harder than it should be.

The future of the PCT depends on many factors, but none more so than the people who walk it. Many in the thru-hiking community are concerned that the trend toward fewer people backpacking will mean less people on the trail, and therefore fewer people advocating for this important resource. ADZPCTKO's Greg Hummel, who works as a geologist in crowded southern California, believes more people from overseas will visit, offsetting the possible slacking of interest here. "On one hand, I hope this is wrong and more people get into outdoor activities, as I know that it is one of the best things for my soul and theirs," he wrote to me. "On the other hand, I sense a great slacking of physical fitness. I walk from Union Station in Los Angeles to my work three days a week and have tried to get others who ride the free shuttle to join me, to no avail."

Part of the problem is that many people see a PCT hike as inaccessible because of time commitment, physical conditioning requirements, or financial cost. The idea that a thru-hike isn't something that normal people should seriously consider, that it's too extreme and too dangerous, is one that I run across occasionally in the outdoor recreation community. Ready to repudiate that idea are Ken and Marcia Powers, who got into backpacking as a couple in their 50s, hiked the Triple Crown (the PCT, the Appalachian Trail, and the Continental Divide Trail), and eventually became the first people to complete the American Discovery Trail—a 4,900-mile trek from coast to coast—within one calendar year.

Other than these accomplishments, Ken and Marcia are perfectly normal people. Ken was a database analyst for an oil company, Marcia taught flute, and they raised two sons before retiring. They both are in good physical shape, of course, but they are by no means extraordinary athletes. Marcia modestly describes her fitness routine as walking with a friend, while Ken admits, "I mostly play with computers." The Powers agree that beyond a physical fitness level that many people can attain, a strong mental outlook is important for a successful thru-hike. If enough people can deal with the mental stress of watching a lightning storm approach while they're trying to get over a mountain pass, and can embrace uncertainty as a positive experience, Ken and Marcia are certain that thru-hikers will continue to push the limits and maintain the popularity of long-distance backpacking.

Yo-yo hiker Scott Williamson is concerned, as I am, that the current generation of Americans in their 20s—traditionally the prime thru-hiker group—isn't producing as many serious backpacking enthusiasts as earlier generations did. "Within the general population, the younger generation definitely is not hitting the trail as much," he says. And he's concerned that today's children—who would ideally be hiking and supporting long trails 10 or 15 years from now—have less contact with the outdoors than any generation in history. When we hiked the trail in 2004, books and magazine articles had begun to focus on the need for modern American children to rediscover strenuous exercise and to re-connect with nature. And the federal government was moving in the direction of a major initiative to get more children involved in outdoor recreation.

There is no end to the things PCT advocates worry about down the road. Will the U.S. Forest Service be able to devote adequate money and staff time toward maintaining and improving the trail? Will enough volunteers resist the lure of Second Life and SimCity to dig real trails and saw up real trees for the pleasure of getting real blisters on their hands?

The future of the Pacific Crest Trail does indeed have many question marks. But one thing is beyond question: Everyone who has had any involvement with the nation's major scenic trails becomes deeply interested in their welfare. If that passionate belief in the value of the long-trail experience that I see at backpackers' gatherings continues in the hearts and minds of enough Americans, then when Mary is ready to take her children on the PCT, it will be there waiting.

GLoSSaRY

ADZPCTKO: Annual Day Zero Pacific Crest Trail Kick Off.

bear box: A large, sturdy, metal container, bolted to the ground or chained to trees, in which backpackers store any scented supplies (such as food, sunscreen, and toothpaste) to protect them from bears.

bear canister: A hard, smooth container for food and toiletries that bears cannot open, but which they have been known to try to roll away.

crampons: Spikes arranged to fit over boots, to provide traction on ice and snow.

flip flop: A thru-hike punctuated by brief periods on the road, where the hiker travels from one section of the trail to another in an effort to avoid impassable snow, forest fires, and other impediments. Flip-flop thru-hikers walk every section, but out of order.

gaiters: Protective sleeves that go over ankles and boots to keep snow and dirt out of boots, and burrs and thorns out of socks.

giardia: The bane of backpackers. A microscopic intestinal parasite that brings on abdominal pain, diarrhea, weakness, and very large motel bills. Filtering water and washing hands seem to offer the best prevention.

guidebook: The three-volume set of guidebooks from Wilderness Press, describing the entire route of the PCT, is read, revered, relied upon, and occasionally reviled by every serious thru-hiker.

hiker box: The boxes in which thru-hikers abandon the food they've grown tired of, and hope to pick up something that never gets old, like Pop-Tarts, Pringles, and Snickers bars. Unfortunately, these boxes are usually filled with the corn pasta and dried beans that backpackers tend to buy in fits of healthy aspirations, and ditch upon completing their first section.

ice ax: A mountaineering tool with a blunt edge for cutting steps in snow and a very sharp, pointed end for digging into the snow in order to stop you from a fatal fall on steep slopes (this technique is called self-arrest).

resupply box: A box (or sometimes a bucket) mailed to post offices or other stops along the way, containing everything the backpacker needs for the next section of trail, from food to boots.

section hiker: A backpacker who hikes one or more sections of trail at a time, usually with the goal of eventually completing an entire long trail.

slack-packing: Hiking with just enough food and gear for the day, while leaving tent, sleeping bag, stove, and so on at whichever point the hiker plans to spend the night.

Tahoe Rim Trail (TRT): A 165-mile trail that circles Lake Tahoe, which lies on the California-Nevada state line, generally following the crests of the mountains. A great practice hike for the PCT. About one third of the TRT shares tread with the PCT on the California side of the lake.

thru-hiker: A backpacker who intends to complete an entire long trail during one calendar year.

town stop: A town, resort, motel, or trail angel's home at which a backpacker gets off the trail and usually resupplies.

trail angel: A person who helps thru-hikers in a multitude of ways—providing sleeping accommodations, showers, laundry facilities, meals, movies, internet connections, rides, and more—usually as a hobby, but sometimes inadvertently.

trail magic: Unanticipated good fortune, generally involving offers of food, lodging, transportation, and other goodies, but also applied to any really nice experience or coincidence that goes beyond what a thru-hiker could reasonably hope for.

trail name: A nickname that a thru-hiker assumes (or is assigned) for the duration of the long-trail experience, and often beyond.

trail register: A notebook or binder kept at sites where thru-hikers congregate, in which they sign in to let others know how they're doing, and to express their thoughts about the trail.

trail section: A length of trail, ranging from about 38 miles to 176 miles, usually beginning and ending with a road and a resupply destination. PCT trail sections run alphabetically from south to north. All of California is divided into sections A through R. The alphabet starts over a little north of the Oregon state line with Section A, and ends at the Canadian border with Section L.

trekking poles: Frequently mistaken for ski poles, trekking poles are crucial for some, a nuisance for others, and one of the most frequently lost items on the trail (right after sunglasses). They take the place of a walking stick, easing stress on the knees and providing balance for stream crossings.

Triple Crown: The Pacific Crest Trail (2,650 miles), Appalachian Trail (2,160 miles), and Continental Divide Trail (less than 3,000 miles at the time of this book's publication, but when complete, the CDT will be 3,100 miles). Someone who completes all three is a Triple Crowner and achieves major bragging rights at any backpacker gathering. Oddly enough, Triple Crowners are usually very modest about their achievements.

vitamin I: Ibuprofen. The only essential supplement for backpackers.

water cache: A place where trail angels maintain a supply of water, usually in plastic gallon jugs, for backpackers' use.

water filter: A lightweight, portable device that uses mechanical or chemical methods to remove contaminants from drinking water.

water report: A list of water sources along the trail, with information on location, flow rate, cleanliness, and other essentials.

Yogi: The process of inspiring trail magic from unsuspecting strangers. Also the trail name used by Jackie McDonnell, a Triple Crowner from Kansas who has written guides to the PCT and CDT and is one of Mary's personal heroes.

OFF-TRaiL ANGeLS AND ACKNoWLeDGMeNTS

Day 52: *The Lucky Shekel, A True Story by Mary*

> *One day, Mary was walking up the PCT. Suddenly, she pointed out a cairn/post-type marker to her mom and dad, next to a faint trail. They discussed, after her dad had seen an H2O in sticks, and concluded that they were at Corral Spring. Mary and her dad walked down and filtered water. Mary stood up to look around. Luckily, her dad noticed her shekel on the ground. She put it back in her pocket. Then, they went back to her mom. But Mary's shekel, to her great dismay, had fallen out of a hole in her pocket. Though she searched, she couldn't find it. Finally, after sadly walking up the PCT, she felt something in her shoe. It was the shekel! She named it Lucky.*
>
> *The End*

—from Scrambler's journal

OFF-TRaiL ANGeLS

BESIDES THE TRAIL ANGELS who help many thru-hikers every year by providing water caches, overnight lodging, resupply opportunities, and many other essentials—including, quite often, a sympathetic ear and a shoulder to cry on—there are the people I think of as off-trail angels. These are the friends and relations who help each individual thru-hiker by mailing boxes, caring for plants and pets, and providing transportation and much other assistance. We had several of these invaluable, behind-the-scenes helpers, and most prospective thru-hikers need to line up a similar list of off-trail angels. My sister Liz, neighbor Nancy, and friend Lipa, in particular, went far beyond what anyone should expect an angel to do. They truly deserve a big pair of feathered wings apiece, about 5 feet long, with gold tips—and shiny halos to match.

My little sister, Liz, was in charge of our resupply boxes. She made certain they would arrive at each town stop about a week before we did, shipping them USPS or UPS as necessary. The timing of resupply boxes is very important. If a box is sent too early, so that it sits in a post office more than two weeks, it may be returned to the sender. And if it's sent too late, by even a day, the thru-hiker will have to buy food, medications, and other gear at exorbitant prices in resort stores—assuming they can even find the things they need to buy. Every one of our boxes arrived within that two-week window. And before sealing them, Liz would add color comics, funny photos off the internet, and birthday cards as appropriate. She also accepted all our mail, which we had arranged to be forwarded to her, paid the bills we couldn't either pay in advance or set up for automatic payment, and made sure there was enough money in the bank to cover everything. When personal letters arrived, she'd open them and then respond, telling the letter writers we were on the trail and would get back to them in the fall. When we wrote to her or called, Liz would phone the rest of the family with a progress report. And when a jury summons showed up for me, she wrote to the court and arranged for a six-month extension. It's no exaggeration to say she took better care of our affairs than we do ourselves. Liz's husband, Marq, also qualifies as an off-trail angel, and not just for carrying all those heavy boxes to the post office. He was the source of the shekel that Mary mentions in her journal entry, thus contributing to one of Mary's most memorable episodes.

My older sister, Carol, my brother, George, and my Dad, Grandpa (his name is George, too, but everyone calls him Grandpa), really got into the hike, as well. They helped us with everything from rides and car storage to food and shelter. But my younger sister was the one we utterly relied on. Every thru-hiker should have a sister like Liz.

Nancy was the neighbor who watched our home, kept the house plants happy, and took care of the cats. Every several days, she walked up to our house, cleaned the cat box, refilled the automatic food and water dispensers, and watered the Christmas cactus and the creeping Charlies. The cats, Hank and Henrietta, ungrateful little things, never did warm up to Nancy, even though she was keeping them alive. I wouldn't have blamed her if we'd come back to find the house plants had withered and the cats had gone feral. But instead, they thrived. The plants were the healthiest and bushiest they'd ever been, and the cats were starved only for affection. Nancy also kept Mary's classmates aware of her progress, and even met us at Ebbetts Pass and treated us to a night in a motel at Bear Valley. I always looked forward to calling her from the trail and hearing her calm, competent voice assuring me everything was fine on the home front.

Lipa grew up in a poor family in a small town in Texas. Her father died when she was 8 years old, leaving her mother to raise four children. Lipa married at 23, leaving Texas for the first time in her life when her soldier husband was transferred to Germany. When we met her, she had recently buried her husband after caring for him for years as he slowly succumbed to Alzheimer's disease. Her children were grown, and she was on the verge of retirement as a park ranger for the East Bay Regional Park District. Of our entire personal trail angel network, she was the only one with extensive experience backpacking and getting around in the wilderness—in fact, she and her husband had once considered hiking the PCT. So when she met us at Sonora Pass or took us to Bend, Oregon, or when she made a quick trip to REI to buy socks and underwear for us, or when she sorted our supplies, she knew better than anyone what we needed.

Her most angelic moment came when I called her from Crater Lake. It was August 31, just a week away from our planned rendezvous with her at a trailhead near Elk Lake Resort in southern Oregon. She would bring us our resupply box, and drive us to Bend. We had planned to meet her on Saturday or Sunday of Labor Day weekend, which meant she had to make motel reservations for one of the busiest weekends of the year. Gary became very ill the day before we got to Mazama Village in Crater Lake National Park, and when we got there, the pay phone in front of the store didn't work, the motel rooms had no phones, and our cell phone had no coverage. When I finally got through to Lipa, I had to explain that we were running late, having taken a zero day while Gary recovered, and wouldn't be able to meet her until the day after Labor Day at the earliest. I expected Lipa to point out the difficulties of getting reservations on a busy weekend and then having to change them, not to mention altering her travel plans, and what a pain in the neck this was getting to be. That's probably what I would have done. But she didn't. She commiserated with our problems, agreed to change the reservations, wrote down the new information on when to meet us, and promised to run over to REI to buy socks. What a gem! And when she met us, she ferried us around town, combed out Mary's tangled hair, sewed a new camera pouch for Gary, and generally made us wonder how we'd ever gotten through life without her. She did, however, acknowledge that helping us on the PCT had cured her of any desire to hike it herself.

ACKNOWLEDGMENTS

EXTRA-SPECIAL THANKS go to my husband, Gary, for providing his wonderful photographs and for his crucial editing of my manuscript; my daughter, Mary, for sharing her journal entries and illustrations and for her invaluable suggestions to improve this book; my volunteer readers, Liz Lipton and Marshall Hamilton; my volunteer proofreaders, Michele Jurich and Stewart Applin; Eva Dienel, Roslyn Bullas, Larry Van Dyke, Laura Keresty, and Emily White at Wilderness Press; and literary attorney Robert Pimm for negotiating my book contract and providing advice about the publishing process.

ABOUT THE AUTHOR

BARBARA EGBERT, a.k.a. Nellie Bly, is an experienced hiker, backpacker, and travel writer. An English major (and proud of it!), she has worked in print journalism for more than 30 years. She lives with her husband, Gary Chambers (Captain Bligh), and daughter, Mary (the famous Scrambler), in the San Francisco Bay Area. Visit their website at www.PCTFamily.com.